G000068904

MEDICAL EXAMINATIONS

Dissecting the Doctor
in French Narrative Prose,
1857–1894

ℭ

MARY DONALDSON-EVANS

University of Nebraska Press

Lincoln and London

Acknowledgments for the use of previously
published material appear on page xiii.
© 2000 by the University of Nebraska Press
Manufactured in the United States of America
⊗
Library of Congress Cataloging-in-Publication Data
Donaldson-Evans, Mary.
Medical examinations : dissecting the doctor
in French narrative prose, 1857–1894
Mary Donaldson-Evans
p.   cm. "A Bison Original."
Includes bibliographical references and index.
ISBN 0-8032-6628-6 (pa: alk. paper)
1. French fiction — 19th century — History and criticism.
2. Physicians in literature.   I. Title.
PQ653 .D66 2000   843'.80935261 — dc21   00-037427

For Lance

Contents

ℭ

Illustrations

_ɡ_

Acknowledgments

Those readers who have spent excruciatingly long hours in physicians' waiting rooms will appreciate that *Medical Examinations* has been in my cerebral waiting room for well over ten years. Indeed, it was not only the subject but also the seemingly endless nature of the project that inspired my title, and although I shall avoid a facile pun on the word *patient*, let me just say that my pathological obsession with this study is one illness I am glad at long last to call "terminal."

During the ten-plus years that this particular obsession had me in its grasp, I incurred debts to many people. Let me mention first, not last, my husband, Lance Donaldson-Evans, whose sense of humor has lightened many a discouraging day. Without his moral support, his generosity, and his good-natured willingness to listen, discuss, read, reread, and read yet again, this study would never have seen a printing press. To him I dedicate this book.

My now-grown children, Catherine and Andrew, read parts of my manuscript and offered pertinent suggestions for stylistic revisions. Mostly, though, they have contributed to this project by the laughter and the joy they bring into my life. Along with Lance, they are my "reality check" when work threatens to overwhelm me and causes me to forget my priorities.

Frank Paul Bowman was the first person outside of my immediate family to whom I dared show the manuscript. Reading it with characteristic thoroughness, alacrity, and kindness, he saved me from some embarrassing omissions and errors. If errors remain, I take full responsibility. Gerald Prince followed. For his suggestions and his guidance in helping me place the manuscript, I am deeply grateful. Ross Chambers, who first became aware of my project several years ago and offered support and encouragement then, played an important role when he read the manuscript for the University of Nebraska Press. His comments were gracious and helpful. Allan Pasco, Nebraska's other reader, was equally encouraging. He too is part of the history of this project, as he has often pointed out relevant articles to me. Murray Sachs also helped shape my study: the chapter on Alphonse Daudet's *Le Nabab* owes its existence to him. Barbara Cooper's useful advice for revisions to the Goncourt chapter was very much appreciated; even more appreciated are her unwavering friendship and support. Karen Orman also demonstrated her friendship by her insightful reading of various parts of the manuscript. At the University of Delaware and elsewhere, colleagues too numerous to mention by name suggested books and articles they thought would be useful to me. Let me assure them here of my gratitude. I would also like to thank my chairman, Richard Zipser, for his invaluable assistance in arranging my teaching and administrative schedule to allow me the time needed for a book-length project.

As Director of Graduate Studies for my department over the past six years, I have benefited from the help of several graduate assistants. My gratitude for helping me with the more tedious aspects of preparing a manuscript for publication goes to Bree Dallmeyer, Victoria Douglas, Heather Garton, Stephanie Hopwood, Christina Joligard, Susan Klute, and Laura Quinn.

My work was supported by a General University Research Grant from the University of Delaware in the summer of 1990 and by a fellowship from the National Endowment for the Humanities in 1993–94. For this help, without which my project would probably still be scattered across an array of diskettes under unrecognizable file names, I am deeply grateful. I am grateful too to Jack Tracy, who did a superb job of photographing the illustrations, and to Daniel Simon for copyediting the manuscript with care and discretion. Finally, I would like to thank the friendly and patient staff at the University of Nebraska Press.

A few of the chapters are revised versions of previously published articles, and I would like to thank the publishers for permission to reprint them. Chapter 1 originally appeared in *Symposium* 44.1 (spring 1990): 15–27, published by Heldref Publications, 1319 18th Street N.W., Washington DC 20036-1802, and reprinted with the permission of the Helen Dwight Reid Educational Foundation, copyright 1990; chapter 3 in *Literary Generations*, edited by Alain Toumayan (Lexington KY: French Forum, 1992), 150–62; chapter 4 in the *Stanford French Review* 13:2–3 (fall–winter 1989): 193–210. Chapter 5 was presented as a conference paper during Maupassant's centenary year, 1993, and published subsequently in *Maupassant conteur et romancier*, edited by Christopher Lloyd and Robert Lethbridge (Durham, U.K.: Durham University Press, 1994); I would like to thank Professors Lloyd and Lethbridge, who organized the conference from which this publication grew. Chapter 7, on *Mont-Oriol*, was originally presented as a conference paper that same year, at a one-day colloquium organized by Micheline Besnard-Coursodon. To her, too, I extend my heartfelt gratitude.

Note on the translations: Unless otherwise indicated, all translations from the French are my own. Page references are to the French editions listed in the bibliography. In cases where high quality, easily procurable English editions of the fictional works exist, I have listed them in the bibliography in the hope that they will be helpful to the non–French-speaking reader.

MEDICAL EXAMINATIONS

Introduction

ʒ

Iatrogenic *adj* [Gk *iatros* + Eng *-genic*]: Induced in a patient by a physician's activity, manner or therapy. Used especially of an infection or other complication of treatment. — *American Heritage Dictionary, Third Edition*

Iatrogenic: Induced by a physician. Used chiefly of imagined ailments induced in a patient by autosuggestion based on a physician's words or actions during examination. — *Webster's Third International Dictionary*

The seemingly paradoxical notion that the medical practitioner may cause illness rather than cure it has a factual basis. From the well-known dangers of hospital confinement in the pre-Pasteurian era to contemporary tales of horror concerning the transmission of the AIDS virus by doctors and dentists, the danger inherent in surrendering oneself to the medical profession has long been recognized, and in our times the many lawyers who make a specialty of medical malpractice lawsuits foment the widespread public mistrust of the physician. In recent years, the concept of iatrogenesis has even been expanded to include social and structural iatrogenesis, as defined by the Catholic cleric and historian Ivan Illich in his *Medical Nemesis,* an acerbic attack on the medical profession published in 1975. Illich's study begins with the provocative statement that "the medical establishment has become a major threat to health."[1] Incensed by what he terms the "illusion" of the doctor's effectiveness, Illich thunders first against clinical iatrogenesis, that is, doctor-inflicted pain or injuries.[2] He then turns his attention to social iatrogenesis, the way in which medical practice "sponsors" illness, creating a demand for its services by, for example, helping "defectives" to survive in large numbers through neonatal care and certifying their infirmities so that they may be excused from participating actively in the labor force. Finally, he raises his voice against structural iatrogenesis, the medical profession's alleged tendency to "destroy the potential of people to deal with their human weakness, vulnerability and uniqueness in a personal and autonomous way."³ Illich contends that in a medicalized society, individuals feel helpless and are unable to cope with pain, disease, and death as well as their ancestors did.

The fact that Illich's late-twentieth-century attack against the medical profession contains explicit suggestions for reform does not concern us here, except insofar as this aspect of his work distinguishes it from the vast majority of antimedical invectives that history has bequeathed to us. Not surprisingly, perhaps, constructive criticism is especially lacking in those works that don the mantle of fiction in order to camouflage their principal goal, that of heaping scorn on the field of medicine. Antimedical fiction has a long history, going back to Aristophanes and beyond. In France alone, one could cite satires of the doctor from the Middle Ages (such fabliaux as *Le Paysan médecin*) through the twentieth century (Jules Romains's *Knock*), with many striking diatribes along the way (most notably from Rabelais — himself a physician — and Montaigne in the sixteenth century, Molière in the seventeenth, and Voltaire in the eighteenth). Furthermore, many works that have subjects ostensibly unrelated to medicine feature physicians as episodic characters and work surreptitiously to demean the medical profession. A case in point is Sartre's story "Le Mur," with its characterization of the coldly clinical Belgian physician as the Other.

Such negative portrayals of the medical practitioner transcend not only chronological but also geographical boundaries. In nineteenth-century England, distrust of men of science (often represented as physicians) or anxiety about their potential to harm (rather than help) society found expression in such classic works of literature as Mary Shelley's *Frankenstein* (1818), George Eliot's *Middlemarch* (1871–72), and Robert Louis Stevenson's *The Strange Case of Dr. Jekyll and Mr. Hyde*

(1886). And while one can certainly find physicians in heroic and selfless roles throughout world literature (Dr. Martin Arrowsmith of Sinclair Lewis's *Arrowsmith* [1825], Dr. Thomas Stockmann of Ibsen's *An Enemy of the People* [1882], and Dr. Rieux of Camus's *La Peste* [1947] come to mind), stereotypes of the inept and unskilled physician on the one hand, or the unscrupulous, opportunistic materialist on the other, dominate the collective imagination and populate the pages of both high and low literature. In twentieth-century America, the physician-turned-novelist Robin Cook has written a highly successful series of medical thrillers (*Coma, Fever, Brain, Fatal Cure*, etc.) that play on common fears of the medical profession, and the American humorist Dave Barry's quip—"When the medical community finishes with you, you may actually look back with fondness on your original ailment"—provokes in many a hollow laugh. Similarly, we may be amused by such irreverent proverbs as "doctors bury their mistakes" or—from a contemporary American play—"Doctors kill you. Show me a person who has just died and I'll show you a doctor ten feet away,"[4] but even in the era of modern medicine, such phenomena as the "second opinion," the "malpractice suit," and the newfound popularity of "alternative medicine" testify to the fact that few patients have an unshakable faith in what is deemed to be an "inexact" science. Moreover, Molière's seventeenth-century mockery of the obfuscating language with which his charlatans hide their ignorance still rings true today, as Tristan Bernard's anecdote about one Dr. Iléon, "one of our most distinguished practitioners," reveals.[5] Bernard's fictional surgeon, consulted about a sailor's swollen face, surgically opens up his cheek and removes a wad of chewing tobacco; then, for the instruction of his colleagues, he writes a treatise entitled "Surgical procedure for the removal of chewing tobacco from sailors' mouths without having recourse to opening the lips and the jaws."[6] In these examples, a leitmotif is apparent: the doctor, historically associated with the magician, has lost his "supernatural" power. Medical satires insist instead on the *perversion* of this historical relationship. In their caricaturized literary representations, today's practitioners, fallible mortals, insured to the teeth and therefore not accountable for their errors, no longer intone magical "formulas" in order to perform miracles, as did medicine men of yore, but rather use a professional discourse unintelligible to the general public as a source of power and self-protection. Such stereotypes mirror public perception of the medical doctor: iatrophobia (fear of medical doctors) is no laughing matter, as any psychologist can attest.

The practitioner who is cavalier about his failures is a stock character throughout world literature. "Right! Another one!" exclaim Victor's American physicians after bleeding their patient to death in Flaubert's "Un cœur simple." Even more frequently represented is the physician who places his own material needs above the health of his patient. Indeed, for centuries fiction writers have exploited the possibilities of the profession's inherent paradox, amusingly summed up by George Bernard Shaw in the preface to his five-act play *The Doctor's Dilemma*:

> It is not the fault of our doctors that the medical service of the community, as at present provided for, is a murderous absurdity. That any sane nation, having observed that you could provide for the supply of bread by giving bakers a pecuniary interest in baking for you, should go on to give a surgeon a pecuniary interest in cutting off your leg, is enough to make one despair of political humanity. But that is precisely what we have done. And the more appalling the mutilation, the more the mutilator is paid . . . I cannot knock my shins severely without forcing on some surgeon the difficult question, "Could I not make a better use of a pocketful of guineas than this man is making of his leg?"[7]

The notion that physicians are ambivalent souls, in large part because illness, the very condition against which they struggle, is their bread and butter—it is said that at professional banquets they avoid the classic toast to health—is not just the stuff of fiction. In his sensitive and penetrating study of twentieth-century physician-authors, *Le Corps souffrant*, Gérard Danous alludes to this paradox. He further contends, after analyzing the complex emotions that drive practicing physicians to take up the pen, that the rarer and more difficult (and hence the more hopeless) the case presented to the medical practitioners, the happier they are: "They combat illness with courage and tenacity, but I must confess that they probably also like it."[8]

UNE HEUREUSE TROUVAILLE.

Parbleu je suis ravi   vous avez la fièvre jaune   c'est la première fois de ma vie que j'ai le bonheur d'en soigner une !

1   The physician's insensitivity and his excitement at rare or tenacious diseases are illustrated in Honoré Daumier's "A Lucky Find," from *Les Beaux Jours de la vie*, September 1844. The caption reads, "My gosh, I'm delighted! You have yellow fever. . . . It's the first time I've been fortunate enough to treat this disease!"

The present study deals not with the twentieth century but the nine-teenth, not with flesh-and-blood physician-authors but with physician-characters and physician-narrators who are linguistic constructs. In spite of their apparent insubstantiality, they have much to tell the modern reader about the extraordinary coalescence of the medical and literary perspectives that defined late-nineteenth-century France. Furthermore, an analysis of the period's medical discourse—or more precisely, the literary transposition thereof—is highly revealing. Drawing upon such sciences as evolutionary biology, anatomy, physiology, physical anthro-pology, and psychology, and such pseudosciences as phrenology and physiognomy, medical discourse overflowed its traditional banks and inundated nineteenth-century French literature. Its ubiquity in literary texts offers clear evidence of the literati's enthrallment with medical phenomena.

Beginning in the early years of the century, French writers had encouraged their readers to equate literary production with scientific endeavor. Balzac appropriated for himself the title "doctor of social medicine." Sainte-Beuve said of Flaubert that he wielded the pen as surgeons do the scalpel, a pertinent analogy given the fact that Flaubert's father was chief surgeon at Rouen's general hospital.[9] Zola, referring to his novels as laboratories, held that scientific research could be performed as successfully and legitimately in naturalist fiction as in the workplaces of the medical community. What these literary titans shared with many other, less imposing literary figures of nineteenth-century France was a tendency to represent life in a way that was heavily influenced by the biomedical sciences. Among the reasons for this influence were the increasing prestige of the medical profession and the consequent desire, on the part of the literati, to give legitimacy to their enterprise by allying themselves with science. Furthermore, many nineteenth-century writers were sons of medical doctors (Flaubert, Nerval, Fromentin, Sue, Proust), health officers (Mirbeau), or men of science (Bourget) or had undertaken medical studies of their own (Louis Bouilhet, Léon Daudet, Maurice de Fleury, Sue). However, the rush to appropriate medical discourse and to give literary texts the patina of scientific documents was not simply a case of adulation on the part of

2   The identification between the realist writer and the surgeon is caricaturized in A. Lemot's "Flaubert Dissecting Emma Bovary," from *La Parodie*, 12 December 1869. Note Emma's blood dripping into the author's inkwell, emphasizing the pen/scalpel metaphor and suggesting that the author draws his inspiration from his protagonist's suffering.

the literati, nor was it merely a reformulation of the traditional desire of the writer of fiction to pass fictional production off as "real" stories with "serious" content. Many writers, particularly in the latter part of the century, had a "hidden agenda," that of undermining the authority of the medical profession. Hence it was not always admiration or a desire for legitimacy that led a whole generation of French writers to privilege the medical detail, to cast physicians in narratorial roles, to present characters as pathological specimens, and to adopt a medical lexicon even in describing nonmedical phenomena. An analysis of selected works of fiction in which the medical perspective is salient will illuminate not only the texts themselves but the ideological biases of their authors, as well as the cultural/historical context that nurtured them.

The impressive rise in the status of the medical practitioner in France during the course of the nineteenth century occurred in tandem with a number of important scientific advances. From the crude and often fatal battlefield surgery of Revolutionary times to the birth of modern clinical medicine, progress in medical knowledge, diagnostic expertise, and therapeutic intervention had been dramatic.[10] The practice of medicine was transformed by a new and more sophisticated understanding of disease and the resultant changes in the system of medical education. But the transition did not occur overnight. Long after they had been discredited, ancient theories of humoralism dating from Hippocrates and spread in the first century by Galen continued to dictate such medical treatments as bleeding and leeching, and these treatments were not widely abandoned until well into the nineteenth century, when the development of cell theory, a better understanding of blood composition, and the discovery of bacteria caused physicians to turn to other forms of therapy and prophylactic procedures such as vaccination. The period also witnessed some important medical inventions, most notably those of anesthesia, antiseptics, and the stethoscope. Already existing instruments, such as the microscope and the clinical thermometer, were considerably refined and improved. One is thus not surprised to learn that the balance of power between patient and physician was reversed: under the Ancien Régime, it was the wealthy or noble patient who told the physician what was wrong with him, whereas, under the new order, the physician had authority, and he exercised it most notably in teaching hospitals, where the indigent provided the necessary *materia medica* for experiment and demonstration.[11] Even though itinerant charlatans and other illegal practitioners (nuns, pharmacists, folk healers, unlicensed midwives, etc.) continued to compete successfully with licensed medical doctors and health officers, particularly in the countryside,[12] and the retrograde practice of diagnosing illness and prescribing medication by mail—a practice ironically revived in our electronic age—persisted throughout the century, orthodox practitioners were taking steps to remedy what they saw as a deplorable situation.[13] Professional societies were formed, subspecialties developed, medical journals proliferated. Many physicians became involved in issues of public health, thereby advancing their professional status and contributing to the dissemination of medical views on a large number of topics. The Third Republic saw an astounding number of medical practitioners run for public office, Clemenceau being no doubt the best known.[14] By the century's last decades, the medical community had succeeded in convincing a large segment of the population that medicine, once cynically branded "the most conjectural of arts,"[15] was indeed an experimental science, fully worthy of its respect. The physician's prestige was enormous, not only in the political realm, but in such fields as urban planning, education, and criminology, in which he became the consultant expert.[16] In France, the roll call of illustrious men of science, most of them physicians, included Bichat, Bernard, Broca, Broussais, Charcot, Laënnec, Littré, Lucas, Pasteur, Pinel, and Ricord. The names of two eighteenth-century physicians, Guillotin and Marat, associated more with death and violence than with their life-sustaining profession, were eclipsed, if not forgotten.

This growing recognition accorded the medical profession was accompanied by the widespread diffusion of a medical view of reality, or what some have termed the "medicalization" of society. To take but a single example, the late-nineteenth century witnessed an appropriation, by the ruling bourgeoisie, of medical discourse to describe the state of the French nation following the disastrous events of 1870–71. France was diagnosed as "sick," while Germany was associated with vibrancy and good health. While this use of the physiological metaphor can be traced back to the organic model of Saint-Simon and his followers, its popularity was a characteristic of the latter part of the century.[17] Robert Nye has pointed out that the secularism of the Third Republic encouraged this form of social and political analysis.[18] Whatever the case, the linguistic hegemony exercised by medical discourse permeated nearly every aspect of French life. There is an interesting irony in this fact, for, as recent medical historians have noted, this unparalleled dominance of the medical perspective came at a time when, despite numerous advances in the field, the efficacy of therapeutic treatments had yet to be demonstrated. In other words, it was a time when medical *practice* lagged significantly behind medical *knowledge*.[19] Yet the medical profession had been so successful in promoting itself that the general public was unaware of the gap between theory and praxis. It is significant that daily newspapers of the period regularly featured columns authored by physicians alongside serialized fictions by well-known writers. It was inevitable that a certain cross-fertilization would occur.

And so it did. As might be expected, the strongest influence by far was that of medicine on literature, and not the reverse. Although there is ample evidence to support the contention that literature also influenced medicine—one could point for example to Freud's use of Greek myth in the elaboration of his best-known theory and to the reliance of the medical case study on emplotment and on a narrative logic of cause and effect[20]—late-nineteenth-century physicians, especially psychiatrists, often admonished their peers not to base their observations on literary models and took pains to flatten and condense their discursive style and hence to distinguish it from the more amplified and rhetorical style of the novelist.[21] Writers, on the other hand, whose stories and novels drew upon a rich nosology of contemporary ailments, were only too happy to cull plots, characters, and descriptive terminology from their medical sources, and they openly acknowledged their debt to science. Their deferential posture with regard to the physician is eloquently illustrated by the following statement from Michelet: "Our physicians are an extremely enlightened class of men, *the* most enlightened in France, in my opinion. No other class knows as much; no other has as many certainties. No other is as strong in intellect and character."[22] Physicians themselves, having no reason to doubt the sincerity of the writers' adulation, congratulated themselves on their high standing in the intellectual community and pointed, as proof of this standing, to flattering literary portrayals of the medical practitioner. In a speech to his colleagues in November 1875, the medical professor A. Rey made the following claim: "In novels, plays, studies of manners, or works of the intellect intended to portray the different groups that make up society, the physician appears as a superior being, familiar with humanity's weaknesses and miseries. Kind, affectionate, sometimes tender, he always intervenes in order to do good."[23] Rey was not likely to find disagreement among the members of the professional confraternity to whom he addressed his remarks. Convinced of the nobility of their calling and the superiority of their knowledge, physicians took for granted that their fictional counterparts would be cast in heroic roles.[24] In the context of the heady progress of their discipline, such hubris is not surprising. What is perhaps more difficult to understand is the wholesale acceptance of this viewpoint on the part of literary critics. So pervasive was the sycophantic courting of the medical practitioner in the second half of the nineteenth century that, until very recently, no one has thought to question its sincerity. An unpublished Cornell University doctoral dissertation dating from 1936, dealing with novelistic representations of physicians in late-nineteenth-century French literature, is typical. Although the author concedes that "medical satire does occur in some [French] literary works," his extensive catalog leads him to conclude that "the novelist reflects the more and more favorable opinion society comes to have of the doctor."[25]

This long-held opinion no longer stands up to scrutiny. Poststructuralist reading practices, a wider familiarity with relevant texts, a new willingness to read works outside the traditional canon, and a more sophisticated understanding of medical history have rendered such a monochromatic interpretation problematical.[26] Similarly, studies on discourse formation and analysis have given us the tools with which to penetrate the literati's superficial docility with regard to the medical profession.[27] A more nuanced picture comes into view when we enlarge our study to include representations not only of the medical doctor but of his discourse, when we look beyond the *apparently* honorable place reserved for medicine in the fiction of the period. In a large number of works published in late-nineteenth-century France, one finds traces of a subtle resistance to medicine's growing power. Some writers make use of strategies that could be qualified as "counter-discursive," a term coined by Richard Terdiman to refer to the use of the dominant social discourse with apparently subversive intent. Terdiman regards "dominant discourse" as something imposed from without, and he identifies the counter-discursive strategy as the effort — generally on the part of writers and artists — to gain control of its power for their own ends.[28] Thus, counter-discourse can be seen as an oppositional technique on the part of the writer, exposing in the text an alienation with regard to its sociohistorical context. The seemingly subversive use of medical discourse in some of the works under consideration here appears to conform to Terdiman's paradigm. In others, however, the resistance appears to be almost inadvertent, and the concept of "oppositional" writing that Ross Chambers develops in his elegantly argued *The Writing of Melancholy* seems more applicable. Analyzing works published during the reign of Napoléon III, when writers frequently exercised self-censorship, either consciously or unconsciously, Chambers contends that the oppositional status of such works is a "product of reading" that emerges only when one compares the narrative function of the text, which may actually reinforce the prevailing ideology, with the textual function, which "call[s] for a more subversive reading."[29] Between them, Chambers and Terdiman cover roughly the same period that I treat in this study, that is, the second half of the nineteenth century. I would like to examine a group of stories and novels that manifest the same sort of textual duplicity that Chambers found in works published during the heavily censorious Second Empire and that Terdiman identified during the Third Republic. Using the concepts they developed, I intend to reveal the ambivalence behind the writers' ostensible infatuation with the medical profession and the ambiguity of their apparently straightforward language.

The scientific basis of literary realism has long been recognized. Unfortunately, for the better part of the twentieth century, critics were content merely to outline the relationship between science and literature, pointing (for example) to Geoffroy Saint-Hilaire's influence on Balzac or to Claude Bernard's imprint on Zola. In 1991, Jean-Louis Cabanès added detail to the diagram with his magisterial two-volume study of the intersection between medicine and realism.[30] His study, an exhaustive compendium of medically-inspired descriptions in realist fiction, investigated with impressive thoroughness the realist movement's tendency to conflate the physiological with the pathological.

A year later, Lawrence Rothfield adopted a different angle of vision in his *Vital Signs*, a study of late-nineteenth-century English and French literature.[31] Equipped with a thorough knowledge of the history of medicine, Rothfield argued for a new understanding of the ties that connect the scientific and literary praxes of this period, distinguishing between clinical and experimental medicine, which he identified with realism and naturalism, respectively. In his view, the crumbling of the realist/naturalist movement and the rise of modernism can be attributed to "the decline of medicine's epistemic and ideological authority [and] the consolidation of medicine as a safe and unexciting bourgeois career."[32] Like Rothfield, I believe that the professionalization and "bourgeoisification" of the medical profession contribute to what he terms a "new wave of antagonism" against medicine. And, like him, I detect an evolution in the way in which medical paradigms inform the literary text. However, whereas Rothfield focuses on cognitive authority and generic issues, establishing a relationship of causality between what he sees as medicine's loss of prestige and the collapse of the realist/naturalist movement, I am more interested in interpretive issues and the explicit representation of medicine, medical discourse, and the medical practitioner in the literature of the period. Rothfield himself has suggested that a "purely thematic approach to the medical content in . . . novels would be valuable in itself, opening onto important cultural issues relating to the doctor's social status and professional role as well as the patient's relative subjugation or interpellation through stereotyping."[33] Although my approach is not "purely thematic," it makes no attempt to grapple with the thorny theoretical issues highlighted by Rothfield's study. For this reason, we reach somewhat different conclusions. It is my contention that institutionalized medicine continued until the very end of the century to hold sway over public opinion, professionally, politically, and socially, and that this enduring prestige of the medical professional in the absence of reliable therapeutic results was a source of considerable annoyance to the literati. Notwithstanding the presence of such ideal physicians as Balzac's Bianchon, I believe that we can find evidence of a resistance to medicine's hegemony even in the earliest and most ostensibly "respectful" realist writers. Like Rothfield, I certainly detect a tension between these two professional bedfellows, but I part company with him by situating the disintegration of the marriage at a much earlier date and by attributing it to different factors.

Although, as Bob Mitchell has shown, French poetry from the mid-nineteenth century on gives evidence of a preoccupation with the medical, I shall limit my study of medical presence in nineteenth-century French literature to prose.[34] Through a close reading of seven novels and two short stories published between 1857 and 1894, I shall first demonstrate that a familiarity with nineteenth-century medical texts can offer new hermeneutic possibilities and enrich our understanding of the literature in question. I have deliberately selected narratives that invite a "medical reading" by their almost ostentatious foregrounding of medical paradigms or by the prominence of physicians in their fictional worlds. The discovery of a simmering hostility toward the physician was an unanticipated side effect of my own reading of these texts. Thus my second goal is to show that these works, shot through with medical assumptions, which they vulgarize and appear to disseminate without ulterior motive, in fact can be read "oppositionally." From the apparently deferential to the playfully parodic and finally to the profoundly hostile, their representations of medical discourse and the medical practitioner show that what is at stake here is a campaign on the part of the literati to subvert the authority of the medical professional and in so doing to reappropriate the prestige and power they themselves formerly enjoyed. The works in question, all of which feature a significant medical presence, whether personified by a physician-character or represented by medical discourse, are Flaubert's *Madame Bovary* (1857); the Goncourts' *Madame Gervaisais* (1869); Zola's *L'Assommoir* (1877); Alphonse Daudet's *Le Nabab* (1877);

Huysmans's *En ménage* (1881); Maupassant's "La Relique" (1882), *Mont-Oriol* (1886), and "Le Rosier de Madame Husson" (1887); and Léon Daudet's *Les Morticoles* (1894). I have endeavored to select works that are representative of an era that was deeply preoccupied with degeneration in all its forms. This said, I am fully aware of the incomplete and arbitrary nature of any selection and of the risk that inductive reasoning will lead to reductive conclusions. Thus, I shall take care not to indulge in generalizations but simply to present my findings.

The works selected span nearly half a century. Why is this period of particular interest? My hypothesis is that, contrary to appearances, the tradition of antimedical literature reaches new levels of intensity between 1857 and 1894. No less virulent for being veiled, the attacks against the medical practitioners came at a time when the literati regularly rubbed shoulders with members of the medical establishment in their salons — when, in their eagerness to win approbation from these power-ful members of society, writers pored over medical textbooks, attended lectures by well-known medical figures, and consulted physicians so that their descriptions of medical phenomena would be clinically accurate. I have found an escalation in the level of cynicism and alienation expressed by the writers over the period I wish to examine, an escalation that is directly proportionate to the rise in stature of the medical practitioner. I postulate that this growing cynicism results, not only from a resentment against a social/professional group, but also, at least in part, from the ineffectual therapies that gave the lie to medicine's brash promises. It is not irrelevant that several of the writers in this group suffered from syphilis, a disease that struck particular terror in the hearts of late-nineteenth-century Frenchmen and for which there was at the time no known cure.

This study is divided into two major sections, with a transitional chapter between them. The first section (chapters 1–4) examines the novel's incorporation of medical discourse, the second (chapters 6–8) analyzes fictional representations of medical practitioners as characters. The link between the two sections is provided by a chapter on the physician-narrator (chapter 5). I shall proceed chronologically within each section. The first part begins with three novels that have in common their principal subject (female decline and degradation) and their adoption of a medical perspective. In *Madame Bovary*, it is not so much the medical profession per se that is targeted, at least not overtly, although Flaubert's contempt for the two-tiered system of medical education is manifest in his creation of the health officer, Charles Bovary. Less widely discussed is the novel's representation of an inflated medical discourse. The class responsible for this discursive inflation, the bourgeoisie, is here caricaturized in the person of Homais, who as a small-town pharmacist is identified with a professional class that supplied many of the nineteenth century's illegal practitioners. A knowledge of medical texts contemporary with the writing of the novel allows us to measure the depth of Homais's quackery and to better understand the function of the blind beggar, a character who has been the object of numerous critical studies. *Madame Gervaisais*, the Goncourts' patently anti-clerical novel, adopts a misogynistic medical model for the study of a woman's decline, while at the same time undermining the traditional opposition between science and religion and suggesting that physicians have collaborated with clerics to bring about the degradation of a socially and intellectually superior member of what Simone de Beauvoir was later to call the "second sex." *L'Assommoir*, a novel structured by oppositions, is preoccupied with filth and cleanliness. This opposition assumes new meaning when the heroine's demise is analyzed in the light of hygiene manuals, contemporary views on disease transmission, and medical studies of occupational hazards. Although there is no solid evidence that Zola intended to indict a medical profession for which he had considerable (and well known) esteem, Gervaise can be seen, at least in part, as the victim of a clichéd discourse that is medical in origin. Such an interpretation—"a product of reading"—is no less valid for being at odds with the prevailing view, according to which Zola's novels bear witness to their author's wholesale acceptance of medical hypotheses. Nevertheless, one must distinguish between the apparently unconscious resistance one uncovers in *L'Assommoir* and those subversive appropriations of medical discourse by the other authors in this study against which Zola's deference stands out in sharp relief. Indeed, the last novel to be analyzed in this section, Huysmans's *En ménage*, commonly thought

v. listy
Reads like a thesis ...

to belong to the author's "naturalist" period, reveals itself upon closer inspection to be both irreverently antinaturalist *and* antimedical. Unlike the first three novels in this section, *En ménage* exploits the medical perspective to examine the decline, not of a woman, but of two men, an artist and a writer.

The transitional chapter examines two short narratives filtered through a medical perspective, Maupassant's "La Relique" (1882) and "Le Rosier de Madame Husson" (1887). In this chapter I argue that the physician-narrator, far from the objective and reliable observer of human foibles he has often been thought to be, is himself subject to a diminishing pathologization that makes his own narration of events tantamount to a recital of his own symptoms.

In the second section, I return to 1877 to examine the first in a series of extended portrayals of the medical doctor. Alphonse Daudet's *Le Nabab*, published the same year as *L'Assommoir* and set during the same period (the Second Empire), contrasts sharply with Zola's novel in that it describes, not the working class, but the privileged high society. This novel inaugurates a new series, so to speak: in the first place, it features a physician not in an episodic role but as protagonist; in the second, it introduces a theme that will become increasingly popular, that of the physician as foreigner. Just as *Madame Bovary* had "displaced" and camouflaged the criticism of the medical establishment by focusing on a second-class doctor (the inferior grade of health officer was established in 1803 to deal with the "simple" illnesses of the peasantry and the working class) and an illegal practitioner, the pharmacist; just as the Goncourts in *Madame Gervaisais* had effected a geographical displacement by setting the action of their narrative in Rome; *Le Nabab* "decenters" its criticism by making its villainous and parasitic physician Irish.[35] However, a close reading of the novel reveals the charismatic Dr. Jenkins to be a generic "Other" who appears to be identified—at least metaphorically—with the Jew, thus uncovering a carefully concealed anti-Semitism on the elder Daudet's part. An analysis of Maupassant's *Mont-Oriol*, published in 1886, the same year as Edouard Drumont's *La France juive*, reveals a similarly disturbing xenophobia and an even more pronounced tendency to associate the physician with the foreigner in general and the Jew in particular. As disquieting as this novel's anti-Semitic, anti-medical subtext may be, it appears harmless indeed when compared with the overt anti-Semitism of Léon Daudet's *Les Morticoles*, regarded by some critics as more a tract than a novel.

In my conclusion I explain the rather widespread contempt for the medical practitioner that one finds among fiction writers, and the often ruthless mutilation of his discourse "sous le scalpel des gens de lettres" ("under the scalpel of the literati"), to borrow a partial title from a recent doctoral thesis at the University of Toulouse.[36] More importantly, I analyze the curious and unexpected conflation of anti-Semitism and anti-medicine that took place with increasing vehemence during the last decades of the nineteenth century. For, together with the hypocritical display of humility vis-à-vis the medical practitioner, the most distinguishing feature of the anti-medical literature of this period is its anti-Semitic and xenophobic flavor. The injection of what Natalie Isser refers to as "the poison of antisemitism"[37] into the fin-de-siècle debate between conservative nationalists eager to uphold religious tradition and the secular apostles of the Third Republic who placed their faith in the god of Science was clearly detrimental to literature, as examples such as Léon Daudet's *Les Morticoles* and André Couvreur's *Le Mal nécessaire* vividly demonstrate.

It would be a mistake to deny that there are positive portrayals of the physician and his discourse in nineteenth-century French realist literature. Balzac's Benassis and Zola's Pascal Rougon come to mind. Yet even in these apparently flattering portraits, there is ambiguity, as recent criticism has pointed out. Benassis, "the incarnation of the good doctor," is nevertheless powerless to cure tuberculosis, and the cretinism against which he struggles "disappears only with the last cretin's death." Despite the physician's many qualities as a man of progress, he is "without great curative powers."[38] Pascal Rougon, who, in Zola's words, was to be "brimming over with self-denial and tenderness" is not without hubris, that of believing himself to stand outside the curse of heredity.[39] Here, as in Zola's other novels, "a kind of hesitation can be felt sometimes, cutting against the grain of the medical positivism simultaneously espoused, unsettling the scientific assurance of the accusing subject."[40] It goes without saying that the hint of ambivalence towards medicine that one occasionally finds in Zola lacks the anti-Semitic flavor that can be detected in some of the other authors in this study. Indeed, it is not by chance that the author who drew his principal inspiration from science also defended Dreyfus. Nevertheless, because the positivistic faith of even the celebrated naturalist wavers at times, it seems appropriate to include him here. Whether subtle or blatant, the fears, doubts, and antipathies that characterize the literati's attitude towards medicine and its practitioners informed a large number of literary works published in the second half of the nineteenth century.

It is important to understand that this attitude did not arise in a literary vacuum. Although this study focuses on works published in the mature nineteenth century and is particularly concerned with phenomena that occurred during the early Third Republic, it is impossible to discuss this subject without at least a passing reference to Balzac, whose immense *œuvre* had a lasting influence on many of the authors treated here. As Graham Falconer points out, Balzac introduced "massive doses of physicality into a genre that had hitherto concerned itself primarily with the analysis of mental states."[41] Nor is it by chance that the longest chapter in Lucienne Frappier-Mazur's monumental study on Balzac is devoted to the human body. The role of pathology and hence of physicians in *La Comédie humaine* is simply too large to ignore.

Among the many physicians who populate the pages of Balzac's stories and novels, Horace Bianchon is the best known. Introduced as a medical student in *Le Père Goriot* (1834), Bianchon completes his medical studies under the tutelage of Despleins (said to have been inspired by the surgeon Dupuytren) and reappears either with or without his mentor in more than thirty works as the stereotypical liberal physician, a sensitive, moral scientist who inspires confidence and is summoned repeatedly for consultations. Often a skeptic where religion is concerned, he nevertheless defends its importance in one of his last incarnations when he attributes society's evils to "lack of religion . . . and the invasion of finance, which is nothing but the solidification of egotism."[42] The fact that Balzac, confusing fiction and reality as he lay dying, called for Bianchon bears eloquent testimony to his importance in the Balzacian imaginary.

Despleins himself plays a role as surgical consultant (see *La Messe de l'athée*). Halpersohn, a Polish Jew who is regarded as something of a charlatan, manages nevertheless to cure an esoteric illness in *L'Envers de l'histoire contemporaine*, and Benassis (*Le Médecin de campagne*) and Roubert (*Le Curé de village*) represent the archetypal country doctors. A few physicians lend a somber hue to the otherwise sunny landscape of Balzac's portrayal of the medical profession, among them the mediocre Dr. Poulin (*Le Cousin Pons*); the malicious Dr. Rouget and his self-important and unscrupulous colleague, Dr. Goddet (*La Rabouilleuse*); and the three indifferent physicians called to Raphael's bedside (*La Peau de chagrin*) who are more interested in diagnosis than cure. Balzac, in a word, was not blind to medicine's limitations, and the judgment expressed in *Ursule Mirouët* that "Medicine is one of the professions that require talent and luck, but more luck than talent" no doubt reflects his own opinion.[43] Jacques Borel, who emphasizes Balzac's ambivalence with regard to medical practitioners, nevertheless distinguishes between the generally honorable place reserved for them in his work and the ignominious role played by physicians in Proust's fiction.[44]

In addition to his fictional physicians, often inspired by real physicians of his time who can be identified rather easily, Balzac regularly cited the names of famous physicians in his work, thus obtaining a "reality effect" and anchoring his work in its historical context. Jean-Louis Cabanès has shown convincingly the way in which Balzac's representations are nourished by the medical and scientific controversies of his day.[45] In this, he quite obviously paves the way for Flaubert, Maupassant, Huysmans, and Zola, among others, but there is an important difference: Balzac's enthrallment with science—and with such pseudo-sciences as magnetism, physiognomy and phrenology—stemmed from his belief in organicism and his genuine desire to find in science a system that might support his own intuitive understanding of the functioning of the physical and social body. As Cabanès points out, none of the writers of the second half of the century shared this "totalizing ambition." Yet if their motives for incorporating medical discourse in their works were different from Balzac's, and their portraits often drawn with a rancor unknown to him, they did inherit his tendency to emphasize (and to link) social and physical pathologies and hence to give a prominent place to physicians in their fiction.

Let me close with a disclaimer. When I began my examination of "medical presence" in late-nineteenth-century French literature some ten years ago, I did so with no preconceived notions and certainly with no inkling that my research would take me not only through the *P* section in the Library of Congress catalogue system (especially the *PQ* section, where French literature is housed) and the *R*, *RA*, and *RC* sections (medical history and practice) but also through *QH* (biology), *QP* (physiology), *D* (history), *DS* (Jewish studies), *HQ* (feminism), *HV* (social pathologies), *N* (visual arts) and *ND* (painting), and many other letters of the alphabet as well. I learned quickly that the deification of the medical professional, a phenomenon that became especially common in the later years of the nineteenth century, and the growl of iatrophobia that resonates through the fiction of the period had to be set against the cultural forces that shaped the century. Such seemingly unrelated phenomena as the Industrial Revolution, the stunning rise in literacy and the concomitant development of the mass media, the birth of finance capitalism, the emergence of a French feminist movement, the increasing secularization of society, all of these forces, and others as well, had their role to play. However, let me stress the fact that I am not a historian, medical or otherwise, and that my excursions into the other disciplines interrogated in this study have had an overarching goal: to contextualize and I hope to illuminate the medical dimension that figures so prominently in the late-nineteenth-century texts on which this primarily literary meditation is grounded.

1

Madame Bovary's Blind Beggar
A Medical Reading

ℓ

There is no caste that I despise as much as the medical, I who come from a family of physicians from father to son, including cousins (since I'm the only Flaubert who is not a doctor). But when I speak of my disdain for the caste, I make an exception of my dad.—Gustave Flaubert

Flaubert's contemptuous comment about the medical profession, made at one of the famous "Magny dinners" and duly reported by the Goncourt brothers in their journal, may appear somewhat incongruous in view of the extent to which he drew upon medical knowledge in the creation of his characters and their stories. Yet there exists a relationship between his cynicism and his enthrallment, his condescension toward the medical practitioner and his respect for medical science. Although any one of his novels or stories could be used to stake out the parameters of his ambivalence—the unfinished *Bouvard et Pécuchet* offers a particularly rich source of medical allusions—scholars interested in what Lawrence Rothfield terms Flaubert's "medicalized realism" have typically turned to *Madame Bovary*. Rothfield, taking issue with Michael Riffaterre's reading of Emma's hysteria, contends that, in order to understand fully Flaubert's text, a knowledge of contemporary ideological presuppositions is insufficient and that a more technical understanding is required, specifically a familiarity with the discursive assumptions of medical science.[1] Rothfield illustrates the use to which such understanding can be put by studying the *Dictionnaire des sciences médicales* and other early-nineteenth-century medical essays, most notably those authored by Xavier Bichat. *Madame Bovary* itself suggests a study of these sources, since the novel alludes both to the medical dictionary and to the celebrated pathological anatomist, the former a symbol of Charles Bovary's relative ignorance, since its pages are uncut, the latter associated with the single competent representative of the medical profession mentioned in the novel, Dr. Larivière. Rothfield's Bichatian reading of Emma's hysteria leads him to postulate that Flaubert has projected his own distressing medical experiences onto his heroine, based upon the anatomist's contention that hysteria and epilepsy were gendered variants of the same disease. Rothfield concludes that Flaubert's motives in making extensive use of medical discourse in his novel are both biographical and sociological—biographical because Flaubert shared Larivière's medical knowledge as well as Emma's symptoms, sociological because the incorporation of medical assumptions allowed him to affiliate himself with a rising professional class "for whom technical skill rather than ideological purity or personal authority [was] fast becoming the relevant measure of value."[2] Rothfield's approach has much to recommend it, and although I do not believe that the passage describing Larivière's eleventh-hour appearance at Emma's bedside succeeds in mitigating the novel's unremitting pessimism with regard to nineteenth-century medical practice, my own analysis of the novel from a medical perspective makes use of many of the same reading strategies.

Medical readings of Flaubert's famous novel are not in short supply.[3] Nor are studies focusing on the function and symbolism of the blind beggar.[4] Oddly enough, however, the graphic details of the beggar's condition and the peculiarities of Homais's suggested therapies have never come under close scrutiny, despite the plethora of attention accorded to the novel's other medically inspired descriptions (Emma's hysteria, her poisoning, the clubfoot operation). Yet scholars have clearly been troubled by the grotesque nature of the beggar's malady, and William Paulson goes so far as to suggest that we cannot piece together the seemingly disparate elements in the description unless we place it in the context of "prior discursive and textual treatment of the blind."[5]

Flaubert, clearly, had departed from the tradition that equated loss of sight with wisdom, a tradition that in the nineteenth century produced such inspirational figures as Chateaubriand's Chactas. Nevertheless, most critics agree that Emma's encounter with this hideous figure is a "recognition scene" of sorts and is associated with insight. Variously interpreted as a symbol for reality, the devil, nemesis, conscience, "the hound of fate," or love in a bourgeois culture, the beggar is routinely reduced to his two most salient characteristics: his blindness and his general repulsiveness. With few exceptions, he is just as routinely ignored by modern scholars, who, in the wake of deconstructionism, focus their attention on Flaubert's unraveling of the realist enterprise, his subversive use of language.[6]

Flaubert's preoccupation with language is well known, as is his penchant for the medical metaphor. Indeed, the two phenomena, closely related, become fused in the figure of the blind beggar. The evidence for this assertion is both intra- and extratextual. To comprehend the beggar's role, it is necessary first to pinpoint the beggar's position in the complex network of relationships connecting the characters and then, making use of biographical and historical data, nineteenth-century medical writings, literary antecedents, and Flaubert's correspondence, to arrive at a diagnosis for the beggar's illness. Proceeding in this way, we will be able to understand how the creation of this complex character is consistent both with Flaubert's linguistic project and with his cynicism concerning the medical practitioner of his time, a cynicism that is also demonstrated by the novel's tongue-in-cheek incorporation of clinical discourse. To date, those who have accorded their critical attention to the beggar's role have emphasized his singularity and have tended to assume that he is, in his striking monstrosity, an original creation. However, a close examination of the passages in which he is described reveals him to be a collage of characters presented earlier. His physical blindness recalls the metaphorical blindness of Emma, Homais, and Charles (to name but three of Flaubert's characters who are blinded by one form or another of stupidity). As the recipient of Emma's last five-franc coin, he is the degraded ersatz of Léon and Rodolphe, who had been the beneficiaries of her sexual and economic largesse. As a living spectacle of disease, he becomes the incarnation of Emma's moral corruption. He is, finally, a social outcast and a mental deficient and, as such, the hyperbolic counterpart of the isolated schoolboy, Charles, whose lack of intelligence is a leitmotif of the novel.

In addition to setting up conspicuous parallels between this decrepit figure and the novel's protagonists, the text also undercuts the notion of the beggar's originality by establishing precedents for nearly all of his activities. He is identified with the organ grinder by his begging and the evocative quality of his music, with Charles's flaking plaster curate by his fall from a moving vehicle and his skin condition, with Hippolyte by his role as Homais's victim, with the novel's dogs by his grotesque mime, and with the novel's lovers, real and imagined, by his position as the last male for whom Emma spares a thought. From the bungling health officer who makes her his wife to the crucified Christ on whose effigy she bestows her last kiss, Emma's quest for the Incarnation of Love, for the real-life equivalent of dashing heroes encountered in her reading of eighteenth-century sentimental literature, ends with the beggar, recalling Candide's search for happiness, which ended in the company of a toothless and repulsive Cunégonde. Desire gives way to disgust, and the euphoria that Emma experiences when she believes she has found, in "the Man-God" (399), the Lover of her dreams, is replaced by a more sobering recognition: Love's last incarnation assumes the shape of the Beast of Concupiscence. Emma's final convulsion, as she sees the face of the beggar rising before her in the eternal darkness of death, is a hideous mockery of the convulsions that precede the "little death" of sexual intercourse.

To reach this savagely cruel climax, the narrative has led us (and Emma) through numerous "false incarnations," of which the most obvious ones are Charles, Rodolphe, and Léon. As we have seen, the *bad links* beggar's links to these characters are solid and highly visible. However, if we continue to interrogate the text more fully, we can also uncover links of a different sort connecting him with other men who awaken a certain prurient curiosity in Emma but with whom sexual contact remains metaphorical. For example, while the Duc de Laverdière and Edgar Lagardy are socially and economically antithetical to the downtrodden vagrant, they in fact prefigure him in numerous ways. The signifiers of decrepitude that characterize the debauched old aristocrat (his red-rimmed eyes, his deafness, his "pendulous lips" [109] from which fall drops of sauce, his childlike dependence upon others to help him eat) are transformed and recycled by Flaubert to describe the beggar's condition. And the agent of this transformation is disease: the infirmity is now blindness, resulting not from a natural decline in faculties brought on by age (as was Laverdière's hearing loss) but rather from an unspecified illness. The same may be said of his other characteristics: from red-rimmed eyes to bloody orbits, slack lips to skin hanging in shreds, dripping sauce to oozing sores, the mechanism of the transformation is identical. The aristocrats had seemed to Emma paragons of health and virility, and indeed, when confronted with the duke, she sees not the pathetic old man he has become but the dashing lover he used to be. In a serial substitution typical of this narrative, the old aristocrat is replaced by a younger avatar of himself, the viscount, who is in turn effaced as an object of Emma's interest by Rodolphe, himself finally superseded by Christ in a short-lived renewal of religious fervor. And then the cycle begins again with the opera singer, Lagardy, occupying a position parallel to that of Laverdière who, as unseeing object of Emma's contemplation, serves as a catalyst for her dreams of love. Like the Duc de Laverdière, Lagardy captivates Emma's imagination by his reputation as a capricious womanizer. However, as an itinerant performer, one who quite literally "sings for his supper" and whose song can be interpreted as a *mise en abyme* of Emma's story, he also anticipates the beggar.[7] Once again, the chasm that separates these characters appears at first unbridgeable—the healthy complexion ("one of those splendid pallors" [292]) and mellifluous voice of the former versus the skin eruptions and alternately thin and raucous voice of the latter—until a juxtaposition of the two passages reveals startling similarities. And, as was the case with the Laverdière/beggar doubling, the latter appears as a debased version of the former. To the languorous rolling of Lagardy's eyes corresponds the beggar's flickering pupils; to the former's tale of a tragic romance corresponds the latter's bawdy song; to the pathos of Lagardy's gestures of despair corresponds the beggar's "act" (374), which has been interpreted as a lewd mime of copulation.[8] The description of Lagardy's performance also has strong sexual overtones, from its allusion to the singer's "bel organe" ("beautiful voice" but literally "beautiful organ" [293]); the orgasmic cry, uttered by Emma, "that blended with the vibration of the last chords"; the phallic "unsheathed sword" (295) brandished by Lagardy; to Emma's reflection that the tenor must have an inexhaustible love "to be able to pour it out onto the crowd so abundantly." This reflection is followed by her fantasy of traveling the theaters of Europe with Lagardy, waiting backstage like a modern-day "groupie" to gather, "open-mouthed, the outpourings of this soul who would be singing for her alone." When the curtain falls, she sinks back into her seat, palpitating, exhausted.

The sexual innuendoes of this scene are of course not gratuitous. In fact, the opera scene, marking a kind of awakening for Emma in which she becomes—at least for a moment—painfully aware of the deceptive nature of art, functions also as a transformation of her romantic malady.[9] Thereafter, her "illness" takes on a more explicitly erotic cast: she is dominated, not by melancholy, but by a new kind of depraved sensuality. No longer credulous, as she had been with Rodolphe, she seeks in her relationship with Léon (who replaces Lagardy) not the ineffable pleasure of romantic love but the more earthy thrills of carnal possession.

If the opera had stirred in Emma bitter memories of her wedding day when, on a small path in the middle of a wheat field, she had walked toward the church "without noticing the abyss into which she was flinging herself" (294), the beggar's song offers a less romanced version of her downfall:

> Souvent la chaleur d'un beau jour
> Fait rêver fillette à l'amour
>
> Pour amasser diligemment
> Les épis que la faux moissonne,
> Ma Nanette va s'inclinant
> Vers le sillon qui nous les donne.
>
> Il souffla bien fort ce jour-là,
> et le jupon court s'envola!

[The heat of the sun on a summer day
Warms a young girl in an amorous way.
To gather up the golden stalks
After the scythe has cut the wheat,
Nanette bends down and slowly walks
Along the furrows at her feet.
The wind was blowing hard that day
And Nanette's petticoat flew away.]
(400–401)[10]

Here, the agricultural metaphor serves to tie together two of the novel's most important thematic strands, Eros and Thanatos. Virginal and unsuspecting on her wedding day, stooping only to pick thistles from her trailing wedding dress, Emma is transformed, in the course of the narrative (and by the beggar's song), into a loose woman, whose provocative posture and short skirt signal her sexual availability; whereas by her diligent gathering of the phallic sheaves of wheat she hastens her own demise, harvesting the products of the Grim Reaper.[11] From this perspective, the abyss she had failed to see on her wedding day is the dark continent of her own sexuality, consubstantial with the gaping maw of Death.

Early in the novel, Emma had dreamed of finding a real-life referent for words encountered in her reading: *ivresse, félicité, passion* (intoxication, felicity, passion). The beggar is blind, diseased, and imbecilic, the cruelly grotesque incarnation of a related trio: *amour-cécité, amour-maladie, amour-folie* (love-blindness, love-sickness, love-madness). As such, he serves as a monstrous cliché, the ironic conclusion to Emma's quest. However, when we examine his symptoms with the diagnostic tools available at the time the novel was written, we begin to see the outlines of an even more cynical picture. One such diagnostic tool is the multivolume *Dictionnaire des sciences médicales*. Useless, even dangerous, to the obtuse Charles, the dictionary is a rich source of documentation for today's critic.

The medical dictionary distinguishes between two types of feminine pathologies of love, *l'érotomanie* "which is simply the melancholy caused by an unhappy love, from which nothing can distract the patient"; and *la nymphomanie*, "uterine madness or metromania . . . hideous illness which transforms a previously modest woman into an unrestrained bacchante."[12] It is my belief that Emma's novelistic progress takes her from the first to the second, from *le mal romantique* (romantic malady) to what one could term *le mal vénérien* (carnal malady). I shall not linger on a discussion of the psychological foundation for such a transition, the studies devoted to Emma's hysteria being numerous enough already. Rather, I will focus on the physical representation of her degradation, the beggar, whose condition was intended to evoke the awful specter of venereal disease.

Perhaps the most significant feature of the lengthy first paragraph devoted to this nameless character (one of the few in the novel) is that it does not contain a specific reference to his blindness, although subsequently the narrative will privilege the epithet *aveugle* (blind man) over all others. In fact, the alert reader is given the information necessary to diagnose the beggar's condition even before the text has done so by the allusion to his cane, the orbital motion of his head, and the constant movement of his cloudy pupils. But there are other, more anomalous features: his eyelids are atrophied, his corneas blood-injected. Facial skin hangs in shreds around the eyes, mirroring the ragged clothing covering his shoulders, and a pus-like liquid oozes from the diseased flesh as far as the outer edge of his convulsively sniffing nostrils. When he speaks, he throws back his head with an "idiotic laugh" (340), and his voice has a peculiar quality, "soft and moaning at first, [then] piercing." Medically, this is a very complex picture, and the blindness appears to be no more than one symptom among many of a systemic disease affecting not only the eyes but other organs—the skin, the brain, the larynx—as well. Generations of literary critics have mocked Homais's attempts to cure the beggar with a diet and ointments, but none to my knowledge has reflected on the fact that, for the pharmacist, the diagnosis is not amaurosis (simple blindness) but scrofula. In the nineteenth century, this term was an all-purpose designation for skin pathologies of uncertain origin and presenting somewhat varied characteristics. Indeed, *Le Dictionnaire des sciences médicales* appears to confirm Homais's diagnosis, listing among the symptoms of scrofula cutaneous eruptions of various forms, especially on the head, inflammation of organs that contain many glands, such as the eye, tumors that develop on the eyelid, and secretion of mucus from the eyes. Advanced scrofula is characterized, among other things, by cretinism. At first glance, the beggar's condition appears to conform to this description.

But then what of his blindness? Even in its most advanced stages, scrofula alone was not believed to lead to sight loss. Furthermore, the campaign that Homais wages against the beggar after his failure to cure him is based upon the assumption of contagion: scrofula was not considered contagious. Moreover, scrofula, although of long duration and improperly understood, was considered curable. Flaubert's correspondence leaves no doubt that he intended the beggar's illness to be regarded as incurable. And finally, the scrofulitic's characteristic cough was missing from Flaubert's description. Such a departure from clinical accuracy was clearly not typical of Flaubert. How did it come about? And why?

Flaubert sought the help of his friend, the writer and former medical student Louis Bouilhet, for the beggar's symptoms, and the correspondence between the two men on this subject bears witness to the difficulty he had in the creation of this character, originally intended as a *cul-de-jatte* (legless cripple). But Hugo had already used a similar figure, so Bouilhet suggested instead "a big strong fellow with a canker under his nose, or an individual with a bare stump or one oozing blood."[13] Before writing his passage, Flaubert sought further suggestions ("Should my man have a facial sore, bloodshot eyes, a hunchback, a nose missing? Should he be an idiot? lame?").[14] Interestingly, Bouilhet's response is unknown, although Benjamin Bart believes that "its tenor can be inferred, as the final form of the Blind Man is an amalgam."[15] If Bart is right (and I believe he is), then Flaubert's choice of details testifies less to his concern for referential accuracy in portraying a specific illness than to his desire to evoke a certain etiological category. In fact, the beggar appears to be a medical composite, a "living" counterpart to that often-cited composite object at the other end of the text, Charles's cap, which with its disparate assemblage of forms and fabrics was an insignia of its owner's stupidity, its "mute ugliness [having] depths of expression

like a moron's face" (62). In the same way, the diseased and filthy
beggar, with his mime and song, and above all his peculiar collection of
medical symptoms, was meant to evoke a specifically sexual pathology.
Many of his symptoms—the loss of the eyelids, the ophthalmia, the
strange alteration of the voice, the skin eruptions—were associated just
as readily with syphilis or gonorrhea as with scrofula, and in fact the
distinction between these illnesses was often blurred. Although syphilis
had not yet been clinically proven to be a cause of blindness (in fact, the
syphilis virus was not to be isolated until 1905), it was, with gonorrhea
(more commonly known at the time as blennorrhoea) associated with
various ophthalmic conditions, some grave enough to lead to complete
loss of eyesight.[16] Indeed, gonorrheal ophthalmia is characterized by a
pronounced redness of the eye, herniation of the eyelid, and a secretion
that is described as follows by *Le Grand Dictionnaire universel* of Pierre
Larousse: "It's a pus-filled mucus, liquid at first and streaked with
blood, which thickens, becomes greenish and indistinguishable from the
blennorrhoeal secretion."[17] The condition, which when untreated leads
quickly to blindness, could well have been Flaubert's inspiration for
the description of the beggar. Furthermore, skin pathologies, especially
those that featured various types of eruptions, were widely associated
with sexually transmitted diseases in the nineteenth century, as the
alliance of the two medical specialties, dermatology and venerealogy,
shows.[18] Scrofula itself was associated with venereal disease, and the
Dictionnaire des sciences médicales lists, among its numerous predisposing
causes, "parents infected with syphilis, the premature exercise of the sex
organs, masturbation, syphilis."

The next question, of course, is why Flaubert would have brought
to Emma's bedside a sordid victim of venereal disease. Aside from
the obvious symbolic importance of such a figure, the extratextual
motivation was no doubt strong indeed. Venereal disease caused a
generalized anxiety in nineteenth-century France, somewhat akin to the
pathological fear of AIDS characteristic of the late-twentieth century.
According to Theodore Zeldin, 180 books were published on syphilis
alone between 1840 and 1875, and he does not include in that figure
"obscure theses, innumerable articles, works on other sexual illnesses,

the vast literature on female diseases."[19] Zeldin points to the immense popularity of a treatise on diseases of the sexual organs, marketed for "men of the world," which sold 7,000 copies each year between 1853 and 1862. The remarkable success of Debay's well-known *Hygiène et physiologie du mariage* (172 editions between 1848 and 1883) also suggests a preoccupation with the physical elements of human sexuality and the related topics of disease and dysfunction, although it did not include a section on syphilis. As Zeldin puts it very aptly, "It did not take Freud to make the French worry about sex. On the contrary, it might be argued that they became interested in obscure, unconscious and invisible sexual problems only when their directly physical troubles in this connection ceased to be overwhelming."[20]

The vulgarization of medical knowledge, which led, later in the century, to a truly medical view of reality, had already begun in Flaubert's time, and although he was later to poke fun at his compatriots' phobia ("Just about everybody is infected with it," he says of syphilis in the *Dictionnaire des idées reçues*), he himself had reason to share their concern.[21] Biographers agree that, by 1850 at the latest, he had contracted a serious venereal infection, most likely syphilis. Some believe that the onset of the illness occurred during his trip to the Middle East. A letter to Bouilhet dated 14 November 1850 offers compelling evidence: "I must tell you, my dear Sir, that in Beirut I picked up seven cankers, which spread together to form two, then one. Finally, they healed."[22] Flaubert's optimism was short-lived. A month later he was again suffering from syphilis's characteristic skin lesions. In accordance with its standard clinical development, the skin condition was followed first by impotence and hair loss, then by the secondary effects of the mercury treatment, swelling of the tongue and tooth loss. His physical appearance was repulsive, and although the symptoms clearly differ from those of the blind beggar, the evidence that Flaubert intended his character to be suffering from a related venereal infection is overwhelming. The fact that the passage describing the purulent flow of mucus from the beggar's eyes was suppressed by *La Revue de Paris* lends weight to this hypothesis. Although the journal that serialized Flaubert's novel excised passages for a variety of reasons and without explanation, the editors were particularly sensitive to those descriptions that might attract the attention of censors, and in view of the fact that they left intact the graphic account of Hippolyte's gangrene, it is reasonable to assume that their objection to the description of the beggar's eyes was founded on "moral" issues.

In 1836, with the publication of his influential *De la prostitution dans la ville de Paris,* Parent-Duchâtelet had performed a veritable autopsy of what has become known as the "oldest profession in the world." His study included a discussion of the link between prostitution and venereal disease and a proposal for hygienic reforms to solve what was rapidly becoming a national health problem. In his chronicle of a woman's downfall, Flaubert had seen fit to end his heroine's amorous odyssey on a particularly somber note by making her attempt (unsuccessfully) to prostitute herself. After evoking the economic debasement of love, it is thus not surprising that he would turn to that other scourge of sexual exchange, the "poison" that his contemporaries feared more than any other: venereal disease.

The reduction of love to a hideous pathological condition spread by genital contact recalls the famous scene from *Candide* in which the still-innocent hero meets his tutor after several months' separation. When asked about the deplorable state of his health (for Pangloss has been transformed by syphilis), the tutor replies: "It's love; love, the consoler of mankind, the perpetuator of the universe, the soul of all sensitive beings, tender love."[23] *Le Père Goriot,* Balzac's literary portrayal of the destruction of love by Restoration society, had featured a similar image in a crumbling, flaking statue of "l'Amour" that graces the courtyard of the Maison Vauquer: "Looking at its chipping surface, those who are fond of symbols would perhaps see in it a representation of Parisian love which is cured just a few feet from the spot."[24] The reference is to the Capuchins Hospital (also known as l'Hôpital des Vénériens). Into the base of the statue are inscribed the following words from Voltaire: "Whoe'er thou art, thy master see; He is, he was, or he should be."[25]

Considered in the light of these two antecedents, Flaubert's arresting personification of love's pathology may seem less than original. Indeed, this patent lack of originality may well be the most important feature of this ambiguous creation. If the beggar is, on the one hand, a composite,

Tim Unwin

the grotesque fusion of characters and images met not only by Emma within the novelistic space but by the reader in prior texts, then he becomes a perfect figure for the déjà-vu/déjà-lu experience that so distressed his creator. Furthermore, his scabrous exhibitionism and his salacious song solidify his identification with sexuality and with the most banal aspects of this widespread preoccupation. Nor is it by accident that the words to the beggar's song are borrowed from a story by Rétif de la Bretonne, that eighteenth-century profligate who was known as "le Rousseau du ruisseau" ("The Rousseau of the Gutter") and "le Voltaire des femmes de chambre" ("The Chambermaids' Voltaire"). Rétif, who had himself died of syphilis, was known for his inordinate appetite for a dazzling array of sexual perversions, especially incest, and the titillating details of his erotic exploits had only recently come to light, two biographies having been published in the early 1850s, one by Gérard de Nerval, the other by Charles Monselet. Flaubert himself, no doubt influenced by the medical environment of his childhood, had elected a clinical perspective in recounting his tale of an adulterous woman. Yet, for all of its realistic detail, *Madame Bovary* is but a variant on the age-old tale of the fatal consequences of feminine lust, figured so succinctly by the agricultural metaphor of Rétif's ditty. In one way or another, all of "Emma's men" have sown their oats: it is in gathering the product of this activity, in the harvest, that Emma marches steadily toward the tomb (*le sillon*, "the furrow"). It may not be coincidental that the term *sillon* was also a common item in the lexicon of dermatologists, used to describe certain forms of skin lesions. This brings us back to the specific nature of the beggar's condition and to his relationship with Homais.[26]

The incarnation of stupidity and blind faith in what have been called the nineteenth century's twin deities, Science and Progress, Flaubert's pharmacist is also the most ardent Voltaireian in the novel, pompously citing the Enlightenment *philosophe* at every opportunity. However, his utopian ideals put him quite at odds with his spiritual "mentor," and his own naiveté (symbolized perhaps by the fact that the first letters of his children's names can—with the addition of a diaeresis—be arranged to spell *naïf* [naive]) leads him to misread and misunderstand Voltaire, so that, for the reader, he is associated less with the author of *Candide* than with its protagonist. It is thus a sneering indictment of the pharmacist's stupidity that, while for Emma the beggar is clearly a devastating reminder of something incurably horrendous (whether it be her own corruption or that of love), the opportunistic Homais decides to cure him. As earlier in the novel with Emma, his diagnosis is simplistic, for he is as incapable of distinguishing between invisible cause and visible symptom as Emma had been of separating reality from illusion.[27] Furthermore, by attributing to his pharmacist the arrogant conviction that he can cure a blind man infected with what he believes to be scrofula, Flaubert is setting up a double contrast, burlesque in nature, between Homais and Christ, who cured the blind with his spittle, and between the pharmacist and French kings from Louis IX to Charles X, who performed ritualistic cures of scrofula merely by touching the afflicted.[28] Homais is neither Christ nor king, and his proposed remedy is as foolish as his diagnosis. Aside from the inappropriate prescription of a diet high in meat, beer, and wine to an alcoholic beggar who lives on scraps, the anti-inflammatory ointment would treat the external symptoms only, not the cause of the beggar's "horrible infirmité" (to borrow Homais's words). Statistics cited by contemporary medical studies testify to the poor results attained by such ointments, which, significantly, had attained a certain notoriety as a widely prescribed but ultimately useless treatment for venereal disease. An experiment involving ten thousand syphilitics, conducted in 1833, had proved its inefficacy.[29] Even if we accept as accurate Homais's diagnosis of scrofula (which is rather difficult to do, in view of the text's insistence on his incompetence as a diagnostician) the smug complacency with which he promises to heal the beggar must have been seen as laughable, given the mystery in which the disease and its etiology were shrouded. During Flaubert's time, a wide array of skin ailments, routinely diagnosed as scrofula, were subjected to a vast range of remedies, prompting the author of the *scrofules* entry in the *Dictionnaire des sciences médicales* to write, after listing numerous remedies, one as useless as the other, "if the reader isn't sick of reading such a farrago, I'm sick of writing about it; this is a hideous monument to the most revolting empiricism."

The failure of Homais's treatment is visible testimony to his quackery, making of the beggar a mirror image of the sign outside his shop, his blood-red eyes and oozing green pus a derisive complement to the pharmacy's ostentatious red-and-green display. And just as he had represented for Emma the last in several incarnations of love, the beggar stands at the end of a series for Homais as well. A potential obstacle to the pharmacist's social ascension and a threat to his reputation, he is the incarnation of disease, the eloquent emblem of the dishonesty of medicine's brash promises, as promoted by the most notorious of its (illegal) practitioners, the country pharmacist.[30] In this role, he is one of three victims of what might broadly be termed "medical malpractice" in the novel (the other two being Hippolyte and Emma) and one of several in Flaubert's fictional universe.

What then does he represent for the reader? A monstrous incarnation of concupiscence and disease, Flaubert's beggar simultaneously exposes the charlatanism of the novel's archetypal bourgeois and serves as a mime, repeating by gestures and words (the words of *another*) the tale of Emma's demise. Functionally, he may thus be identified with Flaubert, who chose to tell Emma's tale (and in so doing to mock the bourgeoisie) in the borrowed language of the cliché.[31]

The notion of *cliché* can scarcely be overemphasized. The beggar is, so to speak, a living indictment of banality, himself a composite figure who exposes through his morbidity, his poverty, and his vulgarity the meaningless clichés of sentimental and scientific discourse. The fact that his symptoms may point to venereal disease, that category of illness particularly common among the literati and which accounted for one of the nineteenth century's most pervasive phobias, solidifies his link to banality.[32] As Huysmans's decadent hero Des Esseintes was to say later in the century, "Everything boils down to syphilis." But the beggar's symptoms may also be said to symbolize the monstrous petrification of language. Victor Brombert, noting "a great deal of oozing, dripping and melting in Flaubert's fictional world," expressed his belief that Flaubert used liquid imagery to convey a sense of boredom and despair.[33] The observation is all the more pertinent when one realizes that this flow of fluids generally follows some kind of tumescence, whether it be the gush of blood and pus from Hippolyte's tumefied leg, the rush of sentimental clichés from Rodolphe's lips, or the grandiloquent flow of scientific commonplaces from Homais's pen. In this light, the mucus that oozes from the swollen membranes of the beggar's unseeing eyes is doubly significant. In the first place, it becomes the perfect figure for love, cynically reduced to the tumescence and detumescence of coitus. But it also becomes Flaubert's most eloquent metaphor for language, conceived as the ludicrous result of a pathological swelling, a putrid seepage, destined to congeal in the repulsive form of the *lieu commun*.

It is especially pertinent that medical discourse provides the source of one of the novel's most pervasive forms of banality. In this respect the beggar, who by his symptoms personifies the trite and the trivial, is but one of several characters who expose the foolishness of the novel's principal purveyor of clinical terminology, Homais. The other two principal "patients," Hippolyte and Emma, also furnish opportunities for the mockery of clinical language. Three examples will suffice to illustrate Flaubert's derisive treatment of medical discourse. The first occurs when Charles labors to comprehend textbook descriptions of the various malformations that produce the clubfoot:

> While he was studying talipes equiaus, talipes varus, and talipes valgus, i.e. strephocatopodia, strephendopodia, and strephexopodia (or, to express it better, the different deviations of the foot, downward, inward, or outward), along with strephypopodia and strephanopodia (in other words, downward or upward torsion), Monsieur Homais, using all sorts of arguments, exhorted the stableboy to submit to the operation. (242)

If the alliterative names of the clubfoot variations were not enough to provoke hilarity during "l'épreuve du gueuloir" (the oral reading test to which Flaubert submitted his fiction), the narrator's parenthetical "correctives" to the textbook language ("to express it *better*") leave no doubt as to Flaubert's intention to ridicule scientific terminology. Moreover, the structure of the paragraph establishes parallels between Homais and the medical textbook, while Charles is equated with the imbecilic stableboy as the object of a "solicitation." Despite his failure to understand the medical textbook, Charles will proceed with the operation, just as surely as Hippolyte, incapable of comprehending Homais's "reasoning," will finally acquiesce and agree to the surgery.

The second example of a calculated deflation of medical language is the narrator's often quoted reprise of the pretentious question that Homais asks upon learning that Hippolyte is in excruciating pain: "So what's the matter with our interesting taliped?" The narrative reply pairs Homais's clinical noun with a distinctly non-clinical verb: "The taliped was writhing in horrible convulsions, to such an extent that the apparatus in which the leg was enclosed kept hitting against the wall, hard enough to put a hole in it" (245). The use of the verb *se tordre* ("to twist" or "to writhe") is cruelly ironic: now it is not the stableboy's leg that is twisted but rather his entire body, as he writhes in pain. Furthermore, besides serving as a vehicle for the mockery of the pharmacist's pretentious use of a clinical lexicon, the question-answer and verb-noun juxtapositions underline the contrast between the subjective reality of the boy's unbearable suffering and the objective stance of the pharmacist, who regards the patient merely as an object of scientific experimentation ("our *interesting* taliped").

A final example of Flaubert's depreciation of medical discourse, one which simultaneously illustrates the ambivalence to which we alluded at the beginning of this chapter, can be found in the words of Dr. Larivière who, summoned to Emma's bedside as she is dying, realizes immediately that it is pointless to try to save her, the poison having already spread through her system. Yet he must endure the pharmacist's expatiations on her symptoms and the measures he took to diagnose and treat them: "First we had a feeling of dryness in the pharynx, then excruciating pains in the epigastrium, superpurgation, coma. . . . I wanted to do an analysis, Doctor, and *primo*, I carefully inserted into a tube . . ." (396–97). Larivière's curt reply betrays his impatience with such medico-babble: "You would have done better . . . to insert your fingers into her throat" (397). The fact that Flaubert elected to make the surgeon propose a commonsense solution in straightforward, unscientific language lends weight to the hypothesis that Larivière was inspired by the only physician for whom Flaubert professed respect, his father.

Hence Flaubert's expression of disdain for the medical caste, quoted at the outset of this chapter, is carefully camouflaged in *Madame Bovary*. Is Flaubert in fact ridiculing medical discourse, or is he mocking rather the wholesale purchase of a vulgarized medical discourse by the bourgeoisie? *Le doute est permis* (doubt is permitted), as Balzac would say. Ross Chambers, in his own "oppositional" reading of *Madame Bovary*, writes of the invasion of discourses in the novel, discourses which are "identifiable as *alien* to the text . . . ascribable to the characters themselves and not to the literary enunciation that is a kind of empty vehicle for them."[34] It is precisely this close identification between language and character that enables Flaubert to mock without appearing to mock, to "have it both ways" or, to use the words Jonathan Culler used two decades ago, to maintain the *uncertainty* of his text.[35] A remarkable tour de force, Flaubert's decision to make his foolish bourgeois pharmacist the principal supplier of contemporary medical discourse in the novel allowed him to mock the bourgeois infatuation with medical science while simultaneously appearing to join forces with medical practitioners of his day in decrying the unlawful practice of medicine. Similarly, Charles's inability to bridge the gap between theory and practice (his failure to comprehend the scientific jargon of the medical textbook and the resultant fiasco of the clubfoot operation) may be seen as an indictment of the profession at large or as a demonstration of the limited abilities of those who reached only the rank of health officer. The role played by the conservative provincial physician, Canivet, brilliantly conceived by the self-censoring Flaubert, can likewise be read in diametrically opposed ways. Like the beauty of Victorine Taillefer (Balzac tells us in *Le Père Goriot* that she is "pretty by contrast"), Canivet's competence depends upon who's in the neighborhood, so to speak. A full appreciation of the subtlety of Flaubert's portrait would require a juxtaposition of the two passages in which he appears, that of the amputation, which insists on his bombastic self-sufficiency and condescension vis-à-vis Bovary and Homais, and that of the unsuccessful purge, in which the groveling provincial doctor is scolded into submission by Larivière. Only Larivière himself appears as a positive representative of the medical profession, and the flattering portrayal of this physician is neutralized by the fact that, through no fault of his own, he is unable to save Emma. Thus, while our examination of the beggar's role and condition from a medical perspective provides us with insight into Emma's degradation and gives us a glimpse at Flaubert's carefully concealed antimedical agenda, the creation of this character is but one of the myriad ways in which Flaubert succeeded in belittling a profession from which he had been excluded by paternal decree.

2

THE DOCTOR AND THE PRIEST

A Case of Collusion in *Madame Gervaisais*

℥

Cliniciens-ès-lettres. Such was the designation that Victor Segalen used for Edmond and Jules de Goncourt in the title of his 1902 medical thesis. The unusual term, with its juxtaposition of the medical and the literary, points to a connection between the brothers' clinical perspective and their professional practice as writers. Indeed, the persistence with which the Goncourts illustrate medical hypotheses in their fiction, together with their tendency to present their heroes (and more often their heroines) as pathological specimens, suggest that they fully deserved the *honoris causa* degree that Segalen bestowed upon them. With the possible exception of *Germinie Lacerteux*, which is regarded as one of the founding texts of naturalism, their six co-authored novels are today valued more as medical curiosities than as literary achievements.[1] Furthermore, in their *Journal*, the Goncourts themselves summarize their accomplishment in medical terms: "We were the first to write about nervous ailments" (2:187).

Given this emphasis, it is somewhat surprising to note that a strong antimedical bias runs through their work and that, despite their reliance on medical sources and their apparent adoption of a medical perspective, the Goncourts felt themselves superior to and even in competition with medical practitioners. This supercilious attitude explains what Patrick O'Donovan has termed the "highly negative portrayal of clinical medicine" in *Germinie Lacerteux*, *Renée Mauperin* and *Soeur Philomène*.[2] Understandably, perhaps, critics have tended to ignore the antimedical dimension of their last co-authored novel, *Madame Gervaisais*, in which it is infinitely more subtle, but present nonetheless. Even Marc Fumaroli, who brilliantly exposes the duplicity of the novel's narrative techniques in his genetic study of 1987, asserts that the brothers are "acquiescent where the vocabulary and the formulae of medical discourse are concerned," although he does concede, based upon comments in the *Journal*, that they considered medical science to be nothing more than an "infra-littérature."[3] Through a close reading of *Madame Gervaisais*, I hope to explain the reasons for the Goncourts' antagonistic stance vis-à-vis the physician as well as the subtle mechanisms by which it is revealed.

Published in 1869, the year preceding the premature death of Jules, the younger brother, *Madame Gervaisais* has been regarded as a Janus-like text, doubly autobiographical in its anticipation of Jules's demise and in its retrospective interpretation of the death of a beloved aunt, Nephtalie de Courmont, after whom the eponymous Madame Gervaisais is patterned.[4] During their childhood, the Goncourts had spent many happy hours in the company of their aunt, an intelligent Parisian woman of means and a refined freethinker, to whose influence Edmond would later attribute his career as a writer as well as his passion for collecting. Nephtalie de Courmont had contracted tuberculosis, that archetypal Romantic sickness, and had traveled to Rome on the advice of her physician, in hopes that the more temperate climate might hasten her recovery. Instead of finding a cure for her physical malady, she had succumbed to the more insidious "disease" of religion, breathing her last on the very day on which she had been granted a private audience with the Pope. The Goncourts decided as early as 1856 to use their aunt's story as the basis for a novel, and they traveled twice to Rome (in 1856 and 1867) to gather information for their work. The influence of contemporary medical discourse on their rendition of Courmont's story is palpable, first in the strongly anticlerical tone of the novel, and second in their insistence on the pathology of their heroine's religious experience. Although the links between religious mysticism and hysteria were not to be fully explored until Charcot's work in the 1880s, Alexis Favrot had posited a connection as early as 1844 in his medical thesis, *De la catalepsie, de l'extase et de l'hystérie*.[5] Treating ecstasy as a morbid state, he had identified two nearly indistinguishable varieties of the illness, *l'extase mystique* and *l'extase cataleptique*, both with the same predisposing causes: "an exaggerated love of poetry, science, fine arts, and especially of religion."[6] Favrot had insisted on the body's withdrawal from contact with the outside world, using the classic example of Saint Theresa's mystical experiences to outline the symptoms: "One experiences a sort of dimming of intellectual activity—understanding, memory, will—[and] a kind of sensual delight not unlike that felt by a person in the last throes of agony, happy to die in the bosom of God."[7] Favrot's contention that women were particularly susceptible to these conditions, together with his evocation of the sexual nature of the ecstatic state ("a kind of sensual delight"), inspired the Goncourts, who, like many of their contemporaries, were convinced that women were especially vulnerable to religious influence. In addition to the work of Favrot, other medical monographs provided them with a descriptive model; indeed, as Marc Fumaroli has suggested, the narrative's evolution is largely determined by the successive descriptions of a series of pathological symptoms (61).

The Goncourts' belief, noted in their *Journal* on 11 April 1857, that "religion is part of woman's sexuality" (1:248) colors their description of Madame Gervaisais's religious conversion, and those few critics who have deemed the novel worthy of analysis almost invariably comment on this aspect of the work. Most recently, Emily Apter's provocative essay on what she terms the Goncourts' "mystical pathography" considers the way in which the maso-fetichistic heroine succumbs first to the visual seduction of Rome's opulent Catholicism, and then, as she listens to the dramatized chanting of Christ's Passion according to Saint Matthew on Palm Sunday, to an acoustic seduction, "a kind of orgasm of the ear," which finds its ultimate expression in the confessional, the locus of "a more violently sexual encounter [. . .] between ecclesiastical Voice and female Ear."[8] Like others who have commented on *Madame Gervaisais*, Apter focuses on the representation of the heroine, ignoring the role of the novel's other main character, her son Pierre-Charles.[9] Yet the child is present from the first scene to the last (in fact, it is to him that the Goncourts give the last word), his relationship with his mother provides one of the novel's principal dramatic interests, and his

Calvary is, by Edmond's own admission, the authors' only significant departure from biographical accuracy, thus their only true invention. (Although their aunt did indeed have a mentally deficient son, Arthur, this child died of meningitis before his mother's departure for Rome, and it was his younger brother, Alphonse, who actually accompanied Nephtalie de Courmont to Italy.) Few scholars would deny that Madame Gervaisais's decline into mysticism would be less poignant were it not for the fact that it causes her increasingly to ignore and abuse her small son by isolating him from friends, forcing him to spend long hours with her in church and eventually starving him, refusing him needed medical attention, and denying him even the smallest displays of maternal affection. Any understanding of the novel's subtleties must take into account the role played by the aphasic child who is related to his mother, not only biologically, but thematically, through a series of parallels and oppositions. Indeed, mother and son are part—perhaps the most important part—of the novel's vast network of binary pairs. In chiastic fashion, the novel records not only the mental and physical deterioration of Madame Gervaisais but also the painful cure of her son. The description of these contrary itineraries relies heavily on the medical knowledge of the time.

As a first step toward placing the novel in its historical context, we need to remember that *Madame Gervaisais* reflects in fictional form the medical profession's increasing frustration with the hierarchy of the Catholic Church. Despite their scientific pretensions, Parisian physicians, whose therapeutic results were not yet consistent enough to win the confidence of the populace, were finding it exceedingly difficult to replace the Church-supported "vitalist" view of health and disease with the "materialist" view that they espoused. The supporters of the "vitalist" view attributed the failure of individual organs to an alteration in the *principe vital* or "soul": suffering and pain, seen as punishment for sins committed, therefore had a redemptive function. A cure of the body required first a cure of the soul, with the priest playing an important role as healer, a role inherited from Christ himself. For the "materialists," on the other hand, disease was located in the organs, and its cure depended upon the physician's, not the priest's, early intervention. The debate that raged around the subject of the use of anesthesia in childbirth (weren't Eve's daughters *meant* to bring forth life in pain?) provides an example of the practical implications of such a philosophical difference.

In light of this struggle against what they considered to be the superstition of the church, a superstition that often retarded the physician's intervention until it was too late to be effective, the Parisian physicians' anticlericalism and their demand for autonomy from metaphysical concerns is understandable.[10] As the age of positivism dawned, the medical community was at first hopeful of victory in its battle against religious superstition. Encouraged by a number of important medical advances that took place in the 1860s, the physicians had good reason for optimism. This decade saw the publication of Claude Bernard's *Médecine expérimentale* (1865), a study that established the scientific basis for the "art" of medicine by emphasizing the importance of observation and experimentation. It also saw Lister's development of the antiseptic method (1867), which resulted directly from Pasteur's research on fermentation and eventually produced a dramatic decline in postoperative mortality. However, in counterpoint to these scientific achievements, the decade also witnessed the revival of an ancient belief in the curative power of religious pilgrimages, as evidenced by the immense popularity of Lourdes following Bernadette Soubirous's visions of 1858. Clearly, the battle was not yet over. A curious epidemic that had broken out in the Savoie mountain village of Morzine in 1853 and continued throughout the 1860s dramatized the clash: religious authorities interpreted the sickness as diabolical possession; physicians characterized it as *une épidémie hystérico-démonopathique.*[11]

When examined in the context of such events, the stance adopted by the Goncourt brothers in *Madame Gervaisais* is predictable, and Marc Fumaroli is correct in observing that the novel lends itself, like *Madame Bovary* (of which its title is an echo), to "an anticlerical interpretation" (47).[12] However, the undeniably strong influence of contemporary medical discourse, present throughout *Madame Gervaisais*, is deceptive. Just as Flaubert delivered his most stinging attack against religion, as well as his most ardent defense of science and progress, through the intermediary of one of his most ridiculous characters, so the Goncourts, whose skepticism extended not only to religion but also to contemporary scientism, exploited in *Madame Gervaisais* a number of revealing counter-discursive strategies. In adopting a medical perspective and incorporating the numerous clinical and postclinical discourses that contributed to that perspective (evolutionary biology, physical anthropology, degeneration theory, Social Darwinism, etc.), the Goncourts were using tools that justified their own prejudices (most notably, their anticlericalism and their misogyny) while simultaneously demonstrating that such tools could be weapons of destruction.[13] Perhaps the most intriguing aspect of *Madame Gervaisais* is that even as it "speaks" the language of medicine, it undercuts the authority of the physicians from whom this language emanates.[14]

Between the poignant depiction, in *Soeur Philomène*, of a medical resident who bungles a mastectomy (the patient dies), assaults a nursing sister, and succumbs to a fatal drug addiction, and the subtle caricature of the medical practitioners in *Madame Gervaisais*, there is a stark difference in tone. Thematically, however, there is a continuity between the two novels that may escape the careless reader. The following passage from *Manette Salomon*, published midway between *Soeur Philomène* and *Madame Gervaisais*, reveals the source of the Goncourts' cynicism with regard to the medical practitioner:

> On the second day, Anatole saw that [Coriolis] was so sick that he went to get a doctor, the practitioner who regularly ministered to the artsy crowd and whom half of the literati and the artists treated like a friend. He was a strange man, with the nasty yet smiling face of a hunchback, a twitching eye, and lizardlike eyelids. When he was seated at the foot of a patient's bed, he looked disquietingly like an old judge watching the suffering. He seemed happy to have a talented, moral person in his clutches, happy to explore the patient's fears and cowardice in the face of sickness, and his benevolent, unctuous facial expression was belied by a cold glimmer in his eye that revealed both the callous rancor of someone who had had an aborted career and a disappointing life and who was annoyed by the good fortune of others, and the curiosity that came from

his impious and pitiless study of humanity, which was trying to come to grips with the instinctive desire to heal inculcated by his medical studies.[15]

Redeemed only by his intellectual curiosity and his curative instinct, the physician is portrayed here as a rancorous enemy, at once father, judge, and reptile. By implication both immoral and without talent, he is a failed artist who finds relief from his acute jealousy when he watches the artist suffer. The Goncourts' projection of their own jealousy onto the physician, manifest here, also informs their representation of the medical practitioner in *Madame Gervaisais*. Cleverly adopting a biomedical model in their description of a woman's exploitation by the clergy, they maliciously juxtapose cleric and doctor and suggest that in spite of the antagonism that existed between these professional groups, they are collaborators at heart.

It has often been pointed out that *Madame Gervaisais* is the only one of the Goncourts' novels that is not set in Paris. The novel's principal theater, Rome, appears in fact as the antithesis of Paris. City of Faith, crucible of civilization, teeming with the uneducated indigent, dominated by the Roman Catholic clergy, Rome is the icon of the primitive. Paris, by contrast, is the city of science, high culture, Reason, capital of "Voltaire's country" (160). To Rome's reactionary clergy correspond the physicians of Paris, prophets of progress, resolutely turned toward the future. But Paris is also a city of "gloomy mornings" (78) that contrast sharply with the eternally blue sky and brilliant sunshine of Rome. Moreover, as a "museum city" to which many real-life nineteenth-century artists (Corot, Rodin, etc.) made pilgrimages, Rome speaks to the artist in Madame Gervaisais, who, having left Paris, "the city without art" (85), on the advice of her physician, Monsieur Andral, seeks the "rebirth" of good health, an appropriate goal to be carried out in a city that is associated not only with antiquity but also with the Renaissance. The humiliation she feels as she listens to the banalities proffered by her compatriots in the dining room of l'Hôtel de la Minerve serves to establish not only her own superiority as a Woman of Reason but also the deceptive nature of the contrast between Gallic intelligence and Roman stupidity.[16]

If the binary opposition between Rome and Paris, the Italians and the French, is blurred in the novel's opening chapters, so also is the distinction between Science and Religion and their two principal spokesmen, the doctor and the priest. Quite aside from the fact that Dr. Andral, her French physician, becomes an unwitting accomplice of the clergy when he urges her to go to Rome for the sake of her health, Madame Gervaisais's cynicism with regard to his prescription for a potion immediately calls into question the efficacy of the proposed "cure."[17] In fact, she takes the medicine, reluctantly, only because it may "stop me from feeling the fleas of the Minerva" (73). The medicinal remedy is thus reduced to the role of a mere soporific. Dr. Andral is credited with the ability, not to cure her body, but to anesthetize her mind, thereby rendering her insensitive both to the irritating fleas of her Roman hotel and, by metaphor, to the "nibbles" of the Goddess of Wisdom and Reason. Later in the novel, this task of stripping Madame Gervaisais of her reason will fall to the Roman Catholic clergy.

Madame Gervaisais's medically prescribed departure for Rome is the first step in a process of "dispossession" that had been inaugurated long before, when, following the wishes of her dying father, she had married an important government official. Increasingly aware of his wife's intellectual superiority, her husband had belittled her publicly. After ten years of marriage, his only contribution to her happiness was his final acquiescence to her request for a child. The fruit of this unhappy union, Pierre-Charles, having incurred brain damage during a forceps delivery, is incapable of producing meaningful speech throughout much of the novel. An example of the limits of nineteenth-century medical technology,[18] this botched delivery also raises questions about the competence of the physician, since Madame Gervaisais, whose difficult parturition was very nearly fatal to her as well, is restored to health by her maid, Honorine, "who stayed by her bedside for ten consecutive nights and saved her" (80), rather than by her doctor. Later, when she contracts tuberculosis, Madame Gervaisais is forced to abandon painting, "one of the most cherished pleasures of her life," an act of self-denial "that the doctors had successfully demanded of her" (85). Exiled by her physicians into a foreign land where she is constrained to play the alienating role of foreigner as well as the passive role of spectator, she who had once presided over elegant Parisian *soirées* and taken pleasure in artistic creation of her own, Madame Gervaisais suffers a fate that is strikingly parallel to that of her son, dislodged from his own "mother-country" by the physician's "brutal instrument" (101) and condemned to a role of silence and passivity. Indeed, one might say that, like him, she is from the start a victim of medical misjudgment. Betraying their own cynicism, the Goncourts highlighted the most futile of nineteenth-century remedies, and the fact that they observed the strictest accuracy in their portrayal of nineteenth-century medical practices does not imply that their goal was merely mimetic. The etiology of tuberculosis being unknown at the time, the most commonly prescribed therapy was a rest cure in a temperate climate, hence the credibility of Madame Gervaisais's sojourn in Rome. Similarly, women were believed to be prone to neurosis, a condition thought to be exacerbated by excessive mental or creative activity. The injunction of Madame Gervaisais's physicians that she cease painting is thus also entirely consistent with contemporary medical wisdom, all the more so in view of the widespread medical prejudice against female intellectual activity of any kind, which was said to interfere with the reproductive process.[19] In short, the medical practitioner, as catalyst both for the child's linguistic retardation and the mother's eventual fall into what the Goncourts see as the trap set by religion, is hardly an innocent bystander.

With a symbolism some might consider heavy-handed, the Goncourts time their heroine's arrival in Rome to coincide with the Feast of Corpus Christi. A slight, pale woman of thirty-seven, Madame Gervaisais represents the ideal consumptive beauty of the period, "a beauty that is superior in style and character to a woman's human beauty" (92–93). In addition to establishing a relationship between her physical illness and her "otherworldliness," the Goncourts' description of their heroine emphasizes her androgynous nature.[20] Ironically, it is upon her "flat-chestedness" and her "sexless and almost seraphic thinness" that her powers of seduction depend. Moreover, as an example of a highly intelligent breed of women "almost extinct today," Madame Gervaisais is the product of a motherless childhood. Reared by her father and nourished by his "masculine ideas and . . . liberal principles" (94), she had books in place of dolls, and she acquired self-knowledge through her reading of philosophy, scarcely a woman's pursuit at the time. Despite the maternal deprivation of her own childhood, Madame Gervaisais is characterized as a warm, loving mother. Indeed, descriptions of her relationship with Pierre-Charles bring to mind the Madonna and child paintings that proliferated in Italy during the Renaissance.

Contrary to the cerebral Madame Gervaisais, who is characterized upon her arrival in Rome as *surhumaine*, a "purely cerebral being" (93), Pierre-Charles is portrayed as a completely sensual, almost subhuman creature. His mutism offset by a keen sensitivity to the language of the body, he kisses his mother "on her face, her eyes, her arms, her hands, on different parts of her nightgown, with the caresses of a tender little animal, with kisses that almost licked her" (78). Besides anticipating Freud, this passage sets up the classic nature/culture dichotomy in the relationship of son to mother. In fact, the novel will ultimately record the destruction of "culture" by "nature," an operation which is prefigured by the image of the Coliseum:

> The ruin was returning to nature, as it happens in Rome, with stone that turns back into rock, marble that turns back into stone, communal baths that are transformed into grottos, palaces leveled by the soil, domes that are split open by the root of a bush, and blocks of stone that fall apart when a seed dropped by a sparrow becomes lodged in them. (83)

Philippe Hamon has noted that the ruin, "like all fragmented objects, . . . requires an intense effort at semantic completion on the part of the . . . reader."[21] In the case of the Goncourts' description of the Coliseum, the recuperative effort is not difficult. Madame Gervaisais's eventual capitulation to her emotions and nerves (i.e., to her [feminine] nature), makes her the nineteenth-century human analogue of antiquity's proud Forum. Her evolution conforms to a medically inspired belief in an immutable feminine nature that could be disguised, but not fundamentally altered, by cultural acquisitions.[22] Nature in the end triumphs: just as the smallest seed, dropped from a sparrow's beak, can sprout and grow and ultimately destroy massive blocks of stone, so also will Rome's religious spirit penetrate and transform the Goncourts' intellectually and socially superior heroine. As Martine Mathieu points out, "It's . . . not only the ghosts of childhood that are freed . . . but also the most primitive urges that deliver her up to a regression characterized by unbridled naturalness."[23]

Madame Gervaisais's "renaissance" is not a rebirth to health, but rather a rebirth to womanhood. And since, as a woman, she is by definition ill according to nineteenth-century medical thought, her "feminization" is a "pathologization." The transformation is the culmination of a lengthy process that begins shortly after her arrival in Rome. Having rented a furnished apartment near the Spanish Steps, she visits Rome's ruins, discovers "floral Rome," and experiences a sensual awakening that is coded as a morbid lust for death. Excited by the "fragrant good-byes" (88) of dying flowers, she had never before felt "this emanation of a flower's soul," which she now experiences as a "jouissance" (extreme pleasure, often orgasmic). Critics have noted the banality of Madame Gervaisais's Roman peregrinations and have accused the Goncourts of constructing a "hybrid" novel, part touristic guide to Rome, part mystical autobiography, part medical case study. Although Italy had inspired similarly composite works of fiction in earlier writers (e.g., Madame de Staël, Stendhal), the Goncourts were criticized harshly for what was considered to be a particularly indigestible mixture. The novel's early chapters, with their lengthy descriptive passages, may indeed try the reader's patience. Nevertheless, they have an important semiotic function. The heroine's first contact with Rome's Catholic pageantry, transcribed in the first person in the form of a letter from Madame Gervaisais to her younger brother, is a case in point. As "directress of his upbringing" (96), who had carefully led her younger sibling to a philosophy that rejected the supernatural, she describes with disgust a religious procession that features a military regiment, an embroidered banner of the head of Christ, blood raining down from the crown of thorns, an enormous cross carried by a sweating, groaning monk, and an altar held aloft by sixteen men. Expressing her repugnance for the "materiality" of religion, Madame Gervaisais nevertheless ends her letter on what is presumed to be a "light" note with a reference to a Catholic periodical: "They treat us rudely. The other day I read that freethinkers and philosophers were descended from orangutans" (100).

This hypothesis, however facetiously presented, fulfills two functions. In the first place, it suggests that the clergy are capable of appropriating scientific theories, twisting them to their own purposes. (Darwin's *Origin of Species*, first published in 1859, had been translated into French by Clémence Royer in 1861.) Second, it prepares the reader for Madame Gervaisais's return to a primitive, almost simian nature.

There is some irony in the fact that the decline of her intelligence and the mimicry to which she will be reduced, first through the influence of the Catholic faithful and finally through that of the clergy, is set into motion by her efforts to teach her son to read. The drama provoked by this effort, which causes the child to experience life-threatening seizures, is in fact preceded by a parallel drama involving Madame Gervaisais herself. Venturing out unwittingly on a day when the sirocco is blowing and the sky has a yellow cast reminiscent of "African paintings" (an image that reinforces the association of Rome with the primitive), she falls ill and has to summon a physician. Dr. Monterone, the liberal Roman "foreigners' doctor," functions not to introduce medical discourse into the novel but rather to satirize Roman morals and customs. A comic character, he is "the storyteller," "the chatterbox who jumps from one subject to another" and who punctuates every utterance, excuses every weakness, with a dismayed allusion to the power of the clergy: "Che volete? Siamo sotti i preti!" [What do you expect? We're under the control of the priests!] (105). Nevertheless, he does manage, through repeated bloodlettings, to restore Madame Gervaisais to a semblance of health, when the "malaise that he wasn't taking seriously" (106) reveals itself to be more grave than he had initially believed. Considering that bloodletting had already been proven inefficacious by midcentury and was no longer practiced by enlightened physicians,[24] Monterone's treatment reveals his ignorance—error is after all inscribed in his name—and the reader is justified in wondering if Madame Gervaisais's improvement is merely a fortunate coincidence, owing as little to his intervention as to the prayers of Pierre-Charles, who "writes" daily letters to God pleading that the life of his mother be spared.[25]

A striking structural similarity links this episode with that of Pierre-Charles's illness, which follows it several chapters later in the text. Victim at birth of the physician's forceps, which had compressed his "delicate little cranium" (101), the child is mentally incapable of responding to his mother's pedagogical efforts, and he becomes not just a "martyr of love" (107) but a martyr to her vanity. The novel records both her sustained efforts to teach him to read and the ensuing seizure, describing with clinical accuracy the orbital rolling of the eyes, the contraction of the mouth, the clenching of the teeth, the fever—symptoms culled from various medical sources, most notably J. L. Brachet's *Traité pratique des convulsions des enfants*, published in 1837. Once again Monterone is summoned, and his first question ("Would my little friend have had some upset, a cerebral fatigue perhaps?" [152]) reflects a common medical belief of the time that parents could provoke convulsions in their children by submitting them to "forced study."[26] Thus apprised of her own role in her son's illness, Madame Gervaisais falls into a state of delirium, then, regaining her reason, makes a pact with the physician: "À nous deux maintenant, Docteur" [It's up to the two of us now, Doctor!] (153). The intertextual allusion to Rastignac's pact with Paris in Balzac's *Père Goriot* enables us to see Madame Gervaisais's statement in a properly ironic light. Ostensibly nothing more than an agreement with the physician that they will collaborate to restore the child to health, her words evoke both the sacrifice of the ideals that had led to her misguided attempt to force literacy on her brain-damaged child and her first surrender to the materialism she had earlier found so offensive. The five chapters devoted to the child's illness and recovery chronicle the first stage in Madame Gervaisais's conversion, a conversion that had been slowly prepared in the preceding chapters by references to her Roman wanderings, her reaction to the events of Holy Week, and her progressive disillusionment with the Rome of antiquity. Her gradual rejection of the ideal of pagan beauty, associated in her mind with the strength, health, and bestial cruelty of ancient man, in favor of the Christian ideal of universal brotherhood, represented by a Christ she conceives as Healer of a sick humanity, is at first an intellectual, *reasoned* "conversion." However, thanks to the intervention of her two Italian landladies, Pierre-Charles's illness will engage her *emotions* and bring her to a "suspension of disbelief" from which she will never recover.

It is of course not coincidental that the episode of Pierre-Charles's near-death coincides with Madame Gervaisais's first, spontaneous lapse into faith. To the mortal risks associated with learning and hubris are contrasted the life-giving powers of instinctive behavior and humility. Madame Gervaisais's spontaneous decision to accompany the Italian women to San Agostino, where in the sordid, dusty obscurity of a poorly maintained church stands a jewel-encrusted Madonna credited with saving the lives of children and pregnant women, is clearly a turning point in the novel. Silently watching Roman women of all classes fall to their knees before the holy icon in order to kiss "this foot that had been worn away, devoured by kisses, half of its toes, recast in gold, having become webbed through the action of the adoring mouths and lips" (156), Madame Gervaisais, at first shocked by the idolatry, is suddenly "propelled as if by a spring" (158), throws herself upon the foot, which she kisses "madly" as she recites a childhood prayer, and then dissolves into sobs. Once again, in this description of a woman's conduct, one discerns two medical assumptions, first, the triumph of emotion over reason that defines the Feminine, and second, the imitative nature of feminine behavior. Madame Gervaisais reverts to an infantile state, a regression that will subsequently be encouraged by her confessors but is also consistent with the prevailing medical judgment regarding the fundamentally childlike nature of women.[27]

The sudden disappearance, two days later, of Pierre-Charles's symptoms, facetiously attributed by Dr. Monterone to a miracle that could never have occurred "if the Madonna hadn't given a little push to the unworthy Doctor Monterone" (159), is a source of great joy to Madame Gervaisais, who experiences this rebirth of her child as an intense pleasure even as she suffers the embarrassment of knowing that her son's "resuscitation" is being attributed in the neighborhood to her faith and to the Virgin's intervention. Her Balzacian pact with the doctor assumes new meaning in the context of her child's "miraculous" recovery.

More pointedly than the intertextual reference, however, an iconographic allusion seems imbued with a semiotic value that transcends the limits of this episode and offers a key to the interpretation of the entire novel. I am referring to the allusion—the second—to Raphael's *Transfiguration of Christ*. The first reference to this painting, Raphael's final work, comes early in the novel, when Madame Gervaisais, her maid, and her son take up residence in their first Roman apartment. Splashed with sunlight, the apartment nevertheless has its dark corners, and the Goncourts' description of this space is a literary chiaroscuro of which the canvas, hanging in the shadows, becomes a *mise-en-abyme*. Madame Gervaisais's feeling of well-being in the presence of this work of art is highly significant: "She felt as if she had found her special place, that beloved spot that every woman chooses, which she inhabits in order to claim it for herself, to be happily and quietly *in her own company there*, to read, write, and dream there" (75; emphasis mine). In order to appreciate the ironic dimension of the implicit identification between Madame Gervaisais and the Transfigured Christ—an irony that will become apparent only at the novel's conclusion—the reader needs to have some familiarity with Raphael's painting and the Goncourts' opinion of it. The canvas represents the Gospel story of Christ's Transfiguration, as recounted in Matthew, Mark, and Luke. Elijah and Moses float on either side of Christ, and Peter, James, and John crouch below, dazzled by the radiant light in which their Master is bathed. To this Biblical narrative, Raphael has joined, in the lower part of the canvas, a representation of the possessed boy who is cured by Christ when he descends from the mountain after the Transfiguration, a story that follows the Transfiguration narrative in all three Gospels. In Raphael's portrayal of the boy, however, we do not see the cure but rather the despair that precedes it. Raphael freezes in space the euphoric experience of the Transfiguration and the dysphoric tale of the disciples' *failure* to cure the child, "the rapt theophany of the mountain and the woebegone suffering of the valley."[28] An agitated crowd that includes the afflicted child, his parents, and several other figures, presumably the disciples, fills the lower part of the canvas. Several of the painted figures reach toward the Transfigured Christ, thus linking the two narratives. From the Gospels we know that Christ will heal the child, attributing His disciples' inability to do so to their unbelief. But in Raphael's version, the boy is made to wait.[29]

3   Raphael, *Transfiguration of Christ*, 1517.
Original held by the Vatican Museum, Rome.

I would like to suggest that the Goncourts, who despised Raphael, intended nonetheless to use his painting as a unifying symbol, juxtaposing Madame Gervaisais's fate with that of her son. This hypothesis is supported by the fact that the *Transfiguration* is again evoked in the chapter describing Pierre-Charles's seizure, when his mother, observing the manifestations of his terrible illness, "the most barbaric of childhood illnesses" (154), recalls the painting: "Suddenly, the image of the possessed little boy of the *Transfiguration* flashed across her mind and terrified her: she saw his mouth when she looked at her son!" (154). The allusion to the contorted grimace of the convulsing child is convincing enough; however, for the reader familiar with the Goncourts' comments on Raphael's masterpiece in their *Journal*, the passage is even more suggestive, for it evokes the extent to which the refined and artistic Madame Gervaisais is being captivated by the grotesque materialism of the Holy City. The Goncourts accused Raphael of degrading a supernatural experience, vulgarizing "the *Sursum corda* of Christianity": "That's Christian? I don't know a single painting that disfigures Christianity by the use of a more blatant material image, and I know no canvas that has represented it in a more ordinary idiom, in a more vulgar beauty" (3:95).[30] For the Goncourts, Raphael's prosaic distortion of Christianity is but a metonymy of Rome's, and Madame Gervaisais's fascination with the painting is premonitory. In the remaining chapters, she succumbs increasingly to the seduction of the material; her evolution, more akin to a *disfiguration* than a *transfiguration*, follows its inexorable course. Monterone disappears from the scene, to reappear only briefly when Honorine summons him to bleed her mistress. The Italian women who initiate Madame Gervaisais into the mysteries of Mariolatry are replaced by the Countess Lomanossow, a Russian mystic who, by her example but more importantly by her gift—a small notebook entitled *Pensées religieuses* that contains the name of a Jesuit priest—propels Madame Gervaisais toward mysticism. The Goncourts insist on the sexual nature of this experience: a "tender, almost moist orifice" (172) is opened in her heart, and this opening is penetrated by the little book, with its "loving style, enveloping language, with the familiarity of the ideas and the words, the benign naiveté, easy-going simplicity, pretty, and graceful images that are at once piquant and comfortable" (173). However, the book speaks to her, not in the tender idiom of the lover, but in the language of a nursemaid, addressing "the Christian childhood of a soul" (172). The gentle persuasion exercised by this book, which awakens her senses to "the intoxication of heaven and earth . . . of a loving animality . . . of a nature full of vigor" (173), is completed when she begins to visit the seductive Gesù church, the quintessential example of Jesuit architecture, built in the Baroque style during the Counter Reformation to bring the faithful back into the fold through its openly sensory and emotional appeal. Here, her "lazy intellect" abandons itself to the "tenderness of this Jesuit art, as soft and caressing as the touch of a lover's hand" (174). An allusion to the ecstasy of Saint Theresa (175), which, particularly since the appearance of Bernini's famous sculpture, had been considered to have an erotic dimension, leaves little doubt as to the nature of Madame Gervaisais's pleasure, and while it is true that mystical love had borrowed the vocabulary of erotic love since the Middle Ages, the Goncourts' hyperbolic exploitation of this topos is at best irreverent. Madame Gervaisais's susceptibility to this kind of seduction is ascribed to her age, the action of this kind of spiritual sensation being "so powerful in a woman's body when she's reached her change of life" (176). She is, in short, undergoing "a sort of 'turning around' of her nature" (176), a kind of spiritual and intellectual menopause.

Madame Gervaisais's metamorphosis, involuntarily initiated by her Parisian physician and encouraged by her Italian landladies and the Russian countess, cannot be completed without the direct intervention of the Roman Catholic clergy who are, in fact, the principal actors in this drama. The theatrical metaphor is not gratuitous. A sermon heard in the Gesù, in which she feels personally attacked and which she experiences as a public disrobing of her soul, is delivered by

> one of the Order's most talented members; an actor, a mime, *com-mediante, tragediante*, whose gesturing, ambulatory eloquence paced up and down the platform, and whose dramatic passion brought the house down from his pulpit. He ranted, he cried, he sobbed, he raised his voice, he made it break, he groaned and he thundered, in

a sermon that gave to his public all the emotions and the illusions of a theatrical performance. (179)[31]

Like Emma Bovary at the opera, Madame Gervaisais participates fully in the drama and feels herself to be the object of the actor's message and gaze. But whereas Emma had experienced Edgar Lagardy's words as a seduction, Madame Gervaisais feels deeply violated—raped—by the priest's angry invective against a faithless woman and has the sense that her very conscience has been penetrated, a suspicion that will find expression when she accuses her domestic, Giuseppe, of stealing her diary. The presentation of Madame Gervaisais as a soul in turmoil, the passive victim of an auditory penetration, is essential to an understanding of the Goncourts' anticlerical message. For if all of Madame Gervaisais's senses had been excited by the grand seduction that is Rome, it is through the ear that the clerics themselves will gain access to her soul, through the ear that she will become truly penetrated by "religion" as personified by Christ. The figure of Christ first manifests itself, for no apparent reason, "when her mind is unoccupied" (147). Much later, after she has succumbed to the violent emotions awakened within her by what Apter terms the "acoustic register" (first the plainsong, then the violent sermon, and finally the exhortations of her two confessors), she will experience the "inexpressible pleasure" (234) of having her "young Master" within her. Her mystical experience, encoded in sexual terms as an "insinuating penetration" (235), brings her to a union with Christ that is so complete that in the silence of her soul she hears words which, emanating from Him, "seemed to her . . . not to enter through her ears, because they resonated so strongly in the depths of her being!" (235). The irreverent nature of the Goncourts' representation lies not only in the profanation of the mystical experience (which they assimilate to coitus) but also in what might be interpreted as a veiled allusion to the Biblical account of the Annunciation. The Virgin, "impregnated" by the words of the angel Gabriel, will give birth to the Word. Madame Gervaisais will likewise be "penetrated" through acoustic channels, and will find Christ within her. But she is no longer presented as a latter-day Virgin, for now the Christ who penetrates to the depths of her being is not Son but Lover, "this Lover God" (234) who pays her nocturnal visits and robs her of her sleep. Indeed, her hesitation to implore the intercession of the Mother of Christ is mischievously attributed by the Goncourts to "the wife's natural jealousy for her husband's mother" (247), a banal comparison that calls to mind the comic image of the Virgin as possessive mother-in-law.

"Vast embrace, immense holy contagion: this is Religion in Rome" (183). The Goncourts' provocative metaphor, which suggests that ecclesiastical Rome has an influence at once erotic and pathological, is at the center of their interpretation of religious conversion. We have already seen how mystical union with Christ is reduced to carnal possession. Similarly, the sacraments are shown as metaphors for sexual intercourse, and this from their earliest novels onward.[32] What is perhaps less obvious is the insistent suggestion that the priest is to Rome what the physician is to Paris. This leads us to the second part of the Goncourts' formula. To what degree does their novel justify the contention that religion in Rome is an "immense contagion"?

In the first place, it is worth recalling that the Rome of *Madame Gervaisais* functions semiotically as a hospital, a space to which the sick and dying are sent for a cure. And like nineteenth-century hospitals that in the popular imagination were identified—and for good reason—with death, Rome is inhabited by the Grim Reaper. To the visitor dazzled by the pomp and pageantry of Rome's religious festivals, the presence of death may not be immediately apparent, but just as the young nursing sister in *Soeur Philomène* had come to detect, beneath its apparent calm and order, "what the hospital hides so admirably from first glances," so does Madame Gervaisais grow to recognize the myriad faces of death that haunt the Eternal City, from the wilting roses of the flower markets to the catacombs through which she drags her long-suffering son.[33] In this *ville-hôpital*, priests, like pre-Pasteurian hospital physicians, are carriers of disease. However, whereas physicians, in their ignorance of hygiene, unknowingly transmit disease from one patient to the next, the clergy, putative healers in the lineage of Christ, spread the sickness of religion with full awareness of what they are doing. It is in the intimacy of the confessional that they infect the faithful, and the Goncourts' use of a medical metaphor to describe their relationship with their penitents is imbued with a malicious irony. Madame Gervaisais's first confessor, Father Giansanti, diagnoses her illness as "scruple sickness" (199) and laments that the prognosis for one afflicted with this malady, "the most difficult one to cure" (198), is poor. His prescription, delivered "in the deep tones of a physician of souls who would like to engrave a prescription on a sick mind," requires that she obey her spiritual director in all things because "he is replacing God" (200). While it is obvious that the extended metaphor is intended to heap scorn upon the priest, this allusion, not to *le sacerdoce de la médecine* (the priesthood of medicine) but rather to *la médecine du sacerdoce* (the medicine of the priesthood), is a double-edged sword.

Both physician and priest seem to possess a power over life and death. Both are associated with God. Both, finally, minister to the "faithful." In *Madame Gervaisais*, the equation between these two upholders of patriarchal tradition is strengthened by methodological similarities: Giansanti "purges" the Goncourts' heroine when he demands her complete submission. His penitent, who balks at first at his demand, comes to feel a curious pleasure in the moral suffering required by the sacrifice of one's will, and in a clearly masochistic surge of faith, she decides to seek a less indulgent confessor. Her choice of the sadistic Trinitarian, Sibilla, whose prophetic function is onomastically determined, allows the Goncourts to extend the medical metaphor still further. Sibilla, a violent man who had devoted himself to the conversion of black Africans, had agreed to accept Madame Gervaisais as penitent only after the Holy Father himself had intervened:

> In Father Sibilla's spiritual direction, Madame Gervaisais found a brutality similar to that of those great surgeons from the lower classes of society, humane and gentle with their hospital patients but severe with high society, with those they sense are different from them and who bring to them the annoyance of an education, a superiority. (216)

Besides recalling her jealous husband, whose oppression had taken the form of "a hypocritical persecution, the stubborn, incessant and tiresome persecution of a small mind" (136), this passage again links the priest with the medical practitioner, in this case the surgeon. As Marc Fumaroli points out, the Goncourts were not the first to have made this comparison: in *Le Prêtre, la Femme et la Famille*, Michelet had drawn an analogy between the two professions, both of which, in his view, lead to insensitivity, but had pointed out that this insensitivity may be salutary for the surgeon who needs a steady hand, whereas for the priest an unsympathetic attitude could impede the "cure" of the penitent. The Goncourts, however, introduce a new element into the comparison: both priest and surgeon—and they refer specifically to "those great surgeons from the lower classes," a formula that evokes the barber-surgeons of an earlier era, when surgery required less, not more, training than internal medicine—abuse their power, taking a perverse delight in humbling the exalted. If, at the time the Goncourts wrote *Madame Gervaisais*, crude surgical procedures, the unavailability of local anesthesia, and the still widespread ignorance of sepsis and antisepsis meant that surgery was regarded as a last alternative, preferable only to certain death, their representation of the priest—and by extension the surgeon—as sadist merits scrutiny.[34]

The brutality of nineteenth-century medicine is well known. Combined with a lack of confidence in their efficacy, the fear of such treatments as leeching, bleeding, and blistering and the administration of such medicines as emetics and cathartics often deterred patients from seeking treatment for their ailments until they were too far advanced to be curable. Unpleasant, uncomfortable, and often painful, these remedies were characteristic of a time that has come to be known as "the era of heroic therapy," an era when the patient, not the doctor, was hero.[35] The Goncourts themselves often experienced suffering at the hands of their physicians, and they record their trials in the *Journal*, complaining most vociferously about hydrotherapy. Their allusion to "the fear of that rain of torture that makes every bone in your body scream in pain" (2:193), contemporaneous with the last stages of the composition of *Madame Gervaisais*, provides strong evidence of their perspective. When placed in the context of comments made about surgery, mostly during the course of their research for *Soeur Philomène*, their antimedical prejudice becomes even clearer. After one of the numerous hospital visits they made in preparation for the writing of this novel, they wrote in the *Journal*: "When you see charts attached to beds with the words 'Operated on (date),' you're really tempted to find Providence abominable, and to look upon the God who created surgeons as an executioner" (1:644). Observing that as a result of their hospital research, they felt "unusually aroused [sexually]" (1:644), they ponder the link between suffering and sensuality: "I read somewhere that people who looked after the ill were more inclined toward sensual pleasures than others. What an abyss this is!" (1:644).[36] Their suspicion is confirmed several years later when, during a conversation with Doctor Philippe, a kidney surgeon, they learn that he considers surgery his "absinthe" because it never fails to stimulate his appetite. Philippe reveals that the attention required by a surgical intervention causes "such a massive effort at concentration that he's famished afterwards" (2:170).

Sibilla, for his part, is conscious that he has "the overabundance of martyrs' blood in his veins" (215), a fluid excess that recalls Chateaubriand's René, a sexually frustrated adolescent who is "overwhelmed by an overabundance of life."[37] The mechanism underlying Father Sibilla's ferocity could hardly be more clearly delineated: just as surgery is accompanied by a fluid expense for the Goncourts' medical friend, Dr. Phillipe, so does Sibilla seek—and find—an outlet for his vascular surfeit in the "surgery" of confession. However, whereas the pathological nature of the surgeon's postoperative hunger is only suggested, the priest's sadism is explicit. The scorn and condescension with which Sibilla treats his willing penitent, the joy he takes in prescribing "things that were repugnant to her mind and offensive to her taste" (216) are but compensation for repressed desires: "This self-torturer, who had had to struggle against the passions and the hot-bloodedness of his native country and who had managed to deaden his violent appetites, had naturally become a moral torturer for others, and for this woman in particular" (217).

Michelet's distinction between surgeon and priest notwithstanding, when the Goncourts describe the "willful harshness" (216) of Father Sibilla, when they use the same grammatical structure, even two of the same verbs to describe his spiritual direction of his eager penitent ("he manipulated [her soul], palpated it, turned it over" [216]) and the medical examination of their physician ("he palpates me, he turns me over, he auscultates me"), the coincidence merits our attention.[38] Madame Gervaisais has in effect replaced her physicians by priests, taken her care out of the hands of the medical profession and transferred it to that of the clergy. Given the association of therapy with suffering, there is some logic in the fact that she abandons Father Giansanti in favor of Father Sibilla because the former doesn't make her suffer enough. By forcing her to sever all human ties, including the one that connects her with her infirm son whom he regards as divine punishment for his mother's earlier skepticism in matters of religion (a classic example of a vitalist position), Father Sibilla continues the work of destruction begun by his comparatively benign predecessor, Giansanti.[39] This "amputation" is accompanied by a metaphorical lobotomy when he attempts to kill all thought within her, to "reduce this learned, arrogant faith to the Biblical simplicity of stories intended for children and Rome's childlike populace" (219), by forbidding her to read anything but the *Imitatio christi* and popular devotional brochures. Dispossessed of her reason, forced to submit even to the most harsh and unreasonable dictates of her confessor, Madame Gervaisais indeed becomes childlike, a transformation that allies the priest with the physician as an empiricist charged with establishing the fundamentally infantile nature of Woman. Her regression is not only emotional but social, the latter figured in her move to a dilapidated apartment in the Trastevere, "an aggressively low-class neighborhood" (220), and by the gradual deterioration of her refined, artistic tastes: "The artist, the woman predestined for refined aesthetic pleasures, had succeeded in transforming her exquisitely refined senses into the senses of the common people" (233).

The arrival on the scene of a second physician, the charlatan Pacifico Scarafoni, is deeply meaningful in the context of Madame Gervaisais's degradation. Attributing his ignorance to the difficulty one has in learning anatomy in Rome, "where, for medical studies, you're only provided with fragments of female corpses instead of the whole cadaver" (231), an allusion to the female dismemberment and objectification that is metaphorized throughout the novel, Scarafoni is presented as an accomplice of the clergy, whose favor he had won by his hypocritical display of religious fervor. In fact, he had been referred to Madame Gervaisais by Sibilla himself, who had misled his penitent into believing that the physician was responsible for the care of Prince Maximiliani's household, when in fact he practiced medicine only on the aristocrat's animals. Madame Gervaisais, fragmented, destroyed, deprived of her reason, has been reduced to the sensual existence of the lower species. It is now she, rather than her son, who is animalistic, and this in more than one sense. No longer capable of describing her own physical symptoms, she listens in silence as her maid explains her mistress's medical needs to a shabbily attired physician who inspires little confidence. Scarafoni, learning that he had been sent for on the recommendation of Father Sibilla, overcomes his patient's initial skepticism by proposing to cure her with "famous powders" that have been mixed with "paste made from Martyrs' remains" (232). The protean Madame Gervaisais, linked by name and nature to the martyred brothers Gervais and Protais, is incapable of resisting this "miraculous" remedy. Her fate is thus sealed through the collaboration of medicine and religion.

It is not surprising, given Scarafoni's incompetence, that Madame Gervaisais's physical state deteriorates in tandem with her mental state, and that this deterioration, in a causal relationship with her experience of religious ecstasy, "contributed in a unique way to her mysticism . . . the yearning of this body . . . for the supernatural" (241). The Goncourts betray a common prejudice of their time, according to which tuberculosis, a "sickness afflicting the high and noble parts of the body" (241), conferred upon its victims a life-enhancing, creative power.[40] However, its physical manifestations were devastating: in addition to the wasting away of the flesh characteristic of tuberculosis, the disease had a particularly pernicious influence on the brain, reducing it to "that original purity in which it has only just enough [matter] to be qualified as a cerebral substance" (241). In this way, specify the Goncourts, "the brain of a forty-year-old consumptive, regressing to the primitive state of a child's brain, returns to the pure thoughts of a twelve-year-old girl, a First Communion brain" (242). Contemporary discourse on tuberculosis furnished the Goncourts with many of the symptoms of their heroine's disease. Here, however, they claim to have uncovered a new symptom, "a heretofore unobserved cerebral activity, unknown by the medical community and which is currently being studied by a distinguished physiologist" (241). Beneath the apparent seriousness of this passage, a playful reductio ad absurdum of clinical discourse can be discerned. Just what is this "minimum," this *degré zéro* of the brain that is necessary in order for it to be qualified as a "cerebral substance"? Is it possible *not* to find irony in the phrase "First Communion brain"? The Goncourts suggest here that religious brutality and physical illness conspire to bring about the return of the primitive in Madame Gervaisais, and to lend credence to the medical model, they observe that in her religious trances, their heroine speaks in "a little girl's voice" (239). We finally have a basis for understanding the implicit comparison between Rome and Africa. Father Sibilla, it will be remembered, had served as an African missionary before accepting the "comfortable vocation" (215) of Madame Gervaisais's spiritual direction. Having labored to "Christianize" and "civilize" an indigenous African population associated with the primitive, the priest's missionary zeal is now directed toward the other end of the cultural spectrum as he attempts to restore his hypercivilized penitent to a more primitive state. Thus, when the Goncourts state that in Rome "piety has a tendency to ferment just as Nature does in the tropics" (185), we understand Madame Gervaisais's conversion as a regression—as inevitable as the chemical decomposition wrought by anaerobic enzymes—to a naive, childlike nature. Used figuratively, the verb *fermenter* (to ferment) suggests agitation and the arousal of dangerous passions, certainly an accurate characterization of Madame Gervaisais's piety. However, thanks to the simile, a more concrete sense of the verb is also evoked, a sense which, for the Frenchman of 1869, would likely have called to mind Pasteur's experiments. Here, the illusory nature of the opposition between science and religion, the material and the immaterial, is suggested at the linguistic level. Conversion is tantamount to infection, and piety foams and boils, transformed and denatured through the influence of *milieu*.

Madame Gervaisais does not play a totally passive role in her own conversion, for she participates in her fate by means of that archetypally feminine activity, *imitation*. Had Madame Gervaisais in her mimicry limited herself to her human Others, her transformation would have made of the novel a somewhat banal narrativization of a well-known medical paradigm. But when, through the mediation of the merciless Father Sibilla, the Goncourts force their protagonist to heed the injunction of the *Imitatio christi*, they liberate themselves from their medical sources and introduce ambiguity into their text. Unlike an earlier heroine, Renée Mauperin, whose body assumes in death "an ecstatic beauty" that is truly reminiscent of the Transfiguration of Christ as described in the Gospels,[41] Madame Gervaisais's pathologized "transfiguration" evokes the materiality of Raphael's painting: "Her unblinking eyes were motionless: a radiant blindness filled her gaze. An indescribable beauty descended upon the thinness and immobility of this figure on the threshold of heaven. . . . At these moments, her pale, sickly hands, raised heavenward, toward her vision, appeared translucent in the daylight" (240). Although the radiance of her expression and the inexpressible beauty of her face seem at first to recall the Gospel descriptions of the Transfiguration of Christ, a closer reading of the passage, which insists on her fixed stare and includes allusions to her anorexia ("thinness"), her sickly pallor ("pale, sickly hands"), her paralysis ("immobility") and her hallucinatory state ("*her* vision) (emphasis mine), reveals that this is not a supernatural event but rather a pathological state. The addition, in surrounding descriptions, of such clinical details as the "trembling" with which she regains awareness of her surroundings, her sense of shame, her fainting spells and the wasting away of her body suggest a *disfiguration* rather than a *transfiguration*. Striving to imitate a Christ she knows only through the intermediary of Raphael's canvas, Madame Gervaisais experiences ecstasy as a sensual pleasure. The ludic nature of the Goncourts' portrayal of this ironic Christ figure becomes manifest when one considers that they irreverently transform Christ's Passion into her passion (lowercase *p*), His pain into her pleasure, His self-sacrifice into her sacrifice of others. Conversion, equated with sin, is pathogenic.

Enslaved by the imperious desires of a body over which she has no control, the once ethereal heroine is metamorphosed into a purely material being. Like Raphael's Christ, confined by the artist's brush to the upper portion of the painting, she remains oblivious to the suffering of the child she has created. Through her renunciation of intellect, her *contemptus mundi*, and her ultimate and painful rejection of her child, Madame Gervaisais has removed herself from the turmoil surrounding her. This self-imposed exile (a psychologist might call it "withdrawal") completes the evolution initiated when she was "exiled" to Rome. Moreover, in her repeated experiences of ecstasy, she stands outside herself (ex-stasis): her very soul has escaped from her body, leaving behind a sordid, mortal shell that is alive only in the strictest biological sense: "At last the day came when Grace finally killed off Nature within Madame Gervaisais. The woman, the earthly being she had been, existed no longer" (255). To appreciate the biting irony of this statement, one must be familiar with chapter 54 of the *Imitation of Christ*, entitled "On the Contrary Workings of Nature and Grace." Here, Thomas à Kempis observes that while Nature is seductive, disobedient, self-interested, and greedy, Grace "resists sensuality . . . seeks to be overcome . . . is kind and generous . . . and esteems it more blest to give than to receive."[42] Except insofar as she has submitted docilely to the dictates of her confessor, the "transfigured" Madame Gervaisais is the antithesis of Grace. As such, she is truly a creation of Rome, and the reader is forced to the conclusion that the heroine's Christ-likeness, mediated by Raphael's painting, is nothing but a sham.[43]

Hence, when Madame Gervaisais, anticipating her audience with the Pontiff, imagines *him* in turn as a Transfigured Christ, the vision appears as a *mise en abyme* of the novel's central image: "Before reaching his chambers, she imagined him transfigured; she would approach him as if he were an image of God, His reflection, His terrestrial presence. A light flashed before her eyes, and in a dazzling vision she saw a shining chamber, similar to heaven's anteroom" (269). Drifting as if in sleep through the hedges of uniformed guards who line the vast, luxurious rooms of the Vatican, Madame Gervaisais stops short on the threshold of the Pope's chambers. The "shining chamber" of her illusions is replaced by "the purple room's dark-red flash of light" (272), an all-too-human opulence that brings to mind her first impression of the Pope, "a face in which human malice could be detected" (132). Significantly, she does not see the Pope. Slipping to the floor through her son's arms in what may be termed an anti-Pietà, Madame Gervaisais dies on the spot, and her death, signaled by the appearance of blood on her lips, is described as a mere sound, that of life emptying itself with "the glug-glug sound of water being poured from a bottle" (272). Dead in the midst of life, her soul having taken flight long before, Madame Gervaisais—or rather the body that was once known as Madame Gervaisais—undergoes a final egress when the sphincter muscles relax as life ceases. This reduction of death to a physiological process, an evacuation having nothing to do with the departure of the soul from the body, might have been the Goncourts' parting shot—one, incidentally, that Zola would recall some eight years later, when he described Maman Coupeau's death in similar terms in *L'Assommoir*—were it not for their decision to enrich the episode of their heroine's death with that of her son's cure. The final passage reads as follows:

> "Mommy! . . . Mommy! . . . " cried Pierre-Charles twice to the corpse that had slid through his small arms and rolled to the ground.
>
> Then suddenly, as if from the child's broken heart a new word sprang forth and intelligence was born, this orphan articulated in a great, wrenching sob:
>
> "My mother!"

We might ask ourselves what purpose might have been served by this conflation of the mother's death and the child's awakening intelligence. Critics have suggested that the Goncourts may have simply intended to illustrate yet another medical cliché of the period, according to which trauma could have beneficent consequences. The explanation, in my opinion, is more complex.

In a novel set in an important Renaissance city, the final image of a child "born again" as Word, cured of his aphasia through his mother's ironic Transfiguration and death, together with the novel's several allusions to Raphael's last painting and to the raising of Lazarus, suggest another interpretation. The Goncourts, by pairing Pierre-Charles's cure

and Madame Gervaisais's "transfiguration" and death, have simultaneously provided an insolent literary version of a painting they disliked
intensely and have subtly suggested that the contempt in which they hold
the clergy extends to the medical profession as well. Seen in this light,
painting and novel enter into dialogue, and the novel becomes an ironic
inversion of the painting's narrative message. For it is Pierre-Charles who
is the true Christ figure of their novel, Pierre-Charles who, mutilated by
the physician's forceps, very nearly killed by his mother's vanity, and
forced to carry the cross of his mother's progressive abandonment,
is the "martyr d'amour," while the apparent Christ figure, Madame
Gervaisais—having been transformed from an ideal mother who recalls
the Madonna into a lubricious female willing to cut all worldly ties and
even to betray her maternal mission in order to experience anew what the
Goncourts portray as a sexually charged mystical union with Christ—is
"possessed." And although, ultimately, the blame for Pierre-Charles's
infirmity can be laid at the door of the medical profession, his mother's
disfiguration, initiated by physicians, abetted by the progress of the tuberculosis, is completed by a clergy defined in medical terms, empiricists
to whom the Goncourts have assigned the task of demonstrating the
validity of clinical theory. In the Biblical narrative that inspired Raphael's
painting, the faith of the disciples is not sufficiently strong to cure the
suffering child, who must wait for help from a Transfigured Christ.
In *Madame Gervaisais*, neither priests, self-proclaimed descendants of
Peter, nor physicians, the secular disciples of the scientific age, function
as healers, and the child's spontaneous linguistic production, the only
promising "cure" registered by this narrative, is a mere accident, the
result of the liberating experience of a denatured mother's death.

By adopting a medical perspective, the Goncourts were able to indulge both their anticlericalism and their misogyny. At the same time,
their problematical portrayal of one French and two Italian physicians,
whose collaboration with Catholic clerics—whether unwitting, grudg-
ingly acknowledged, or joyfully accepted—precipitates their heroine's
demise, suggests that the Goncourt brothers were not the unconditional
admirers of medicine that some thought them to be. Critics have rightly
seen in the Rome of this novel a vampire. Let us extend the metaphor.

The physician who sends Madame Gervaisais into its clutches, the physician who draws her blood, and the physician who seduces her with his primitive pharmacopeia of homeopathic powders and martyrs' pastes are accomplices of that vampire—less active, no doubt, than the clerics, but accomplices nonetheless. There is of course strong irony in the fact that the Goncourts make of clerics and physicians the unwitting collaborators in a woman's dereliction of her maternal duty, in view of the fact that in nineteenth-century France the Church and the medical profession, each in its own way and for different reasons, tended to reduce women to their maternal function.

Madame Gervaisais associates conversion with infection and seduction, the mystical experience with orgasm and pathology. While the last two elements in these trios had been connected often in this syphilophobic era, the recasting of this somewhat trite association in the context of mysticism was of medical inspiration. Yet the Goncourts were not slaves to their medical sources, as their *Journal* entry of 5 February 1869, amply demonstrates. Referring to literary production as a birth, the creation of "this true child of your entrails," they ponder the literary gift that enables them to transform—one might say "transfigure"—their sources, and from the dozens of examples they might have provided, they settle on two which, through their very juxtaposition, are highly revealing. The first concerns the source of the passage describing Madame Gervaisais's advanced tuberculosis:

> This piece, which wouldn't even exist if we hadn't written, refined, and animated it, this piece which we heard over dessert at Magny when it escaped from Robin's confused but insightful mind, full of lofty science but which he can't explain without stammering. These ideas, to which we gave crispness and character, could never have been expressed by him in the bold style of our pen—because in putting them down on paper he would have had the same slobbering scruples and the rather hesitant corrections that he sent to us in the margins of the proofs we asked him to read. (2:197)

The explicit contrast between their lucidity and the doctor's confusion, their courage and his timidity, their flair and his ponderous knowledge no doubt translates their irritation with Robin, who, asked to comment on the passage in proof, expressed certain reservations about its clinical accuracy. But, as Marc Fumaroli has noted, it also offers telling evidence of their disdain for the raw materials with which they had to work and their belief in the superiority of the literary product, the result of a mysterious alchemy that gives form to the formless, animates the inanimate, transforms the prosaic into pure poetry.[44] It is perhaps an unconscious association between Robin (with his "stammering") and Pierre-Charles that causes them to pass, without transition, to the second example of a transformation wrought by their novel:

> Strange roots, encounters, and singular pollination! To be able to extract something sublime from mire! One would never guess that the final passage came from a horrible story that had stayed in our mind's ear, a trashy refrain uttered by a little tramp who, getting home late one night, yelled to her mother who was refusing to let her in, "Mom! mom! unlock the door!" and then, losing her temper, "Oh! this is shit!" That's what you might call a pearl found in the latrine. (2:198)

Robert Ricatte, editing the unexpurgated version of the *Journal* in 1956, is mystified by the Goncourts' pride in the banal ending, and he concludes that the story of the prostitute in fact inspired an earlier episode, in which Pierre-Charles finds his mother's door closed to him and throws a tantrum, "with shouts, appeals, swear words that he stumbled over because they were too big for his mouth" (249). Whatever the case, the mistake is in itself highly revealing. For if while reflecting on the doctor's stammered replies to their questions they are led by association to a consideration of Pierre-Charles's inarticulate mumbling, so too does the thought of the prostitute's vulgar language bring to mind the novel's conclusion. Emitting sounds from opposite ends of the alimentary tract, Madame Gervaisais produces fecal matter and Pierre-Charles speaks. Brought into parallel, linguistic production is tantamount to defecation, as the prostitute's vulgar expression clearly suggests. And the Goncourts swell with pride: "C'est ce qu'on peut appeler une perle ramassée dans les *lieux*" [That's what you might call a pearl found in the latrine].

Suitably polyvalent, *les lieux* (places) refers most obviously to *les lieux d'aisance* (latrines). But the term perhaps also evokes the locus—loci—of the famous dîners Magny, where the Goncourts avidly collected anecdotes and information that would subsequently be transformed into fiction. It was apparently here that they heard the tale of the prostitute, here that Robin responded to their inquiries regarding the symptoms of tuberculosis, which brings us to our final observation. A not-so-subtle devaluation of the physician results from the *Journal*'s summary description of the literary enterprise and its reduction of source personnel to two, the physician and the prostitute. The metatextual anecdote recounted by the *Journal* testifies to the Goncourts' disregard for science and its practitioners, a disregard that is evoked only obliquely in the novel. The Goncourts' most noteworthy achievement in *Madame Gervaisais* was to have exploited the misogynistic medical paradigm in their description of a woman's religious conversion while subtly carrying out a denunciation of medicine itself on four levels: (1) in the narrative framework, where a clear causal relationship between medical practice and physical/mental illness can be established; (2) in the novel's metaphors, which assimilate Rome to a hospital, conversion to infection, priests to doctors; (3) visually, through references to the iconographic representation not of healing but of failing to heal; and (4) through the metatextual comments of the *Journal*, which, together with allusions to physicians and the practice of medicine from other novels, offer strong evidence of their cynicism. If the medical profession's persistent fascination with female religiosity was later in the century to inspire such works as Zola's *La Conquête de Plassans* (1874) and Maupassant's "La Maison Tellier" (1881) and "Miss Harriet" (1883), the Goncourts' narrative of a woman's religious conversion, coupled with the tale of the agonizing "weaning" of her son and the painful awakening of his intelligence, offers ample evidence of their ability to transform their medical sources in order to make them suit their own (destructive) purposes.

3

Miasmatic Effluvia
L'Assommoir and the Discourse
of Hygiene

¶

In *Les Romanciers naturalistes* (1881), published some twelve years after *Madame Gervaisais*, Zola expressed the opinion that the Goncourts' work could not properly be called a novel but was, rather, the simple "study of a woman." Because he underestimated the importance of Pierre-Charles ("hardly the outline of a child"), Zola did not appreciate the subtlety of the final scene. On the contrary, he felt that it weakened the novel's effect. To temper his criticism, Zola found other aspects of *Madame Gervaisais* praiseworthy, and in the words he chose to express that praise we find a strong link with his own novelistic practice and specifically with *L'Assommoir*: "Madame Gervaisais is saturated with that Catholic perfume, that Roman scent that provokes a kind of religious epidemic. Little by little, she is penetrated by it. The Goncourts studied with an infinite art the slow progress of religious contagion."[1] For Zola, the Goncourts' heroine was a victim of her milieu. The olfactory allusions ("that Catholic perfume," "that Roman scent"), associated with the notion of disease transmission ("religious epidemic," "religious contagion"), suggest that even in the Pasteurian era during which he wrote, Zola's imagination was still stimulated by the outdated notion of dangerous miasma. But Zola's comments on *Madame Gervaisais* also bear witness to his belief in the concept of "moral contagion" (a concept that would be explored with particular intensity by the medical profession in the 1880s and 1890s) and to his tendency to conceive of nonmedical phenomena in medical terms.[2] Like the Goncourt brothers, Zola drew heavily on medical science in his creation of literary characters and their environment. Unlike them, he is not generally suspected of having an antimedical bias, and indeed, a writer who compared the practice of his art to that of the physician is unlikely to express a resistance, however subtle, to medical hegemony. Yet a reading of *L'Assommoir* reveals just such a resistance. In this novel, a still-docile Zola, making abundant use of stereotypes culled from the medically inspired hygienist discourse of his time, emphasizes their role in the degradation of his heroine, Gervaise Macquart.

Since its publication in 1877, *L'Assommoir* has been the object of numerous critical articles and monographs, many attempting to come to grips with the question of whether Zola was intending to imply that the working class was responsible for its own fate, a question that arose at least partly from Zola's bold decision to represent the workers in their own words, through dialogue and free indirect discourse. David Baguley links the protagonists' demise with their abandonment of the three cardinal virtues promoted by the novel's bourgeois discourse: work, cleanliness, and abstinence. Colette Becker, on the other hand, believes that the novel offers a catastrophic vision of working-class life as "an inescapable sinking." And Sandy Petrey concludes, after analyzing the novel's "discourse of labor," that Zola's message runs precisely *counter* to bourgeois ideology: "The text describes work, not as a step in the climb towards happiness, but rather as the beginning of a fall towards misery, madness and death."[3] The heroine's metamorphosis from an appetizing young woman to a repulsive *clocharde* (vagrant) has attracted particular attention. While it is clear even to the casual reader that this transformation owes something to both heredity and environment, the precise reason for Gervaise Macquart's decline, and the moment at which it begins, are a subject of some debate. Most critics see in Coupeau's fall from the roof a turning point, and Gervaise's hereditary alcoholism is assigned an important role. Kathryn Slott believes Gervaise to be a victim of gender oppression: "The true focus of *L'Assommoir* is less how Gervaise's weakness ruins her life than how alcohol brutalizes men who in turn abuse women."[4] Joy Newton, while avowing multiple factors in her decline, first lays the responsibility at her own door ("Her ambition to have her own business is the cause of the drama and the tragedy that follow"), then, in a subsequent article, exonerates her, attributing her degradation to "a combination of three . . . factors for which she is in no way responsible: accident, crippling fatigue, and loneliness."[5] Marcel Girard accuses Gervaise of weakness and gourmandise,[6] and Jacques Dubois, without denying the influence of environment, asserts that, "from beginning to end, the heroine is the principal agent of her own ruin."[7]

My own conviction places me on the side of those who see Gervaise as an innocent victim. In proceeding along the track laid by Jacques Dubois, whose socio-critical reading pays special heed to the traces of diverse ideologies to be found in the novel, I would like to examine Gervaise's demise through the microscope of nineteenth-century medical discourse, particularly as it relates to hygiene and the working class. Such an approach seems particularly appropriate when one is dealing with a novel as preoccupied with cleanliness and dirt as L'Assommoir. I would like to argue for a restricted reading of the concept of milieu, one that pays special attention to the work environment of the blanchisserie (the laundry). In short, without denying the influence of ideas culled from Social Darwinism, degeneration theory, physical anthropology, and so forth, I am convinced that Zola intended to expose through his novel the laundry's corrupting influence, an influence so pernicious that it can transform a woman whose every attribute identifies her with thrift, industry, and purity into the incarnation of waste, sloth, and filth. Seen from this perspective, Coupeau's fall, the ultimate occupational hazard of the roofer, has a counterpart in the less dramatic but no less destructive perils of Gervaise's chosen occupation.

Like Madame Gervaisais—to whom she is clearly linked onomastically—Gervaise Macquart sees her troubles begin when she is transplanted to a new geographical space. However, whereas the degradation of the Goncourts' bourgeoise occurs when she leaves Paris, that of Zola's working-class woman appears to be the ultimate consequence of her arrival in the French capital. Encoded as the incarnation of freshness and health when she first arrives from Plassans, Gervaise has the glowing complexion, blond hair, and sparkling teeth that Zola associates with life in the country. She is further identified with whiteness by her moral qualities (she is "as gentle as a lamb, as good as bread") and by her profession.[8] Drawn to those who, like her, are the incarnation of cleanliness (the blond-bearded Goujet lives with his mother in an immaculate apartment), Gervaise makes a virtue of both physical and moral hygiene. She has been chastened by her youthful adventures with Lantier that resulted in a premature maternity, and she tells Coupeau in no uncertain terms that sexual relations no longer interest her. Yet by novel's end she has attempted to prostitute herself, she is described as "a heap of something unclean" (2:731), and, as John Frey so succinctly puts it, "only her odour recalls her to the story" on the last page of the novel.[9] Indeed, she has assumed a shape that assimilates her to *entassement* (piling up), *saleté* (filth) and *odeur* (odor), nouns used repeatedly in hygienist discourse to describe the conditions in working-class neighborhoods.[10]

I would like to suggest that Gervaise Macquart is poisoned by the fetid air of the laundry just as surely as Coupeau is killed by the "poison" of alcohol. Simply stated, the task of laundering clothing is marked not only by its feminine specificity but also by its risks. Zola had represented a different aspect of this danger in *La Fortune des Rougon*, where the death of Gervaise's mother had been associated with laundering duties resulting from "pneumonia that she caught when she went to do the family laundry . . . and then carried it back wet on her back."[11] In *L'Assommoir*, on the other hand, the danger appears to be "in the air." If machines breathe freely in the universe of this novel (the still at Colombe's; the steam machine in the washhouse), the characters cough and splutter with various respiratory ailments (Maman Coupeau has asthma; Clémence suffers from a head cold; Coupeau has a persistent cough, etc.) and the verbs *suffoquer* (to suffocate) and *étouffer* (to smother) are noticeable by their frequency. The fear of asphyxia, a danger to which the medical community constantly alerted the populace in the latter half of the nineteenth century, is evoked twice in the novel. In fact, there is throughout the work a whole network of allusions to the quality of the air (including innumerable evocations of various odors), constituting a subtext that orients our reading of the novel.

It has often been pointed out that Gervaise's universe is inscribed within a space limited by two constructions that in the nineteenth century evoked death, the slaughterhouse and the hospital. However, since the hospital is also associated with the possibility of healing, the more important common denominator shared by these two geographic perimeters is their mutual production of foul and unhealthy odors. In one of the earliest scenes in the novel, Gervaise looks with disgust toward the walls of the old slaughterhouse, "black with killing and foul odors" (2:380). Discussions regarding the generally insalubrious nature of the abattoirs were common currency in the contemporary medical press, and physicians were relentless in their struggle to relocate them to the periphery of the city. If by the novel's end the slaughterhouse is being demolished, the Lariboisière Hospital, that other limit to Gervaise's horizon, which had been under construction in the opening pages, now has its full complement of indigent sick, and its halls reek of a nauseating "sickroom smell that catches at your throat" (2:696). In addition, the more general stench of poverty that hangs heavily in the air of les Batignolles and assumes various forms contributes to what one might term the morbidity of milieu. Zola singles out for special mention the "air heavy with alcohol" of the cabaret (2:410), the odor of onion soup emanating from the workers' kitchens (2:422), and the repulsive smells that permeate the corridors of the huge apartment building on the rue Neuve de la Goutte d'Or, including "the stale odor of the dwellings of the poor, the smell of accumulated dust, rank filth" (2:416) and the stench and "fetid dampness" (2:422) of the plumbing. However, there can be no doubt that the most memorable description of odors in this novel, equal in importance to that of the celebrated "symphony of the cheeses" in *Le Ventre de Paris* or the fatal odor of flowers in *La Faute de l'Abbé Mouret*, is the one that takes as its subject the *odor sui generis* filling the small laundry during a ritual sorting of the linen:

> The sorting lasted a good half hour. In the warm air, a stale stench rose up from all that dirty linen being moved around. Gervaise, who was used to filth, wasn't in the least bothered by it; she plunged her bare pink arms into the pile of shirts yellowed with grime, dish towels stiffened by greasy dishwater, socks eaten away by sweat. However, in the strong odor that hit her in the face as she bent

over the heaps of laundry, she was overcome with apathy. She
was intoxicated by this human stench, and she smiled vaguely, her
eyes misty. And it seemed to her that this asphyxia of old linens
poisoning the atmosphere was the cause of her first feelings of
indolence. (2:505–6)

Zola's use of the verb *se griser* (to become intoxicated) to describe
the effect of the laundry's stench upon Gervaise suggests a parallel with
alcoholism, and the arrival of a drunk Coupeau in the midst of the sorting
process clearly has symbolic value. In a manner similar to Gervaise, his
inebriation is characterized by indolence and a state of sexual arousal.
After resisting his somewhat comical displays of affection, Gervaise
finally allows him to kiss her:

She gave in to him, dazed by the odor emanating from the pile of
laundry, feeling no disgust for Coupeau's winey breath. And the
sloppy kiss that they exchanged full on the mouth in the midst of
the filth of her trade was like a first fall into the slowly increasing
sluggishness of their life. (2:509)

"First feelings of indolence," "first fall": Zola could hardly be more
explicit. As *blanchisseuse*, his heroine has made a business of managing
filth. She is aptly named: Gervaise *gère la vase* (manages slime), so
to speak. But in allowing all of the soiled and malodorous linen in
the neighborhood to invade her private and public space (for the
laundry serves as her home), she is putting herself at risk of infection,
metaphorically speaking. It is common knowledge that Zola subscribed
to Taine's theory on the influence of the occupational environment,
believing, with the philosopher, that "trades create varieties in men just
as the climate creates differences in the animal kingdom."[12] However,
there is more at stake here than the power of an occupation to transform
its practitioners. Dubois comes close to the mark when he writes: "We
recognize . . . the imprint of the positivism inspired by Taine. It becomes
obvious in the famous influence of the environment taken to the extreme
and, in Gervaise Macquart's case, going as far as impregnation, osmosis
and the usual means of duplication."[13]

Indeed, Gervaise is literally impregnated by filth until, in the end, she becomes indistinguishable from it. Hence the episode near the novel's conclusion when she eats "something disgusting" (2:795) on a dare, in order to earn money, represents the final alignment of her personal life with her professional practice. Filth is quite literally her business: it is by taking in filth that she earns a living. And her laundry is penetrated, not only by the literal filth of the soiled linen, but by such incarnations of moral slime as Virginie Poisson and Lantier. The dream of a refuge against the world's ills is illusory: the boutique may keep out the cold but it is not impervious to dirt. What Dubois does not appear to notice, or in any case does not elaborate, despite the detailed attention he accords to ideology and bourgeois discourses on the poor, is the mechanism by which this "osmosis" occurs. Jacques Allard hints at a causal relationship between Gervaise's profession and her decline: "The neighborhood laundry business was founded precisely on the accumulation of dirty linen in the shop, whence the laziness (resulting from the asphyxiating action of the soiled clothing) and consequently, the degradation."[14] I would like to take this observation a step farther by proposing that in order to understand Gervaise's demise, we must see her as a victim of contamination—*contagion*—by her milieu. Gervaise has somehow contracted a moral illness more deadly than the most virulent physical disease, an illness characterized first by indolence, which is experienced as a sensual pleasure, then by an erotic fascination with filth: "Dirt was a warm nest in which she loved to snuggle. But the pleasure that *really* intoxicated her was just letting things go, waiting until the dust blocked up the holes" (2:644). In order to comprehend the means by which this "contamination" occurs, it is useful to have some knowledge of nineteenth-century medical theories of disease transmission.

For the greater part of the nineteenth century, the means by which diseases were communicated was improperly understood. Until the 1880s, some years after Pasteur made the groundbreaking discoveries that eventually resulted in the triumph of germ theory, the prevalent belief, inherited from the eighteenth century, held that disease was the product of noxious odors resulting from decaying matter, effluvia of various sorts, and bodily excretions, especially (but not exclusively) of the sick. As the century wore on, miasma theory (as it was known) came increasingly under attack by contagionists (those who believed that disease was communicated from person to person or indirectly by objects carrying a morbific agent). By the 1870s, the anti-contagionists had conceded with regret that unhealthy air was not always malodorous ("It is most unfortunate that each miasma isn't accompanied by an unpleasant odor that might warn of its presence"); however it was an article of faith that the overcrowding of populous sections of the city always produced unhealthy air: "The accumulation of even healthy organisms in a relatively restricted space poisons the atmosphere in a precise way by spreading what is typically known as the miasma of overcrowding."[15]

In a period wracked by epidemics, such a conviction had enormous implications. The example of cholera alone will suffice to illustrate the fears that haunted the nineteenth-century bourgeois imagination. Asiatic cholera (*cholera morbus*) came ashore in Europe for the first time in 1829 and was to return several times before the century's end, making its last appearance in France in the summer of 1885, in Toulon. The disease, which killed approximately half of those who contracted it, was characterized by uncontrollable vomiting and diarrhea. Although its etiology and means of transmission were unclear, researchers had, by mid-century, identified what they believed to be predisposing conditions for the spread of cholera, including crowded and filthy living conditions, humidity, and lack of sunlight. There was a proliferation of hygiene manuals intended for the general public, and in text after text, bourgeois readers were lulled into complacency by the same comforting refrain: "Miliary fever, cholera, typhus, typhoid fever, etc. don't have aristocratic instincts, and we know perfectly well that these plagues prefer to inhabit the poor sections of town."[16] Observation had borne out the accuracy of this formulation: in the case of cholera in particular, the urban poor were most severely affected. The only problem was that one could not assign limits to the foul air that was believed to circulate in working-class neighborhoods. *La classe laborieuse* was indeed *dangereuse*, not in a criminal sense but as a source of illness.

How could the health of the general population be protected? There were two approaches. With *l'haussmannisation* of Paris, Napoléon III had attempted to widen the distance between the affluent and the destitute, the healthy and the unhealthy, thus effecting a symbolic quarantine of the workers in growing *faubourgs* of the city. This is not to say that the regime was unconcerned with the lives of the working class. Napoléon III's efforts to establish salubrious quarters for workers proves the contrary, and such improvements as the development of a citywide underground sewage system during the Second Empire clearly benefited everyone. Nevertheless, the fear of cholera and the urban poor was the major impetus behind urban renewal. Social reformers and members of the medical profession did their part by pleading for improved hygiene among the proletariat. Attention shifted from the public to the private spheres: concern for the salubrity of the streets had been growing since early in the century, as Parent-Duchâtelet's work on sewers (1836) had demonstrated. Now, however, a link was established between body, home, and street: while the reigning powers had to assume responsibility for rendering the streets more healthful, personal cleanliness and the tidiness of one's home were within the province of the workers themselves. The moralizing discourse of hygiene, directed at all classes but with special urgency at the lower classes, promoted cleanliness as a virtue second to none. Julia Csergo's monograph on nineteenth-century hygiene, *Liberté, Egalité, Propreté*, demonstrates the degree to which cleanliness was valorized as an emblem of worth and moral probity. Her play on the famous national slogan is deeply significant. One was not expected to fraternize with the worker but rather to inculcate in him values that would make him less repugnant, less threatening to bourgeois health. Where would these values be taught? Above all in the home, by wives and mothers. Medical discourse was most insistent on this point: women, who were viewed as the representatives of the medical profession within the home, were to carry the hygienist message to their families. As Alain Corbin puts it, in *Histoire de la vie privée*, "They're the ones who look after the family's health."[17]

In addition to its nefarious role as a cause of cholera, an unhealthy home environment was held to be responsible for the "contagion" of alcoholism. The argument went as follows: after long hours of work in dirty factories, men deserved to return home to a clean house.

Those who were saddled with negligent wives would delay their return, stopping instead for a drink at the local cabaret. This habit would soon lead to chronic inebriation, a condition that became known only in 1852 as alcoholism.[18] Like cholera, then, the specter of alcoholism intensified fears of the class that was known as "the great unwashed." However, unlike cholera, alcoholism was perceived as dangerous, not because it might be transmitted to the upper classes (the contagion of example was felt to be operative only among the poor), but rather that, under its influence, workers would become restless, revolutions would be fomented. In the seventies and eighties, the Commune was cited as an example of mass madness brought on by excessive drinking, and statistics on the number of ex-Communards to be hospitalized for alcohol addiction were tabulated as proof of the phenomenon.[19] To solidify the connection between what were identified as the twin scourges of the proletariat, cholera and alcoholism, it was asserted that alcoholics were particularly susceptible to cholera infection, to which they succumbed more rapidly than those who abstained from drink. Once again the responsibility was placed squarely on the shoulders of womankind. Keep your home clean, Madame, and you will live in health and happiness, if not in prosperity: this was the moralizing message of hygienist discourse. To disobey this bourgeois imperative was to condemn one's family to a demoralizing slide into poverty, filth, and disease.

Contemporary literature on hygiene, particularly when it dealt with the connection between lack of cleanliness and cholera and alcoholism, confirms the hypothesis I have already introduced concerning Gervaise's decline and enables us to read *L'Assommoir* from a new perspective. It is true that Zola made no secret of his direct sources for the novel, such as Denis Poulot's *Le Sublime*, Jules Simon's *L'Ouvrière*, Delvau's *La Langue verte*, and Dr. Magnan's *De l'alcoolisme*. However, scholars who consult only the "official" sources, without taking into consideration the more general context of contemporary medical discourse, are unable to make the connection between Gervaise's demise and her espousal of a profession that grew out of that very discourse.

Although Zola began thinking about *L'Assommoir* as early as 1868, most of the actual writing was done in a twelve-month period between 1875 and 1876. Studies of his preparatory notes show that the idea of making his working-class family victims of the curse of alcoholism came late to Zola, and that his original intention was merely to tell the tale of a working-class woman. However, as early as 1871, Zola's notes reveal that he was seriously thinking of making his heroine a laundress, and by 1874 he had definitively settled upon this profession. Why? Henri Mitterand points to a literary precedent in the Goncourts' *Manette Salomon* and to the well-known series of paintings of the *blanchisseuse* by Degas (2:1541–42). Edmond de Goncourt explains the artist's choice as aesthetic: "It's all pink and white, female flesh in light cotton and gauze, the most charming pretext for soft blond tones."[20] The novelist's choice, clearly, had a more complex motivation, and to understand it we must ask ourselves what the laundress represented for the Frenchman living in the second half of the nineteenth century.

Firstly, the laundress was intimately associated with the hygienist project. Unlike the housewife, whose duty in this domain did not extend beyond the familial sphere, the laundress was responsible for the cleaning and maintenance of the clothing of the entire neighborhood. Alain Corbin has observed that in the lower classes, personal hygiene was for a long time interpreted to mean, not bathing but rather wearing clean clothes, whence the central role played by the *blanchisseuse*. The entry for *blanchissage* ("laundering") in the nineteenth-century Larousse dictionary (published between 1866 and 1890) confirms this view of the laundress: "The laundering industry is intimately related to public hygiene and employs a large class of workers who must be protected against the disadvantages and hazards of their occupation."[21] In fact, sending one's laundry out to be washed, rather than taking it to the washhouse oneself, was a relatively recent phenomenon, especially in the lower classes, and was not without serious disadvantages, since disease was believed to be spread through the wash water. The laundress herself was most at risk, and nineteenth-century medical discourse ranked this profession among the most dangerous for women. Philippe Patissier, in his 1822 *Traité des maladies des artisans*, observes that "shirts and linen permeated with a thousand kinds of filth give off a stench. In this respect, the laundress's occupation is unquestionably one of the most dangerous; these workers can contract contagious illnesses from handling dirty linen, which is impregnated with noxious emanations from the bodies of the ill."[22] Even toward the end of the century, when miasma theory no longer held sway, the fundamental belief in this occupational hazard remained firm: "When washing the clothes of the sick, they [laundresses] are exposed to contagion."[23] Like alcoholics, laundresses were believed to be particularly vulnerable to epidemic diseases, not only because infection was somehow transmitted through clothing, but also because the very conditions in which they were obliged to work were insalubrious.[24] City laundries, generally on the ground floor of multi-storied buildings, had little direct sunlight; the atmosphere within was warm and moist, conditions believed to augment the activity of miasma as well as cause a sense of extreme fatigue.[25] Furthermore, the noxious odors emitted by the laundry, combined with the vapors produced by cleaning agents and the coke-burning stove on which irons were heated, poisoned the atmosphere and caused asphyxia. In short, the air in the typical laundry was polluted to the point of being unbreathable. Laundresses were subject to a host of other ailments as well, resulting from constant exposure to heat and steam, inadequate perspiration because of the moist air, prolonged periods of standing, often on a wet floor, immersion of the hands and arms in hot, alkaline water, and hard physical labor.

Such was the bleak picture of life in the laundries, as painted by a reform-minded medical profession eager to improve workers' conditions. Superficially, at least, it has little in common with the apparently idyllic tableau sketched by Zola. Although the shop is humid and dark ("the walls pissed dampness and you couldn't see clearly after 3 P.M." [2:497]), Gervaise perspires abundantly, contracts no contagious diseases, suffers no rheumatism or other occupation-related illness, and indeed appears to thrive in the hothouse atmosphere of her shop, which is likened on several occasions to an *alcôve* and resembles a boudoir more than a sweatshop. The image of Gervaise and her employees sipping coffee and luxuriating in the cocoonlike warmth as they watch passersby bundled in overcoats on a bitterly cold winter's day, or of the scantily clad employees bleaching and ironing until late into the night as a titillated Goujet looks on discreetly from his assigned place in a corner of the room, hardly seems to conform to the picture of professional misery drawn by the physicians. To be sure, Gervaise's situation is not typical. As the owner, she employs a washerwoman, Madame Bijard, who completes the first steps in the long washing process in the washhouse. Moreover, as a "detail laundress," she limits her practice to certain items of clothing (collars, sleeve guards, men's shirts, ladies' bonnets, scarves, etc.), leaving the heavier work of laundering sheets, towels, and so forth, to others. Finally, as proprietress of her own shop, which doubles as her home, she does not violate her "feminine domesticity" and is thus spared the wrath of physicians who, echoing Michelet's diatribe against women driven to work by the Industrial Revolution ("Working woman, impious expression!") decry the gainful employment of wives and mothers who are of necessity neglecting their domestic duties.[26] Theoretically, at least, Gervaise "has it all."

In practice, of course, this is hardly the case, and despite the positive valorization of the little laundry, which appears to stand in symbolic counterpoint to Colombe's destructive *assommoir*, the domain of men as the laundry is that of women, this textual space is only apparently utopian, as ambiguous a space as is the Louvre in the wedding-party scene.[27] It does offer, like the cabaret, an escape from the misery of working-class life, but this escape is fleeting indeed, and like that of alcohol, it can be seen merely as an artificial paradise that is ultimately destructive. On one level, the novel can be read as a struggle for dominance between the laundry and the cabaret, two spaces to which the narrative gives significant religious connotations, suggesting that they have become the modern substitute for religion, that once-effective "opiate" of the people. At the beginning of the novel, Gervaise worships at the altar of Hygeia, the goddess of cleanliness. She reigns over her laundry while a devoted Goujet admires her "as if she were the holy Virgin," a role she relishes. Her own hygienic standards are irreproachable: she is "clean as a whistle" (2:442), and she takes loving care of her meager possessions, "[having] a religious respect for [her] furniture" (2:465). Gervaise's example illustrates the growing influence of the medical profession and the hygienist movement that it spawned. In this age of scientism, the doctor has replaced the priest as director of public conscience, and cleanliness has become a cardinal virtue. This shift in emphasis from the moral to the physical is accompanied by a blurring of the distinction between the two: the good are by definition clean, and cleanliness is a signifier of goodness. This is not simply an example of the old cliché according to which cleanliness is next to godliness: in hygienist discourse, cleanliness *replaces* godliness.

By the novel's conclusion, however, Gervaise has joined the cult of Bacchus, and it is Colombe's cabaret, "illuminated like a cathedral for High Mass" (2:769), that has emerged victorious in the battle for the souls of the poor. How can we explain the triumph of alcohol that flies in the face of the medical community's repeated warnings of the horrors of alcoholism and its tireless proselytizing on behalf of the "religion" of hygiene? Interestingly enough, an examination of the popular discourse as reproduced by Zola testifies to the fact that the hygienist message *did* get through, for there is a persistent confusion between the moral and the physical that is especially prevalent in the sexual domain. Moral and physical "filth" go hand in hand, and words evoking uncleanliness are repeatedly pressed into service to describe "sins" of a sexual nature. To give but one example, the word *saleté* (filth) is used as an epithet for sexual intercourse. "Vous ne songez qu'à la saleté" [All you can think about is sex] (2:407), says Gervaise to Coupeau in the early days of their courtship. *Saleté* is also used to refer to illicit sexual activity (the relationship between Boche and Mme Goudron is characterized as a "saleté," [499]) and vulgar jokes ("la saleté de Sophie" [2:719]; "[Clémence] lâcha un mot cru, une saleté" [Clémence let out a crude word, a piece of filth] [2:507]). This contamination of the physical and the moral is operative on another level as well, for the most unkempt of this novel's characters, those whose laundry smells the most foul, are the sexually promiscuous. Early in the novel, Virginie is characterized as "une saleté" (2:397). The wanton Madame Gaudron brings in a packet of laundry that is so rank Gervaise vows never to accept her business again, whereas the spinster Mlle Remanjou deposits clothing that is never soiled, "which just goes to show that at her age you might as well be a piece of wood, because you couldn't wring a drop of anything out of her" (2:508).

The result of this coincidence of moral and physical impurity is that the clothing brought in to be laundered tells an often sordid tale of debauchery. In an era when clothing had a marked social value among the bourgeoisie as camouflage for corporeal imperfections and enhancement of (especially feminine) beauty (Philippe Perrot refers to this phenomenon as "the sartorial production of the anatomical mirage"), a scene that features clothing in a treasonous role cannot fail to suggest an implicit contrast between *la bourgeoisie* and *le peuple* (the middle and the working classes).[28] This again evokes the analogy with religion. Semantically inscribed as a meeting point between filth and cleanliness, Gervaise's *blanchisserie* may be likened to a confessional, in which the sins of the neighborhood are revealed and symbolically cleansed. The sorting is the moment of truth, and Gervaise delights in this operation during which "the whole neighborhood . . . was undressed" (2:508). The prurient curiosity of Zola's laundresses is in conformity with the image promoted by the medical press, which, not content to outline the physical risks of various occupations, insisted on providing a "moral profile" of the women who engaged in them. The laundress, according to official wisdom, is particularly fond of "dancing, shows, cafés, and erotic pleasures."[29] Zola — and he is not alone — emphasizes this weakness for "erotic pleasures" in his fiction.[30] It is not by chance that the promiscuous Mouquette in *Germinal* is a laundress, or that the voluptuous Clémence takes special interest in ironing men's shirts. Also in keeping with current stereotypes, Zola's laundresses are characterized by their vulgar language and crude jokes. Before Gervaise acquires her shop, Goujet avoids the company of such women, and he lowers his head when he must pass by their shops: "He didn't like their crude language, thought it was disgusting when women constantly used dirty words" (2:474). Later in the novel, Lantier will take pleasure in the company of these same women, "who are anything but prudish" (2:608).

The vulgarity of the laundress and her preoccupation with sensuality appear as a natural consequence, not only of the knowledge gained through the laundering of personal garments, but also of the sexual availability and indolence engendered by inhaling the bodily odors emitted by the soiled clothing. The role of corporeal odors in the evolution of sexuality has been discussed in detail in Alain Corbin's remarkable treatise on the history of olfaction, *Le Miasme et la jonquille*. Zola establishes an unmistakably causal relationship between the professional duties of the laundress and her immorality; in so doing, he betrays the influence of the discourse of hygiene, which displayed an almost obsessive preoccupation with "the stench of the poor," and a growing repugnance for strong animal smells. Unlike the bourgeois, whose olfactory pleasures had proceeded to more delicate perfumes that masked bodily odors, the poor, with their allegedly primitive sexuality, were believed to be stimulated by the violent smells of corporeal excretions. In *L'Assommoir*, this prejudice finds expression in the character of Lantier, who likes the smell of musk, a perfume that was said to emphasize, rather than camouflage, corporeal odors.

Gervaise is thus "infected" with a languid sensuality that overcomes her energy, her industry, and her moral indignation, and this ultimately devastating influence of the environment upon her suggests an analogy with miasma theory. Although the word "miasma," found so frequently in the works of a Flaubert or a Balzac, does not appear in *L'Assommoir*, the fact that Zola subscribed to this theory is not in doubt.[31] Moreover the text is shot through with allusions to the stench of poverty, as concentrated in the laundry and in the huge apartment building, the spaces that Gervaise is condemned to inhabit and in which the tale of her degradation unfolds. Gervaise herself, reflecting upon her first entry into the apartment building on the rue Neuve de la Goutte d'Or, pinpoints that moment as decisive in the turn her life has taken: "Ever since the day she first set foot there, she had begun to go downhill. Yes, it must be bad for you to be jammed in together in these huge working-class tenements; you caught the cholera of poverty there" (2:778). For the scholar familiar with the medical discourse of Zola's time, the source of Gervaise's speculations is easily recognizable in the clichés regarding the promiscuity of crowded living and the "epidemic" nature of indigence. Zola's heroine has indeed become infected with "the cholera of poverty," an infection that was borne in the acrid air of the little laundry.

A distinction must however be made between the fears articulated by hygienist discourse and Zola's literary transposition thereof. Gervaise does not fear cholera; she fears "the cholera of poverty." She does not contract one of the physical maladies of which laundresses were considered to be at risk but rather a moral one, which takes her from indolence to alcoholism. And if alcoholism is presented as contagious (indeed, Poulot's preface to *Le Sublime* exploits the medical metaphor in laying bare the epidemic nature of this pathological condition),[32] it is disassociated from political activism in *L'Assommoir*, where the most outspoken proponents of labor reform are Goujet and Lantier, both of whom are characterized by their sobriety. Finally, the cabaret and the washhouse, which at the time had the reputation of being centers of seditionist activity, here set the scene for disputes and discussions of a distinctly apolitical nature. In short, the conditions of working-class life deplored by hygienist discourse and faithfully reproduced by Zola are presented not as potentially destructive to society at large but as self-destructive, threatening above all to the proletariat.

The walls of the abattoir, "black with killing and foul odors," had established a connection between death and stench. Death is malodorous. Gervaise, who at first finds the smells repugnant, will eventually be seduced by the animal odors of her customers, then by the odor of death as represented by Bazouge, the undertaker (another example of the "osmosis" that makes one resemble one's occupation). In the novel's final passage, it is death itself that causes the odor that poisons the air. Gervaise *is* that odor. By infecting the air with the stench of her decaying corpse, Gervaise is achieving a posthumous revenge against those who poisoned her with the rancid odor of their vice.

The *Petit Robert* gives, as the first definition of the verb *infecter*, "to impregnate with dangerous and unhealthy emanations." What better phrase to describe the pathogenic force of the working-class community on Gervaise Macquart? In an operation analogous to the spontaneous combustion of old Macquart's alcohol-soaked body, described so vividly in *Le Docteur Pascal*, Gervaise's body self-destructs after being permeated, infected by the filth of others. There is thus a direct causal relationship between Gervaise's work as a laundress — that is, her unwitting involvement in the prophylactic mission of the public health movement — and her sordid destiny. I do not mean to imply that Zola was in any way suggesting that the medical profession willfully contributed to the decline of the working class. On the contrary, his letter to the editor Lacroix detailing his plans for the novel reveals that he had from the start a social agenda that was remarkably consistent with that of the hygiene movement, that of demanding "air, light, and education for the lower classes."[33] Later, defending in his 1877 preface his controversial portrayal of the working class, he claimed to have written "le premier roman du peuple qui ne mente pas et qui ait *l'odeur* du peuple" [the first novel about the working class that doesn't lie and that captures the essence—literally, the *smell*—of the working class] (2:373–74, emphasis added). Zola's use of *odeur* to signify authenticity and his insistence on the need to provide a healthier environment for the working classes offer extratextual support for my thesis regarding the importance of atmosphere, conceived in a *physical* sense, on the heroine's destiny. Through a process that owes much to miasma theory, Gervaise Macquart has been metaphorically infected by the environment in which she lives and works. The iatrogenic role of the medical profession that promoted the values of cleanliness to which Gervaise subscribed at the outset of the novel cannot be ignored. There is a bitter irony here, for the hygiene movement, intended to *prevent* illness, in fact has a causative role in the moral illness that kills Gervaise. Had Zola's entrepreneurial heroine been content to attend to her personal hygiene, instead of participating more actively in the hygienist project through the commercial venture of her neighborhood laundry, a happier fate may have awaited her. Moral contagion plays a role as well, of course, and it is clear that Gervaise's situation is exacerbated by her propensity for imitation. In turning to drink, she is after all following Coupeau's example, and the scene in which she mimes the "dance" caused by his *delirium tremens* raises nearly to the level of caricature the medically inspired motif of the "imitative woman."

It was not until 1880, three years after the appearance of *L'Assommoir*, that Zola published his *Roman expérimental*. From that point forward, and owing perhaps to the acerbic criticism he drew from the medical community, Zola's fictional physicians, including Pascal himself, testify to a certain reticence on their creator's part.[34] Although Zola continued to appropriate scientific discourse for his novels, "a kind of hesitation can be felt sometimes, cutting against the grain of the medical positivism simultaneously espoused," according to Daniel Pick.[35] Véronique Lavielle believes that despite Zola's adherence to the scientific model and the ideology of positivism, these values are "constantly subverted by the creator's imaginary."[36] Dorothy Kelly, for her part, implies that Zola made a distinction between Claude Bernard's "virile, masculine, strong" scientific method and the "weak, soppy, effeminate 'art' of medicine."[37] Whatever the case, it is clear that Zola's admiration for medicine and the medical professional was not unqualified. Already apparent in the coldly clinical comportment of Bicêtre's psychiatrist in *L'Assommoir*, his ambivalence can be gleaned from the creation of such characters as the mischievously named Dr. Porquier (*La Conquête de Plassans*), the unsympathetic Dr. Finet (*La Terre*), the benign but ineffectual Dr. Casenave (*La Joie de vivre*), the ludicrously incompetent "deathbed physician" of "La Mort d'Olivier Bécaille" and the many physicians of *Lourdes*, whose self-interested collusion with the mercenary clergy of that pilgrimage site becomes a distant echo of that medico-clerical collaboration sketched in the Goncourt brothers' *Madame Gervaisais*.[38] This is not to question Zola's loyalty to science and faith in progress through scientific investigation, and one would be ill-advised to attempt to make of him a supporter of the late-nineteenth-century's neo-mysticism, which, as Henri Mitterand points out (5:1572–73), he combated energetically in the last novel of the Rougon-Macquart series, *Le Docteur Pascal*. But it seems clear that his infatuation with science did not necessarily extend to its most ubiquitous spokesman, the medical practitioner. *L'Assommoir* provides an early example of the way in which Zola appropriated medical discourse, ostensibly only in order to lend the authority of science to his fiction but at the same time suggesting—perhaps unintentionally—that the broad dissemination of this very discourse could prove detrimental to society.

4

COUNTER-DISCURSIVE STRATEGIES IN
HUYSMANS'S *EN MÉNAGE*

g

In 1880, Joris-Karl Huysmans contributed a story to *Les Soirées de Médan*, thus becoming part of what was derisively referred to as "Zola's tail." A year later, in an otherwise laudatory review of Huysmans's novel *En ménage* (1881), Zola gently reproached his disciple for "the search for the pathological case study, the love of human wounds."[1] While such an accusation may at first glance appear as a classic example of the pot calling the kettle black, what Zola had instinctively seized upon was an apparently morbid interest in medical minutiae that seemed somehow to exceed the naturalists' fascination with disease: their tendency, in the words of one disapproving physician, "to confuse hospitals and bookstores."[2] Huysmans's later publications were to offer ample proof of the appropriateness of Zola's remark. There was indeed a difference between the latter's portrayal of the metaphorical injuries inflicted upon the proletariat by an increasingly materialistic society and Huysmans's graphic descriptions of human rather than societal wounds, from the blisters of scrofula to the skin lesions of the Lourdes pilgrims described in nauseating detail in his last work, *Les Foules de Lourdes* (1906). One can certainly find painfully meticulous descriptions of physical ailments in Zola's work (e.g., the pulmonary diseases of *Germinal*'s miners, Coupeau's *delirium tremens* in *L'Assommoir*, Pascal's heart attack in *Le Docteur Pascal*, and the infirmities of the Lourdes pilgrims in *Lourdes* [1902], his own novel on the famous pilgrimage site, to which Huysmans's novel appeared as a rebuttal). Likewise, the pathological case study exists in the work of both authors. The difference is one of focus: whereas in Zola's work medical phenomena form merely one part of a vast whole, Huysmans's entire literary universe is conceived from a clinical viewpoint. Charles Maingon makes the following distinction: "In the work of Flaubert or Zola, disease is a drama of limited duration. . . . All of Huysmans's characters have more or less serious illnesses from the beginning to the end of his novels, and the author describes their large and small miseries with the precision of an entomologist."[3] The observation is accurate. Huysmans's best-known work, *À Rebours*, that "breviary of Decadence," to borrow Arthur Symons's unforgettable phrase, can, for example, be read as a case study in neurasthenia. Indeed, as Françoise Gaillard has shown, even the structure of the work derives from the medical monograph.[4] Considering that one could make the same observation about most of Huysmans's other novels, it is perhaps not surprising that two monographs have been devoted to the role of medicine in his work.[5] Moreover, in view of Huysmans's association with literary Decadence, it seems fitting that he should have adopted a medical paradigm in transcribing his view of reality, since the very notion of decadence, with its suggestion that society and progress were pathogenic, implies disease. Seen as products of a culture in the last throes of a fatal illness, Huysmans's so-called "decadent" novels have long been viewed as exemplars of a certain literary fashion. However, they also testify to their author's lifelong obsession with disease. In fact, Huysmans incorporates medical discourse into nearly all of his fiction in a highly idiosyncratic way, shaping and stretching the medical metaphor until it fits his (perverse) design. Small wonder that his perspective has been described not as "a medical *glance*" but rather as "a veritable medical *hallucination*."[6]

Whether Huysmans's persistent preoccupation with illness has its source in his own experience with physical suffering or owes more to literary fashion (specifically, Baudelaire's influence), it is clear that, in the early work at least, his "hallucination" was deliberate. Ruth Antosh's 1986 study, in which the author persuasively challenges the traditional division of his works into three periods (naturalist, Decadent, and religious), provides an excellent context for the study of his incorporation of medical discourse in his work.[7] I am convinced that Huysmans used medical discourse with subversive intent in the allegedly "naturalist" works, and that his target was double. On the one hand, his parodical adoption of a clinical perspective serves to underline his scorn for the medical practitioner; on the other, it appears as a subtle mockery of naturalism's scientific bias. Since it was *En ménage* that first alerted Zola to Huysmans's aberrant interest in medical phenomena, I shall focus on this novel. Generally considered to be derivative and devoid of interest, "a flat epic" in the best naturalist tradition,[8] *En ménage* has been neglected by all but a few critics.[9] Most scholars make only passing reference to the protagonist, André Jayant, who is seen as one of Huysmans's many fictional personae. Even those (few) of Huysmans's contemporaries who lavished praise on the novel made no claims for its originality. Zola himself seemed to take an almost paternal pride in defending Huysmans from his detractors, and the physician H. M. Gallot proclaimed *En ménage* "the biggest success of the Médan school," faint praise indeed for one who prized innovation above all else.[10] A serious reevaluation is in order.

The plot line dangles from a classic hook: adultery. A disillusioned, unsuccessful young novelist, André Jayant, returns home early after an evening spent with his artist friend Cyprien Tibaille (equally disillusioned and unsuccessful) to find his apparently frigid bourgeois wife in the act of adultery. After showing her lover to the door, he lets himself out as well. There follows an aimless bachelor's life in which daily comforts are provided by a maid, Mélanie, while sexual needs are satisfied in turn by streetwalkers; a more refined prostitute, Blanche, who is available to him by appointment only; and a former mistress, Jeanne, who is forced to leave him finally for financial reasons. Jayant's disheartening sexual odyssey is punctuated by abortive efforts to rekindle another spark, that of literary creation. By the novel's end, the hero has returned to his wife, and the misogynistic Tibaille, once the ardent opponent of cohabitation, is living with a fat concubine. Tibaille's cynical conclusion that "marriage and living together are no different" is based upon their effect: "They've rid both of us of our artistic preoccupations and our carnal depression. No more talent, only good health, what a dream!" (347).

The key, of course, is the suggestion that artistic talent and physical

(or psychological) health are incompatible. However, before we conclude that Huysmans was simply offering a corollary to the well-worn
Romantic *topos* according to which suffering is an essential condition
for the Muse's visit, we need to examine in some detail the concepts of
health and sickness as they occur throughout the novel.

At perhaps the most obvious level, that of characterization, the
reader is struck by the fact that nearly all of the characters, both major
and minor, can be categorized according to the state of their health.
Indeed, in descriptions of the two protagonists, the medical detail is
privileged, often to the exclusion of more "mundane" traits. Hence,
we know that André is bilious, but we do not know the color of his
hair; we know that Cyprien is anemic and highly nervous, but in the
brief passage describing his appearance, there is scarcely a detail that
cannot be qualified as clinical: his posture, his pallor, even his peculiar
gait, all contribute to the notion that he is "sickly" (110), and the
portrait that emerges is strongly caricatural. Huysmans attributes his
character's grasshopperlike walk to his "slender tibias" (116), a detail
that is playfully reflected at the onomastic level (Tibaille). Even episodic
characters are not spared the scalpel of Huysmans's diagnostic gaze, from
the pale café waitress who is "drained of energy by a constant vaginal
discharge" (31) to the children playing in the Luxembourg gardens, "with
rachitic complexions and the dried-up pock marks of scrofula on their
necks" (54). Furthermore, the nosology of physical ailments evoked
in the novel is impressive, including syphilis, nervous diathesis, scurvy,
diarrhea, constipation, dyspepsia, gastric catarrh, anemia, rheumatism,
obesity, asthma, and leukorrhea. It is perhaps unsurprising, then, that
the two protagonists would display a preoccupation with health and
hygiene that may be characterized as pathological. When they reminisce
together about boarding school, it is not amorous escapades that they
recall but rather the fetid stench of unwashed feet. The only lesson
they have retained is the one given by the headmaster, who regularly
exhibited a book filled with illustrations of men ravaged by syphilis (48),
warning them as he did that they could look forward to a similar fate
if they continued to "have fun" with their companions. As for their

classmates, they are remembered not for their schoolboy pranks but for their physical handicaps:

> "And do you remember Degagnac?" he continued, "that crank who had poor eyesight because his nursemaid was nearsighted? At least that's what he claimed."
>
> "Degagnac, the guy who suckled the milk of blindness? What in the devil became of him?" (52)

Just as the novel's plot, which incorporates many of the currently "fashionable" topics (frigidity, adultery, prostitution, divorce, concubinage), seems designed to appeal to popular taste, so also do the protagonists' memories seem to be triggered by the medical imaginary that dominated the thoughts, dreams, and phobias of the nineteenth-century Frenchman. The heroes' dialogues reflect the debates that raged in medical journals and monographs of the period: the lack of hygiene in the schools, the dangers of wetnursing, the horrors of onanism, the threat of venereal disease.[11] Indeed, such topics were not confined to professional publications but were standard fare, in vulgarized form, in the popular press. If Huysmans, for whom the commonplace was the abomination of desolation, studded his novel with the tawdry clichés of a medical wisdom that had been diluted and devalued by its appearance in the local rag, it was thus surely with parodical intent. In this light, Cyprien's witty statement regarding his classmate's myopia ("[he] had suckled the milk of blindness") appears as a clever reductio ad absurdum of the position taken by contemporary medical treatises on the risks of entrusting one's child to a wetnurse. However, in order to gain a fuller appreciation of Huysmans's subversive treatment of medicine and its practitioners, we need to take a closer look at the two protagonists.

Superficially at least, in what has been termed a "two-part monologue," André Jayant appears to be at the structural center of the novel. Here, the medical perspective is clearly dominant and patently ironic. Indeed, the entire narrative is subordinated to a clinical model, with Jayant as the patient. His disease is diagnosed (as "the skirt attack"), its etiology explored (beginning with "the illness of his marriage"), and the "accident" that provoked the onset of his symptoms (Berthe's infidelity) fully described. Berthe herself falls ill as a result of her shame; however, it is upon André's disease that the narrative focuses. With mock serious-ness, the condition is followed through each of its phases (appropriately, as with syphilis, there are three), and the amorous encounters that are the very backbone of the novel are assimilated to the search for a cure, successive love affairs being portrayed as so many dressings for the wound first inflicted by the unfaithful wife. As each cure fails, from the "healing parties" (141) of his visits to prostitutes, and the "poultices of the heart" (176) applied by Blanche, to Jeanne's therapeutic caresses "[which] closed the wounds opened by Berthe's betrayals and scarcely bandaged by Blanche's home-cooked meals" (259), André's hope for a remedy begins to fade. When, finally, he returns to his wife, the medical metaphor has disappeared, and the reader is left to interpret the reconciliation as a symbol of his resignation. Jayant thus takes his place among Huysmans's other malcontents, whose various quests Jean Borie has rightly seen as expressions of hope in medicine:

> Each time that André or Folantin or Durtal go out to try a new dish or a new prostitute, it's as if they're filling a prescription. In order to satisfy a need, cure it, regain their equilibrium . . . Blanche, Berthe, and Jeanne are basically tantamount to contracts proposed, diets, treatments, spa visits. . . .[12]

Clearly, there is nothing inherently comical about the tedium of André's existence, nor about his fruitless quest for happiness and stability in the form of a satisfying relationship with a woman. The foreground-ing of the physiological was, after all, a standard feature of naturalist narratives. However, when the rather banal malaise we know as carnal desire becomes the springboard for a metaphysical search and the object of an extended medical metaphor; when the reader is treated to an in-depth description of its cause, its progression, its therapy, as if it were a newly diagnosed exotic illness, an element of the ridiculous creeps in. Huysmans's hyperbolic exploitation of a medical-scientific rhetoric in his narration of the most common subject of literature, the search for "love," is clearly ironic, and his use of such ludicrous formulae as "poultices of the heart" and "skirt attack" leave little doubt as to his intentions.[13] Nevertheless, it is not only in discourse but also in story that Huysmans's irony is manifested, as we will see when we turn from descriptions of the vicissitudes of Jayant's sentimental journey to the professional evolution of his artist friend, Cyprien Tibaille.

A character who had first been introduced as the painter of harlots in *Les Sœurs Vatard* (1879), Tibaille is portrayed as an ardent naturalist who finds more art in "a gillyflower dying in a pot than in a field of sun-drenched roses."[14] He has paid dearly for his unorthodox views, since the doors of official salons have been slammed in his face. By the time he makes his appearance in *En ménage*, he is no longer producing work of artistic merit, although he continues to expound his aesthetic theories and his views on life to any male (he is a hardened misogynist) who will listen, including his neutered cat, Barre-de-Rouille. His vocabulary, drawn from the field of medicine, associates him with the physician. In his view, contemporary artists are "gangrenous with romanticism" (114), and he decries the halfhearted treatment used to halt the spread of this artistic epidemic ("If instead of curing our infection we weren't satisfied with simply covering up the symptoms . . ."), suggesting instead a more aggressive therapy, "an iodine that could cleanse the artistic brain." Through Cyprien's assimilation of a moribund literary and artistic movement to a repulsive, pathological condition, Huysmans appears to be taking aim especially at salon artists and the conservative Establishment that supports them; however, the very linguistic weapons he uses in his attack suggest another target, the medical profession. The discovery of microorganisms was very recent, and the importance, not merely of cleansing wounds, but of sterilizing the site of infection, was a refrain of current hygienist discourse, while antiseptics like iodine were the bread and butter of pharmacists throughout the country. It is true that the characterization of romanticism as a malady that must be cured was a platitude of the period. However, Huysmans's extravagant use of medical jargon to endow the metaphor with all the precision of a truly scientific discourse is patently ironic. The original metaphor has been stretched to the breaking point, held up to ridicule. And the authorial finger of scorn is pointing not only at those who accept and indeed exploit such clichés (such as the naturalist artist) but also at the dominant medical discourse that provides them. It is not improbable that, by suggesting a clinical paradigm of treatment for what he considered a deplorable aesthetic conservatism, Huysmans was also mocking the contemporary practice of consulting the medical practitioner for guidance on non-medical topics, topics as diverse as shoplifting and the construction of slaughterhouses, vagrancy and school curricula. Furthermore, in adopting a hygienist perspective by representing romantic ideals as infectious agents, microbes, of which the brain must be cleansed, Huysmans is subverting a cliché of the period according to which naturalists, not romantics, are associated with filth because of their "perverse" interest in decay and degradation.

The "cure" would restore sight to artists blinded by conventional notions of beauty, would open their eyes to the poetry of the pathological. It would transform their art: the cold stone of love goddesses would be replaced by the flaccid flesh of prostitutes, boringly "natural" still lifes by the dazzling artificiality of storefronts. The products of industrial society, however sordid and diseased, would be promoted to artistic status. Ironically, the cure itself further identifies the artist with the physician, who would be unable to make a living were it not for sickness.

However, as a character in a so-called "naturalist" novel, Cyprien is—indeed must be—treated as a patient. In a description that can be seen as a clever pastiche of the style of medical monographs devoted to the lives of famous men, Huysmans thus portrays his character as a pathological specimen: "Cyprien was truly the man of his painting, a rebel with iron-poor blood, an anemic plagued by jangled nerves, a curious, sick mind obsessed with the gnawing sadness of the neurotic, spurred on by fevers, unenlightened in spite of his theories, ruled by his feelings of sickness" (116). The link established between the man and his work, which effects an implicit reduction of art to symptom, was typical of a certain category of medical treatise that came into its own in Huysmans's time and flourished in the early-twentieth century.[15] The portrait is deftly painted: Cyprien is seen as a passive victim of his fragile health, "plagued . . . obsessed . . . spurred on . . . ruled" by his malady. It has been said of Huysmans that he shared none of Zola's scientific pretensions, that the master's deterministic notions were of no interest to him, a claim that would be hard to justify were we to accept the description of Cyprien at face value. However, the multiplication of redundant adjectives suggests that an interpretation of the passage as parody—either of the conventional naturalist character portrayal or of the textbook description on which it is based—is closer to the mark. Furthermore, Cyprien's own clearly whimsical explanation of the etiology of his digestive ailments appears as a playful mockery of Zola's theories of hereditary determinism: "I really don't know what can be left of a stomach that becomes more and more upset as it is passed through the generations!" (37). Finally, there is a paradox in the statement that Cyprien "was truly the man of his painting." Indeed, what painting? We are led to expect a work peopled with strange visions, obsessive, tormented, hallucinatory, yet Cyprien's artistic production is quite the opposite. For if we are told that his most successful paintings were those in which he portrayed the prostitute, none of these works is described in *En ménage*, and we can only conclude that such canvasses were painted during his former incarnation in *Les Sœurs Vatard*. The artist of *En ménage* is "the man of his painting" in quite another sense: having been reduced to the production of commercial art, he has become, like the subjects he once delighted in painting, a strumpet, shamelessly prostituting his creative talent. Yet even here there is an evolution of sorts, a progressive degradation that serves to measure the depth of Huysmans's cynicism.

Cyprien, an archetype of the starving artist who gives meaning to the popular formula "poor as a painter," sells his talent in turn to a pharmacist, a physician, and a wallpaper manufacturer. The first work to be evoked in *En ménage* is a pharmaceutical advertisement that will be reproduced lithographically for use on labels of medicine bottles. Although the artist confesses readily that his motive is pecuniary, the work is not totally devoid of artistry, and even features a few widely recognized symbols—a bust of Hippocrates, two turtle doves struggling in the coils of a boa constrictor, assorted beakers, distilling containers and syringes, and "a caduceus in the clouds" (152). The drawing includes two medallions, each representing a familiar scene, the first an opera ballet, the second a pair of lovers embracing in a sylvan setting. To the left of the medallions, a scantily clad young woman cries, while to the right, a young man in a bathrobe agonizes over unknown woes. These figures are in turn surrounded by hissing, writhing snakes. For a naturalist who is vehement in his denunciation of the banality of contemporary art, such a florid assemblage of iconographic clichés seems tantamount to failure. Yet Cyprien defends his work. What is the meaning of the symbolism? It is to the artist that Huysmans gives the task of explaining his *œuvre*:

> "First, it proves that if you have the means to pick up women who go to dance school or any other school, for that matter, and if with them you indulge in costly feasts, you'll get sick. And that's the just punishment inflicted on debauchery by God.
>
> "Next, it also proves that if, instead of being lecherous and rich, you are an ethereal soul and you're poor; and if, instead of guzzling alcohol with tarts, you love a young woman you think is virtuous, well! you also fall ill. And that's the just punishment inflicted by God on naiveté." (152–53)

Cyprien characterizes his drawing as "modern and humanitarian," for it alerts society's youth to the dangers of sexual activity at all levels of the social scale, whether for hire or for love. The desperately unhappy young couple pictured in the sketch prove with eloquent simplicity "to the younger generation . . . that, whatever they do, they'll cop it" (153). Ostensibly illustrating the "damned if you do and damned if you don't" dilemma, the prospectus, upon closer inspection, is revealed to bear a misogynistic message that relegates all women, regardless of social class, to the status of strumpets and carriers of disease. The message *does* imply a solution: abstinence from sexual congress. The artist insists with feigned solemnity upon the humanitarian aspects of such a message, and his decision to put aside his work is followed by a spontaneous invitation to André that stands in cynical counterpoint to the significance of his commercial art: "Say, do you want to come and drink in the delicious stench of the street with me?" (153). It is no mere coincidence that their nocturnal peregrinations lead to a carnal release for André (for he meets

Blanche and accompanies her back to her apartment) and a begrudging recognition of his own unsatisfied needs on the part of Cyprien. "If I had gotten paid for my ad, I might also have rented a syncope for a few hours" (171). The derisive formula for sexual orgasm, plucked once again from the medical lexicon, and the metonymic reduction of the prostitute to the physiological reaction she is expected to provoke, further underscore the artist's ferocious cynicism. That he would spend money earned from commercially commissioned, didactic art to perform precisely those acts censured by the message he has labored to deliver reveals either blatant duplicity or total disdain for the work to which his adamant refusal to conform has reduced him.

Nor should we forget that his employer is a pharmacist, and as such associated with the physician. Huysmans's clever choice of a profession whose practitioners were known for their greed and dishonesty ("the biggest swindlers" complains Cyprien [155]) is pointedly ironic. Here, art is in the service, not of society, as Cyprien hypocritically proclaims, but of bourgeois materialism in one of its most visible forms: the burgeoning success of the pharmaceutical industry. It is of some importance that the prospectus was not to be distributed gratis to the man on the street but rather wrapped around medicine bottles bearing the inscription "Medicine for external use only." Tibaille's prostitution of his talent appears all the more reprehensible when one is aware that the dubious efficacy of pharmaceutical preparations and the fictions of their extravagant promises is a subject of considerable derision in Huysmans's work, where they are associated with the stupid gullibility of the bourgeois. The scorn heaped on Berthe's bourgeois uncle Désableau illustrates this point. Finding Cyprien bedridden one day, he suggests a variety of popular panaceas to the artist:

> Monsieur Désableau belonged to that breed of people who immediately propose the most diverse remedies to the sick; hence he suggested that the artist take pills and capsules formulated by such and such a doctor, and electuaries, herbal teas, and medicinal preparations recommended regularly in the newspapers, in the ads on the last page. (276)

The "pharmaceutical advertisement," given prominence by its detailed description and its position at the approximate midpoint of the
novel, had signaled but the first stage of Cyprien's decadence. In the next
of his artistic creations, we witness a passage from preventive medicine
to the description of symptoms, from symbolic art to the purely mimetic,
as Cyprien is now producing watercolor plates of assorted skin lesions,
"a whole gamut of skin ailments, a whole range of rashes and sores"
(277). We see these works through the middle-class eyes of Désableau
himself, who is repulsed by the subject. Amused by his visitor's disgust,
Cyprien explains that he is merely carrying out doctor's orders: "I am
simply doing a job ordered by a physician. I have to go to St. Louis
Hospital, set myself up in rooms next to subjects who are pointed out to
me, force diets on those who refuse to let themselves be painted, and all
that just to earn ten francs a plate!" (277–78). If his studio (the hospital)
and his subject (the ulcers and abscesses of its patients) appear to identify
Cyprien with his bourgeois employer, the physician, the fact that he has
been empowered to "punish" those patients who refuse to cooperate by
prescribing a diet for them may be read as a further attempt to ridicule
the medical practitioners who put patients on diets at the slightest
provocation, for a wide variety of ailments, a custom that Huysmans
had already parodied in "Sac au dos." Furthermore, as we have seen, the
concept of remedy as punishment was hardly foreign in the nineteenth
century because of the harshness of the most commonly prescribed
cures. Huysmans's caustic wit could scarcely be more obvious: on the
pharmaceutical label, sickness had been portrayed as a chastisement for
sexual activity, whether discriminating or indiscriminate. Here, people
under treatment for skin lesions of various sorts (which, perhaps not
coincidentally, are common symptoms of venereal disease) may be
further punished at the command of the physician himself. The patients
are viewed, not as suffering fellows to be consoled and relieved, but
rather as living spectacles of disease, infectious entities to be codified
and defined for the advancement of medical science and the greater
glory of its practitioners. Cyprien's cooperation in this distasteful and
purely commercial enterprise proves to be a homeopathic remedy for

his pathological predilection for the sordid and sickly. This time there is no attempt, even half-hearted, to justify his hackwork at the aesthetic or the humanitarian level, and he openly avows that his poverty has reduced him to this shameful venality.

In addition, the deplorable state of his health has led to a previously unthinkable compromise of his principles: specifically, his digestive ailments, boils, and ear infections have stirred in him a vague premonition of solitary suffering, and he has sought—and found—a remedy, both for his medical condition and for his fear. The cure—it should come as no surprise to those who know Huysmans's later work—is found in a woman, Mélie, who accepts eagerly and with compassion to serve as Cyprien's nurse.[16] A former prostitute, now obese and having long since passed the age of "retirement," she considers herself fortunate "as long as I'm not with a man who's dirt poor and as long as he doesn't beat me" (320–21), a modest ambition that recalls Zola's Gervaise. If, when she first meets Cyprien, her pity for the painter focuses on his "ragged clothing" (291), if, "thinking about the future of his wardrobe," Cyprien has an ulterior motive in forming a liaison with her, he invites her to live with him only after he has fallen ill and she has proven herself a devoted nurse. His "proposal" is a masterpiece of Huysmansian wit: "I'm tired, and the latrines of my soul are full. Say, wouldn't it be a good idea for you to come here to eat and sleep?" (298). Besides providing another example of Huysmans's playful juxtaposition of the concrete ("latrines") with the abstract ("soul"), the formula represents a subversion of Parent-Duchâtelet's popular metaphor according to which prostitutes are seen as sewers for the disposal of seminal overflow. The smug, judgmental bourgeois attitude that condemns prostitutes as the dregs of society and those who take them in as gutter cleaners (Désableau's categorization of Mélie as "sludge" and Cyprien as a "sewer worker" may be seen as an expression of this viewpoint) is wittily overturned by Huysmans. Yet this reversal hardly amounts to a "promotion" for Mélie. Although Cyprien is somewhat embarrassed by this woman "who, despite his protests, insisted on taking care of all of the humiliations and abjections of his illness" (292), his childlike submission to her maternal care reveals a misogynistic complicity with her cheerfully expressed belief in a feminine mission that includes the most repugnant of duties: "Never mind, my sweetie, that's woman's work" (292).

The trajectory that has taken Cyprien from chlorotic prostitutes, with whom he cavorted in the belief that an artist must know his subject, to the jovial healer who mends his shirts, prepares his meals, and carries out his chamber pot, marks a passage from artistic idealism—however debased according to current standards—to a crassly materialistic realism. Mélie (whose name, significantly, recalls that of André's maid Mélanie—indeed their functions hardly differ—as well as being a transformation of the Greek *meli*, honey, often used in elixirs for its reputedly therapeutic qualities) is the antithesis of Cyprien. Her corpulence contrasts with his emaciation, her "elephantine footsteps" with his grasshopperlike movement, her healthy appetite with his dyspepsia, her cliché-ridden speech with his oft-expressed disdain for the banal. And it is precisely in this, his compromise with bourgeois banality in all its forms, that his artistic endeavor finds its ultimate expression. When asked about his current activities by André in the closing pages of the novel, he responds, "I subsist between Mélie and Bar-de-Rouille; I also work for wallpaper manufacturers. Among other things, I make tartan patterns, you know, that paper that has crisscrossing red and green stripes" (346). Cyprien's useless existence, symbolically situated between a woman who administers purges to cure him of assorted ailments and a castrated cat whose impotence is reflected in its name, is thus given to an outrageous violation of his professional calling. In producing scotch-plaid patterns for interior designers, work that requires neither talent nor skill, Cyprien is capitulating to a nineteenth-century bourgeois taste for textile look-alikes in interior decorating.[17] He is also serving to illustrate Huysmans's stinging devalorization of the middle class, who spared no expense in furnishing and remodeling their homes while balking at the modest fees requested by artists commissioned to paint portraits for the adornment of their walls.[18] Thus, Cyprien may indeed have "progressed" from medicine bottles to medical textbooks to walls, but the positive nature suggested by the spatial evolution is illusory. Whereas prior to the Industrial Revolution, wall coverings had in fact often featured nonrepeating landscapes and even historical subjects, mass-produced wallpaper is the banalization of art, purely decorative, a pattern to be repeated ad infinitum, increasingly by machine. A product of the rapidly growing marketplace (there were three hundred wallpaper factories in Paris alone by ca. 1860), expressing no aesthetic ideal, devoid of any redeeming didactic or social value, Cyprien's wallpaper symbolizes his ultimate surrender to industrial society. He is now at the mercy of the factories and shops he had once dreamed of painting: no longer aesthetic objects, to be imprisoned in the two-dimensional space of his canvas, they have become monstrous, engulfing subjects, dominating him, robbing him of his creative powers. In a metaphor that owes much to Montaigne's characterization of his writing as "the excrement of an aged mind" and Cabanis's celebrated definition of thought ("Man's thought is only the excrement of his mind"), Mélie's successful purge of her companion thus symbolizes his trivialized "artistic" production. Similarly, the castrated cat stands as a symbol for the sterility of such labor. Cyprien himself has no illusions about his work, and he willingly admits to his motives for doing it: "It's not badly paid and there's plenty of work" (246).

Huysmans's cynical chronicling of the deterioration of an artist, all the more insolent when one considers that this character serves throughout as the spokesperson of naturalist theory, challenges us to reinterpret the novel, and prevents us from lining up behind the numerous critics for whom the author's originality burst forth unannounced with *À Rebours*. Through his exploitation of medical discourse, Huysmans effected a witty distortion of many current clichés and displayed his own skepticism with regard to the supposedly salutary alliance of medicine and art. In the world of *En ménage*, a topsy-turvy fictional world where relations between men and women, subordinated to a clinical model, are identified as the penetration of the former by the latter;[19] where carnal needs are assimilated to medical conditions and digestive difficulties provide the impetus for cohabitation; where science commissions art and writers don't write, the physician is proclaimed king, only to be pulled from his throne, derided and vilified by that ever-disrespectful subject, Huysmans.[20]

En ménage was, in the words of its author, a "hymn to nihilism." By classifying the novel as "naturalist," we have failed to take his epithet seriously and ignored the numerous hints of a subversive subtext. André Jayant's intention, in the first chapter, to obtain documentation for his novel by visiting a slaughterhouse at dawn (a thinly disguised mockery of the archetypal naturalist subject) is never realized, his novel never written, but the allusion is not gratuitous, for his own fictional existence is hardly less instinctual—or more enviable—than that of beasts being led to the kill.[21] Furthermore, despite this apparently deterministic subject, *En ménage* is not a *roman-laboratoire* (a laboratory novel) but a *roman-abattoir* (a slaughterhouse novel), mercilessly slaughtering all the sacred cows of late-nineteenth-century France with its "bursts of sinister gaiety and expressions of ferocious wit."[22]

The novel's preoccupation with wounds and digestion, art and commerce, builds to one final, startling image, in which the whole of the novel can be said to be contained: that of *la cité Berryer*, an open-air market set up twice weekly in a courtyard on the rue Royale, discreetly hidden behind a closed door. Whereas its location "just near the Madeleine" (312) identifies it simultaneously with morality and immorality (a high-society church and the Biblical prostitute for whom it was named), its "three odorous zones," described as acrid, salty, and "stinking," evoke an anatomical image of the most vulgar sort. Cyprien, waxing lyrical about the presence of this fetid market hidden in a courtyard of the elegant rue Royale, describes it in medical terms: "This vile hole, hidden behind superb façades, evokes the idea of a necessary sore oozing pus on a well-dressed body, a blistering agent, a sort of drain, camouflaged under the opulence of the underwear, that pumps out secretions and keeps the complexion clear!" (313). The verbal painting is reminiscent of Cyprien's vaunted talent for representing the prostitute, with the "shameful rotting of her soul and the opulent corruption of her appearance" (116). Once again, the anatomical comparison proves irresistible for Huysmans, and his reference to blistering agents is simply the last in a whole series of allusions to *materia medica* designed to rid the body of impurities. "Oh! if only there were an emetic that could make you bring up all those old affections you have inside," lamented André earlier in the novel.

And here finally, near the novel's end, the remedy has been found in the nauseating realization that, despite appearances, commercial interests are the lifeblood of society and, by extension, of all human relationships. The disheartening gallop of women through André's unhappy life has been replaced by a new image, that of the jostling, shouting string of plump harpies at the Berryer market. Here, the medical discourse itself appears as a "superb façade," designed to hide the awful truth of commercial exchange, the crude identity of "this vile hole" through which bodily secretions must pass if one is to maintain a healthy complexion.[23]

The marketplace as metaphor for the lower bodily functions; the classic dichotomy of woman translated into the medical idiom (the poisoner, carrier of disease, versus the healer); daily life envisioned as a quest for therapy: with all of this, Huysmans's novel proclaims — and with what bitterness! — the robust health of commerce and the critical illness of art. By inscribing his narrative in the lexical space provided by medical discourse, Huysmans may appear to be pandering to a bourgeois taste that he deplores, but in reality he is attacking it from within, setting it against itself, while simultaneously exposing the folly of naturalism's scientific affectations. He thus provides an excellent example of what Richard Terdiman refers to as counter-discursive strategy.[24] "No more talent, only good health: what a dream!" Indeed, an appropriate dream for an era dominated by the bourgeoisie, an era in which talent was regarded as pathological, and commerce conspired to kill it.

5

VOICES OF AUTHORITY?

Maupassant and the Physician-Narrator

ℭ

The novels examined thus far corroborate the thesis that late-nineteenth-century French literati were acutely aware of the limits of medical science and cynical about the widespread diffusion of a clinical discourse. Yet they exhibit a certain timidity where the medical practitioner is concerned, launching oblique attacks by appearing to target what might be termed today paramedical personnel (*Madame Bovary*), by setting their narratives in foreign countries (*Madame Gervaisais*), or by taking aim at the discourse itself rather than the profession from which it emanates (*L'Assommoir*, *En ménage*). With Maupassant, a new, equally subtle, and equally subversive strategy comes to the fore: the use of the physician-narrator.

Maupassant is not the first to have made use of physicians as narrators. In the nineteenth century alone, Alexandre Dumas's *Mémoires d'un médecin* (1849–60), Claire de Duras's *Ourika* (1823), and Barbey d'Aurevilly's "Le Bonheur dans le crime" (1874) all testify to the popularity of the medical practitioner as narrator. Moreover, this is but a sample of the many works that feature physicians in narrative roles. Although on the surface, Maupassant's exploitation of this popular narrative device does not differ markedly from that of his predecessors, a closer examination of stories narrated by physicians suggests that in bowing to convention, Maupassant had a goal that was in fact highly unconventional.

The corpus, if significant, is not large. Despite the considerable number of mental and physical ailments described in Maupassant's fiction, only a dozen stories feature physicians as narrators. Nor is this paucity of physician-narrators offset by an abundance of physician-characters. While all six of the novels and some fifty stories mention physicians, in all but two instances (*Pierre et Jean* and "Un coup d'état") they play peripheral roles, often as helpless bystanders who misdiagnose, propose ineffectual remedies, and aggravate suffering. One early protagonist who bridges the gap between the physician-characters and narrators is "Doctor" Chenet of "En famille." Called to the home of an old woman, the health officer certifies her death ("Rest assured, I never make a mistake" [1:201]), only to learn the following day that she is alive and well. This early representation of the medical practitioner is rich in innuendoes. Besides his ludicrous incompetence, Chenet is characterized by his indifference to suffering, his *gourmandise*, and his garrulousness. When he manages to extract an invitation to dinner from the newly bereaved family, he becomes jovial and loquacious, recounting "stories of deaths that struck him funny" (1:203), anecdotes that, given the circumstances, are indelicate at best. Indeed, his stories, which revolve around the peasants' legendary nonchalance in the face of death, act both as a *mise-en-abyme* of the principal narrative and as a mirror of his own matter-of-fact attitude toward life and death.

It is precisely this "scientific" objectivity in the presence of human misery that would seem to make of the doctor a credible storyteller in an age during which faith in science was supposedly at its height. It thus seems natural that Maupassant would cast physicians in narratorial roles in several of his best-known stories, "the prestige of their occupation"[1] serving as guarantee of their reliability. Moreover, because like Maupassant himself, they are sophisticated, worldly freethinkers, the physician-narrators appear to be transparent vehicles of narrative authority. As spokesmen for science, they are assumed to present the unadorned truth, no matter how distasteful it may be. Hence Dr. Bonenfant of "Conte de Noël," conscious of his anticlerical bias, promises to tell his story of a Christmas Eve miracle "naively, as if I were as gullible as an Auvergne peasant" (1:689); and the characters of "La Rempailleuse" decide to settle an argument by taking as mediator the presumably unprejudiced doctor. However, a close reading of these (and other) stories narrated by physicians calls into question the doctor's neutrality. Bonenfant's narration of a Christmas Eve exorcism, hardly naive, contains a blasphemous subtext.[2] Likewise, "La Rempailleuse," ostensibly a tale of "true love," may be read as a sly attack on a professional rival, the village pharmacist. Here and elsewhere, the physician's motives for narrating are suspect, his objectivity problematical. Angela Moger, while regarding the physician-narrator as an authorial persona—a metaphor for "non-integration in the life process" in a way that recalls Maupassant's lament about the writer, condemned to be a "spectator of himself and others"—allows that this very impassivity may disturb sensitive readers and cause them to focus less on the story told than on the circumstances of its telling.[3] Moger's readings revolve around these circumstances—the narrating instance—and posit an identity between writer and doctor.[4] However, this identification is deceptive, for it is not difficult to show how Maupassant, even as he exploits a well-known narrative convention, actually undermines it from within, much as Huysmans had undermined clinical discourse by pressing it into service to describe even the most trivial of daily activities. To illustrate this point, I will examine two stories written in a comic register, "La Relique" (1882) and "Le Rosier de Madame Husson" (1887).

The first of these tales, a *conte* (a short short story) rather than a *nouvelle* (a long short story), assumes the form of a letter written by a physician, Henri Fontal, and addressed to his former fiancée's cousin, the priest Louis d'Ennemare. Fontal pleads with d'Ennemare to help him locate an authentic religious relic in order that he might reestablish, with his ex-fiancée, Gilberte, an engagement broken when she learned that he had lied about having stolen for her a bone fragment from a reliquary in Cologne Cathedral containing the remains of eleven thousand virgins. He can redeem himself in her eyes only if he procures a genuine relic, "certified by our Holy Father the Pope as being from any virgin martyr whatsoever" (1:593).

If it is true, as Louis Forestier contends, that "the age, the profession or the experience of the storyteller are determined in light of the subject to be treated" (1:xxvii), then it seems relevant to consider why the doctor was selected for this narrative. First, the story deals with the trade in fake Christian relics that had been occurring since at least the fourth century. Who better than the physician, enemy of religion, could expose the gullibility that made possible this type of exploitation? More central to this story's theme, however, is the issue of feminine character, Fontal being a referentially accurate representation of the misogynistic physician of Maupassant's era. As in many of Maupassant's tales, the narrative moves deductively to illustrate an initial generalization: women are illogical, capricious, and superstitious. Before the discovery of the fatal lie, marvels Fontal, Gilberte is ecstatic to have in her possession what she believes to be a genuine relic, despite the conditions of its acquisition: "Just note this: I had committed a sacrilege for her. I had stolen, I had violated a church, a shrine; I had violated and stolen holy relics. For this she adored me, found me tender, perfect, divine. That's a woman for you, Father. Typical" (1:592). Underlining the superficiality of a religious belief that will accommodate such egregious offenses, Fontal insists upon his "real innocence" with regard to those crimes against religion of which Gilberte believed him guilty. At the same time, he presents his dishonesty as a harmless prank. In fact, however, he has repeatedly lied to her. Not only has he purchased from a peddler a piece of bone that he believes to be a false relic with the intention of presenting it to her as real, but, having lost it, he has substituted a fragment of mutton bone. By this action, Fontal has assumed the role of the relic peddler himself. However, in lieu of monetary payment, he envisions a return in species of another sort: the whole virgin for the fragment. His expectation is consistent with his fiancée's promise, censored to avoid offending the priest's virgin ears: "If it doesn't cost you any money, and if it's something truly ingenious and delicate, I will . . . kiss you" (1:590). Having fulfilled at least one of the conditions (the bone fragment is "truly delicate"), Fontal proceeds to weave an ingenious narrative around its acquisition, thereby granting his fiancée's wish to be "touched by . . . the inventiveness."

The telling of the lie—the narrative act—is richly suggestive. The seductive potential of the gift—and of the story—is immediately seized by Fontal. Teasing his fiancée by withholding the gift until she is "crazy with curiosity" (1:591), he finally offers her "the holy medallion." When

Gilberte asks him for confirmation of the relic's authenticity, he launches into his spurious "confession" of the theft, a successful step forward in the seduction: "Her heart was pounding; she felt faint with happiness." Properly primed, Gilberte is now ready for the story. Her resistance overcome, she listens, "trembling, in ecstasy" (1:592), to the tale of his sacrilegious exploit, his penetration and violation of a sacred space reserved for the mortal remains of eleven thousand virgin martyrs. Declaring her love, "She let herself fall into my arms." Lest the reader fail to grasp the parallel between the story told and the circumstances of its telling, both of which appear to conclude with a *prise de possession* (a possession-taking), we are informed in the following paragraph that Gilberte has converted her bed chamber into a chapel to house the sacred relic, the presumed cause of what she terms "this divine crime of love." Only the naive reader—mirror perhaps of the priest who is the letter's addressee—will miss the ambiguity of that phrase.

Indeed, upon second reading, the story appears replete with ambiguities, all of which cast doubt upon the physician's truthfulness. If Fontal has shown himself to be a seductive liar in his dealings with his fiancée, how can he be a reliable narrator? His self-revelation to d'Ennemare is a plea for help rather than a confession. Here, Fontal's seductive strategies are deployed in order to possess—or perhaps to repossess—Gilberte. He flatters the priest, calling him "my old buddy" (1: 589), alluding to his "magnanimity" (1:591); he attempts to establish the chastity of his fiancée ("She's truly a woman, or rather a girl, more than any other" [1:589]), all the while titillating his presumably celibate correspondent with hints of her sensuality ("[She is] pretty . . . as you know; and more seductive than I can tell you . . . and as you will never know"). In a subtly blasphemous comparison of his plight with that of Christ, he refers to the day on which he told the fated lie: "Oh! watch out for Fridays: I assure you that they're disastrous" (1: 590)! He promises undying gratitude ("I'll be grateful to you until my dying day" [1:589]) and an early conversion ("I promise that I'll convert ten years sooner!" [1:593]), although he cleverly avoids specifics (convert to what? sooner than what?). Describing himself as "sick at heart," Fontal humbles himself ("Forgive me, I'm unworthy") and declares his affection for the priest ("I love you with my whole heart"). Finally, he presents his request, not on his own behalf, but on behalf of "this poor pauvre Gilberte," who may otherwise have to bear the cross of virginity forever: "I beg you: do something so that she won't be the eleven-thousand-and-first." By phrasing his request in this way, Fontal is at once repeating the subterfuge of the inner story, that is, presenting as virginal something that is not, and teasing the priest by suggesting that he has the power to make a woman of a girl.

But why select a doctor as narrator-protagonist? Maupassant's choice was hardly haphazard. In the first place, it is worth noting that this physician is summoned to Cologne to perform surgery on a dying man, and that the surgery is . . . an amputation. Bones, in short, are his business. Fontal's medical intervention is followed almost immediately by a commercial transaction, the purchase of the phony relic. As an enlightened consumer, the physician knows that the object he is purchasing is in itself devoid of value; however, he correctly surmises that its exchange value will be considerable. Thus he is already implicated in the phony relics trade. He becomes even more fully involved when he produces and mounts his own phony relic and then invents a story to explain its origin. Now, considering that the adoration of sacred relics was often linked to spontaneous cures from serious illness, the portrayal of the physician as an enterprising charlatan offering relics to the faithful is filled with an irony all the more delicious in that the "illness" he is attempting to cure is virginity.[5]

There is a final dimension to Maupassant's choice of narrator in "La Relique," and it concerns the fantastic—that is, unbelievable—nature of the legend itself, to which the physician's fictions are analogous. "I took a small bone in the middle of a huge pile," he tells Gilberte, and to the priest he adds, "I said a huge pile, thinking about the number of bones that the debris of eleven thousand virgin skeletons must produce" (1:592). The hyperbolic dimensions of this legend of martyrdom make it comical, not tragic;[6] furthermore, the word *debris*, evoking unwanted remains, conjures up the image of a trash heap of gigantic proportions from which Fontal is valiantly trying to save a potential victim. Yet his enterprise is hardly an attempt to stem the tide of an epidemic; in reality, his "fantastic story" (1:591) and his seductive homeopathic remedy are intended to serve his own very carnal interests. That he seeks as accomplice a priest whose patronym identifies him with the lover of Jeanne's mother in *Une Vie*, a character who is at once paramour, letter-writer, and provider of "relics," contributes to the text's irony. With the collapse of distinctions—or what Charles Stivale might term the "homosocial specularity"—between priest, relic peddler, and physician, all of whom rely on the naiveté of the faithful, we can measure Maupassant's cynicism regarding the medical practitioner of his time.[7] I might add, finally, that the compensatory gesture of acquiring "a small bone" in Cologne after having amputated a limb from a male patient should be given its full symbolic weight. "La Relique" is less a story of female superstition and fetishism than of male desire.[8]

In fully half of the stories that feature physician-narrators, frustrated or unfulfilled sexual desire is derided as contrary to nature. The Catholic doctrine of the Immaculate Conception is assimilated to a demonic possession ("Conte de Noël"), sexual abstinence breeds tragedy ("L'Enfant"), and unfulfilled desire is a curiosity of pathological proportions ("En Wagon"). The medical practitioner is the ideal transmitter of stories that illustrate the body's imperious needs and the pathological consequences of denying them. Eschewing a medical lexicon ("Let's forget the big words, shall we? I'm not talking about medicine or morality, I'm talking about pleasure" [1:450]), Maupassant's physicians are hedonistic *raconteurs*, thrilling to the discomfiture of their listeners, substituting the oral pleasure of narration for the therapeutic power that should be theirs.

This tendency is well illustrated in "Le Rosier de Madame Husson," a framed *nouvelle* and the last of the stories to feature a physician-narrator. Like "La Relique," this story deals cynically with the subject of chastity through the ridicule of a practice dating from the Middle Ages and sanctioned by the Church, specifically the crowning of a town's most virtuous maiden, who is rewarded for her purity and given the title of *rosière* (rose queen). The tale begins when the first narrator, Raoul Aubertin, traveling by train through Normandy, is awakened abruptly just outside the town of Gisors by the sharp jolt of the locomotive's derailment. His journey temporarily interrupted, Aubertin decides to visit his old friend, Albert Marambot, who now practices medicine in this town. Over lunch, Marambot lectures Aubertin on gastronomy; he then guides him on a walking tour of the town, complete with a commentary on "Gisors's glories" (2:954). The appearance of a local drunk serves as transition between frame and embedded story. Marambot proceeds to tell of one particular "glory," a young man who was selected as *rosier* of Gisors in the absence of a virtuous young maiden, only to turn to debauchery and alcoholism thanks to the monetary prize that rewarded his previous virtue. "A good deed is always rewarded" (2:965), concludes Marambot mischievously before continuing his recitation of the list of local celebrities.

Several critics, among them Jean Paris and Frédéric Nef, have conducted cogent structuralist analyses of this story, drawing our attention to the relationship between frame and embedded narrative.[9] However, the symmetries, as Trevor Harris points out, are "difficult to uncover."[10] More than the work of these critics, Harris's own emphasis on ironic repetition in Maupassant's work provides a critical perspective from which to interrogate this apparently uncomplicated text. Beneath the textual surface are some highly revealing parallels that illuminate the physician's role.

It is significant that an auditory clue signals Marambot's presence when Aubertin knocks on his friend's door. Upon being told by the physician's maid that he is not at home, presumably on "doctor's orders" (whence the immediate association of this physician with dishonesty), the skeptical Aubertin, hearing the clatter of cutlery, calls out and brings Marambot to the door. Physically, Marambot's salient characteristic is his corpulence. As Jean Paris has observed, he is thus linked both with the fleshy woman upon whom Aubertin is thrown when the train lurches to a halt and with the derailed locomotive, "the huge crippled iron beast" (2:950). The locomotive in turn is likened to a dying horse that, despite the presence of vital signs, is no longer capable of making even the smallest effort "to get up and begin to move." A similar impotence characterizes Marambot, who is immediately subject to the penetrating gaze of Aubertin:

> I would certainly never have recognized him. He looked at least forty-five years old, and in a split second, I had a vision of provincial life, which dulls, ages, and fattens a man. . . . I imagined the leisurely meals that had given him a paunch, the after-dinner naps induced by the lethargy of a difficult digestion accompanied by cognac, the cursory examinations he gave his patients with his mind on the chicken roasting on the spit. I guessed at the nature of his conversations — about how to cook certain dishes, how to thicken certain sauces — just by looking at the ruddy puffiness of his cheeks, the thickness of his lips, the dull gleam in his eyes. (2:951)

Whereas Aubertin is by implication a bright, sophisticated Parisian, the bloated Marambot is characterized as a self-indulgent provincial gourmand. In contrast to the gaze of Aubertin himself, which is searching, penetrating, in a word, clinical, Marambot's lackluster eyes reflect an intelligence gone to seed. The stupid contentment of a provincial life has anesthetized his mind, as the repeated references to somnolence suggest, and Marambot, reduced to the status of a provincial cow, is shown ruminating his simple pleasures in a way strongly reminiscent of that other famous medical bovine, Charles Bovary, with one important difference: Marambot is unmarried, and the text implies that he is a *célibataire* (bachelor) in all senses of that term, sexual pleasures having been replaced by the gustatory.

According to Jean Paris, the entire story can be read as a struggle between the two narrators, Aubertin's superiority being temporarily overturned when the two begin to engage in dialogue. Here the power of language belongs to Marambot, who monopolizes the conversation, displaying his knowledge of local history and gastronomy, the latter having replaced medicine as an object of "scientific" interest and study. Following the example set by the Greeks and Romans, Marambot has occupied himself with the refinement of his palate. Whereas Aubertin, the layman, has used the powers of his diagnostic gaze in his scrutiny of the physician, Marambot, the doctor, has developed the inferior sense of taste, which is associated with the bestial and plays no role in medical diagnosis. Furthermore, his impassioned defense of gastronomy — which, strongly reminiscent of Brillat-Savarin's *La Physiologie du goût*, is based upon the contention that it is no more acceptable to have "la bouche bête" ["an undiscerning palate," but literally "a stupid mouth"] than "l'esprit bête" ["a dull wit," but literally "a stupid mind"] and that "only fools aren't gourmands" (2:952–53)—is subverted by textual suggestions that his *gourmandise* is a sublimation of the sexual instinct, his "flushed cheeks" (2:953), "gleaming eyes," and the "tenderness" with which he gazes at his wine betraying the substitution of gustatory for coital pleasure. The referential accuracy of Maupassant's portrait of the physician as gourmand notwithstanding, this physician's passion for food is clearly pathological.[11]

As for his patriotism and his fascination with local history, they too become a commentary on his professional "derailment" and are diagnosed as an illness by Aubertin: "It seems to me that you're afflicted with a peculiar illness that you, as a physician, should investigate. It's called parochialism" (2:954). In the frame, Aubertin repeatedly, albeit subtly, mocks provincial life as a source of boredom and mindlessness, only to be rebuked by Marambot, who insists on the superiority of the small town where a single window "keeps you occupied and intrigues you more than a whole Parisian street" (2:952). This evocation of voyeurism adds to our impression of a deviant sexuality. If his decision to recount one of Gisors's ironic "glories" allows him to ridicule chastity, thereby establishing his status as an experienced man-of-the-world, it also has the unintended effect of suggesting parallels with his own situation, gluttony and alcoholism being variants of the same vice of overindulgence (for Marambot is both gourmet *and* gourmand). Moreover, his description of Isidore's metamorphosis from a chaste young man to a debauched derelict lingers on the orgiastic banquet held in his honor:

> Isidore ate and drank as he had never eaten and drunk before. He served himself everything, took seconds on everything, noticing for the first time how lovely it is to feel your stomach swell with good things that first give you pleasure as they pass through your mouth. He had discreetly unbuckled his pants, because the increasing pressure of his paunch was making them feel tight. Silent, although a little concerned about a drop of wine that had fallen on his twill vest, he stopped chewing to raise his glass to his lips. (2:962)

Only a careless reader would miss the significance of the allusions to the unbuckled pants and the scarlet-stained clothing. Even before he has lost his crown of orange blossoms, Isidore has been symbolically deflowered, and Louis Forestier is correct to see in the stain the symbol of his transgression.[12] The direct cause of the *rosier*'s corruption will be money. However, indirectly, the instrument of his degradation is Paris, first because the idea to crown a *rosière* came from Nanterre, just outside the capital;[13] and second because it is in Paris that the *rosier* is transformed from the personification of virtue to that of vice. By implicating Paris, the Provincial would appear to be gaining the upper hand in his battle against the Parisian. But appearances are deceiving, for the metamorphosis he describes mirrors his own, transforming the *rosier* into an unflattering but profoundly revealing double.

Indeed, the passage relating the discovery of the sordid drunk sleeping in a doorway is strikingly symmetrical to the passage in which Marambot himself is described as he appears in a doorway, early in the frame narrative. Like Marambot, Isidore is a distorted remnant of his former self, his "invincible sleep" (2:964) a literal counterpart to Marambot's *inconscience* (lack of thought), his empty brandy bottle the equivalent of Marambot's fork. The analogous destinies of these two characters are also supported by a geographical detail: Marambot lives on the rue Dauphine, along which the town dignitaries process to proclaim Isidore's triumph. The onomastic history of this street adds a further level of irony. In a story that revolves around the description of food and drink, their preparation, ingestion, and digestion, it seems normal that an allusion to bodily elimination would have a place, and the anecdote regarding the princess's procession, interrupted on this street so that she could empty her bladder, fulfills this expectation. More than a mere digression in the narrative, this anecdote encapsulates the narrative situation, specifically Marambot's linguistic incontinence. The pompous Marambot, "his mouth constantly busy" (2:953), now eating, now drinking, now disserting endlessly on culinary pleasures or historical trivia, is, like the princess, the source of an irresistible production. With this variant on what Jean-Louis Cabanès sees as realism's banal evocation of language "in the form of excreted rubbish," Maupassant alludes not to the anus but to a different organ.[14] Ironically, it is not the phallus of Lacanian theory that is suggested here, not the emblem of power, creative energy, and Logos, for there is nothing *seminal* about Marambot's drivel. Like the *rosier* himself, who is likened to "the first seed sown in this field of hope" (2:961) and exhorted to bear fruit, Marambot cannot realize his *potential* for he is as *impotent* as is his namesake in "Denis." In this regard, the confusion between male and female that structures this text (of which the most obvious manifestation is the substitution of a *rosier* for a *rosière*) and the numerous veiled allusions to impotence, from the disabled locomotive to Napoléon's abortive Russian campaign, are highly meaningful. Far from being the learned man of science who discourses knowledgeably about health and sickness, Marambot is a bombastic provincial whose babble is identified with a form of bodily waste. The *rosier* unbuckles his pants to relieve his feeling of fullness; the corpulent Marambot opens his mouth, and the body of the story swells as he speaks.[15] In this light, his criticism of those who have "la bouche bête" assumes new meaning. The single medical function performed by Marambot during the course of this narrative consists in his declaration of the *rosier*'s death. "I had the honor of closing his eyes" (2:965), he tells Aubertin. This brings us full circle: the doctor, like the *rosier*, is blinded by his pride, his verbal delirium a pathological excess, a variant on the *rosier*'s *delirium tremens*. *L'art de la gueule* (the art of the mouth) has replaced both the art of healing and the art of speech.

Maupassant, who tried in vain to find relief from the symptoms of syphilis, was understandably cynical where the medical practitioner was concerned. His ostensibly docile conformity to a well-known narrative convention, the use of the physician-narrator, enabled him to give vent to his frustration, as our reading of two stories has shown. From "La Relique" to "Le Rosier de Madame Husson," the physician-narrator has been transformed from a seductive liar to the personification of impotence and self-indulgence, an aesthete who delights in the sordid and whose flabbiness is a mirror of his discursive style. Considering the prevalence of degeneration theory in the clinical discourse of Maupassant's time, considering also the poetics of disintegration that David Baguley has termed naturalism's "entropic vision," Maupassant's chronicle of the physician's idiosyncratic "degeneration," his iconoclastic presentation of the doctor as pathological specimen, is strongly tinged with irony.[16] The species *homo medicus*, as presented by Maupassant, is more brute- than Godlike, and the texts that feature physician-narrators reveal themselves, upon close inspection, to be profoundly contentious.[17]

6

THE PHYSICIAN AS FOREIGNER
Alphonse Daudet's *Le Nabab*

❡

Of Alphonse Daudet's novels, Roger Williams writes that they "give us life in France between 1860 and 1890 without the political bias that marred Zola's greater novels about life during the Second Empire."[1] Whether or not one accepts the objective/subjective opposition that Williams regards as the defining distinction between Daudet and Zola, it is clear that the works of Daudet, like those of Zola, have documentary value. For the student of Second Empire France, *Le Nabab* (1877) is of particular interest. And for the scholar interested in the intersections between literature and medicine, the study of this novel is vital. Written during a brief respite from the symptoms of syphilis, which, according to Williams's estimates, this close friend of the Goncourt brothers contracted between 1861 and 1863, the novel features an Irish physician, Jenkins, who is perhaps the most striking among the many portraits of physicians in the novels of Alphonse Daudet. A consummate hypocrite whose good looks (he has "the handsome face of a scholar and an apostle" [2:481]) and life-restoring tablets (fatuously named "Jenkins capsules") have made of him "1864's most fashionable doctor," Jenkins comes to symbolize the corruption and materialism of the Second Empire. As the plot unfolds, the reader learns that he has abandoned two wives (the first legitimate, the second common-law), alienated his stepson, and attempted to rape his surrogate daughter. He will continue his work of destruction, murdering the duc de Mora and bringing about the deaths of countless infants, victims of a "philanthropic" plan to replace wetnurses with goats. Published the same year as *L'Assommoir*, *Le Nabab* lays out in excruciating detail not the physical misery of the indigent but the moral bankruptcy of the wealthy. And, just as the influence of medical discourse on Zola's novel finds expression in the ideological underpinnings of the plot, in Daudet's novel, medical presence, here in the form of a physician-character, is oppressive and influential. As a symbol of perverted paternity, the physician plays a central role in the moral decadence of the late–Second Empire society depicted by Alphonse Daudet.

Le Nabab relates the tale of one Bernard Jansoulet, a poor southern Frenchman by birth who makes a fortune in Tunisia and, as "a gigantic parvenu eager to enjoy life" (2:500), returns to Paris with his millions. The fascination he exercises on the Parisian populace, rendered in culinary terms, suggests that the phonetic proximity of his name to the famous southern French specialty known as *cassoulet* is not incidental: "It was he, the Nabab, the richest of the rich, a true Parisian curiosity, spiced by that relish of adventure that gives such pleasure to the jaded crowds" (2:525). Jansoulet, in short, represents not the purebred aristocrat, not the "old money" on which power was bestowed in earlier regimes, but the spicier "stew" of new money, money earned mysteriously and perhaps not altogether honestly by a new breed of adventurers and bourgeois materialists. Setting himself up lavishly in an apartment on the place Vendôme, Jansoulet ("le Nabab") becomes food for all the hungry egotists of Parisian society, from the Corsican Paganetti, who promises him a deputyship in exchange for help in reestablishing the financial health of the Territorial Treasury, to the journalist Moëssard, who expects to be paid for an article praising his generosity. But it is to the physician, Jenkins, who persuades the Nabab to underwrite a charitable project he pompously names "The Bethlehem Society," that the most narrative space is given. Jenkins, flattering the vanity of the naive southern Frenchman, promises him the cross of the Legion of Honor, a recognition he covets for himself as well. Like the others, Jenkins fails to live up to his promise, and Jansoulet, disabused by repeated disappointments, begins denying requests for monetary support. In the end, the humiliated Nabab suffers a fatal stroke that is brought on by the emotional turmoil he experiences when he sees himself derided by former beneficiaries.

Daudet, chronicling Jansoulet's demise, makes extensive use of the theatrical metaphor to expose the hypocrisy of late–Second Empire society. It is not by chance that the novel ends with the successful performance of a play entitled *The Revolt*, written by the physician's rebellious stepson, or that Jansoulet dies offstage on the evening of the première, after failing to respond to repeated bleedings. Having been metaphorically bled by a corrupt society throughout the novel, no longer able to serve a useful purpose in the "theater" of Parisian high society, Jansoulet is left to die in the wings, among the chaotic heaps of old stage props: "Bernard Jansoulet, laid out in the midst of the wreckage with the front of his undershirt torn open, was at once bloody and pale; he had truly been shipwrecked by life, injured and washed up on the shore with the lamentable debris of his artificial luxury, dispersed and broken up by the Parisian whirlwind" (2:850). In this passage, Daudet shifts gears, so to speak, gliding from the theatrical metaphor (Jansoulet as discarded stage prop) to the nautical (Jansoulet as shipwreck). This is neither a mixed metaphor nor an infelicitous afterthought. The maritime imagery had been evoked as early as the second chapter of this twenty-five-chapter novel, in the description of a dinner party given by the Nabab. Although there are no women present, this group of freeloaders, representing "specimens of humanity taken from all the different ethnic groups" (2:500), offers considerable variety. From foreign industrialists to Parisian journalists and southern Frenchmen, "who've landed without a penny to their names" (2:503), all are attracted by the Nabab's immense fortune, as powerful a magnet for them as "the light of a beacon" (2:504) for a lost ship. But if they are ships, the guests are also passengers. A casual observer, noting the exotic fare served at the Nabab's table, listening to the foreign accents, remarking the different physiognomies of the guests, would certainly never believe himself to be on the place Vendôme, "at the very beating heart . . . of our modern Paris" (2:504). The setting—and characters—evoke instead "the luxurious dining room of a transatlantic liner, the *Péreire* or the *Sinaï*" (2:504).

Among the many transatlantic liners to which Daudet might have referred, the fact that these two are cited is highly revealing. The first, evoking Jacob Pereire, a French businessman (1800–1875) who had founded a loan company (*Le Crédit mobilier*) before assuming control of the *Compagnie générale maritime*, is associated with the industrial development of the early Second Empire. *Le Crédit mobilier*, which specialized in long-term loans to industry, was forced to declare bankruptcy, leading to the financial ruin of many small investors. Moreover, Pereire was a Jew and a Saint-Simonian. The second ship, named after a part of Egypt that figures prominently in Hebrew history (for it was on Mount Sinaï that Moses received the Decalogue during the forty-year Jewish occupation of this area) is likewise associated with Jewry. Through these oblique allusions, an anti-Semitic subtext can be detected. Besides suggesting that the Ship of State represented by Second Empire France is a luxury liner aboard which all manner of corrupt, materialistic lowlifes, many of them non-French, mingle for their own benefit, Daudet subtly identifies the foreigner with the Jew. Small wonder, then, that Levantine society ("composed largely of German Jews, bankers, or brokers who, after having made colossal fortunes in the East, continue to do business here so as not to lose their touch" [2:762]) is particularly conspicuous in *Le Nabab*.

The large cast of corrupt characters that populate this novel must of course include the Nabab himself who, as a foreigner in Tunisia, had acquired his wealth in highly suspect ways that parallel those in which the "foreign element" would exploit Paris. Compared on two occasions to a character from *Les Mille et une nuits* (2:482, 2:628), a collection of stories that Edouard Drumont will later qualify as "Semitic," a semantically loaded word in his lexicon, Jansoulet is tainted by his good fortune.[2] However, in *Le Nabab*, he is presented above all as a victim, somewhat akin to Balzac's Goriot who, notwithstanding his own less-than-virtuous past, inspires pity when he is exploited by others. In Jansoulet's case, his apoplectic condition, his "surfeit" of blood, becomes the physiological counterpart of his material affluence. Far from guaranteeing his social and political triumph, his fortune thus leads to his defeat at the hands of characters who, for their part, seem universally defined by a pathological "bloating," either real or metaphoric. His obese, bejeweled Levantine wife, engulfed in folds of flesh, snobbishly refuses to associate with Madame Hémerlingue, a former slave, thus blocking a reconciliation with the latter's powerful husband, who had once been his best friend. The corpulent Hémerlingue (who as a banker with a Germanic surname is associated with the Jew), is afflicted with edema; he contributes to the decline of the Nabab's reputation both in the provinces (when he persuades the bey to snub him) and in Paris, when, by allowing his wife to conspire with the lawyer, le Merquier, he succeeds in preventing Jansoulet from being validated as Corsican deputy.[3] The unscrupulous art dealer Schwalbach (whose name means "swollen stream") takes advantage of the Nabab's ignorance, selling him paintings at inflated prices. The journalist Moëssard, finally, "pallid and puffy like whitlow" (2:683), uses the power of the press to destroy the Nabab's reputation when his (Moëssard's) repeated requests for money are denied.

To the physical inflammation—whether caused by an accumulation of blood, water, fat, or pus—that makes morbid *exemplae* of the Nabab and his antagonists corresponds the swollen self-importance of the Irish physician, Jenkins. With his "large head" (2:484) and his "windbag sentences" (2:506), Jenkins, inflated with vanity, is in fact the incarnation of *bloat*. Moreover, as a foreign invader on French soil, he is also the quintessential opportunist, and is thus the first among the disparate band of parasites hoping for a handout from the Nabab to plead his cause. He is also the first of the novel's numerous characters to be introduced, and the whole of the first chapter is given to a description of his activities. Murray Sachs has noted that Jenkins was imagined by Daudet as "a convenient link among the various characters," an observation supported by Daudet's notes.[4] I would like to suggest, however, that his creation was not dictated by mere technical considerations, that indeed Jenkins plays a pivotal role in the novel. The novel's first sentence—lengthy enough to constitute its own paragraph—amounts to what Jacques Dubois has termed the physician's *curriculum vitae*. Given the importance that recent criticism has attached to the *incipit*, it deserves to be quoted in its entirety:

> Standing on the steps of his townhouse on the rue de Lisbonne, freshly shaven, his eyes shining, his lips parted in a self-satisfied smile, his long, graying hair flowing onto the wide collar of his

coat, square-shouldered, robust, and healthy as an oak, the illustrious Irish doctor Robert Jenkins, Knight of the Medjidjié and
of the distinguished order of Charles III of Spain, member of
several learned or charitable societies, founding president of "The
Bethlehem Society," Jenkins, *the* Jenkins of "Jenkins capsules" (of
which the principal ingredient was arsenic), that is, the fashionable
doctor of 1864, the busiest man in Paris, was getting ready to get
into his carriage one day at the end of November when a window
opened on the first floor overlooking the inner courtyard of the
building and a woman's voice asked timidly: "Will you be home for
lunch, Robert?" (2:481)

Dubois has remarked on the theatrical nature of the scene presented here
and on the parodical tone of the paragraph that, in his view, fails to save
the description from banality. For Dubois, there is nothing subversive
here. A closer examination of this sentence-paragraph reveals a different
scenario.

In addition to the expected markers of health, wealth, and success that
characterize the "fashionable physician" in the Parisian high society of
1864, there are several allusions to what one might term his "otherness."
In the first place, he is associated with the foreign, not only by his English
name, Jenkins, but also by his Irish nationality, his address (he resides on
the rue de Lisbonne), and his distinctions (he is a chevalier of Turkish
and Spanish orders). Combined with this otherness is a vanity that can
be gleaned not only from his demeanor ("his eyes shining, his lips parted
in a self-satisfied smile") but also from the designations by which his
two principal claims to fame are known: "Jenkins capsules" and "The
Bethlehem Society," the second suggesting a disturbing megalomania. In
fact, Jenkins is the antithesis of the Savior. The artifice of his demeanor
is exposed in the novel's first chapter, and by the novel's end we see him
not only as Tartuffe (2:569) but as Antichrist. Revealed progressively as
the plot unfolds, his misdeeds affect nearly every major character in the
novel, from his wife and her son to the sculptress Félicia Ruys, the duc
de Mora, and, finally, Bernard Jansoulet.

In the first place, Jenkins has separated his stepson, André Maranne,
from his mother, his disdain for his stepson's literary ambitions forcing

the young man to leave Jenkins's opulent home and to eke out a living as a photographer while waiting to achieve recognition as a playwright. When, in the first chapter, the physician offers the aspiring writer the opportunity to earn an "honest" living by directing his philanthropic organization, Maranne refuses and is treated with scorn. Jenkins's condescending attitude toward artistic creativity is mimetically accurate: as we have seen, artists were by definition "sick" for many physicians of the era, and their artistic production held interest only because it offered clues to the nature of their illness. Ironically, Jenkins inspires *The Revolt*, the play that will make of Maranne an overnight sensation, just as later another "stepfather," Jean-Marie Charcot, by inspiring Léon Daudet to write *Les Morticoles*, will seal *his* success. Similarly — and equally ironically — Jenkins's betrayal of an assumed paternal role also has the effect of inspiring a young sculptress, Félicia Ruys, to artistic expression. Having won the trust of the young woman by the solicitude with which he treated her ailing father and by his paternal surveillance of her innocence, Jenkins had invited the fifteen-year-old Félicia to dine with him in his home during a period when his wife and stepson were absent, an invitation she accepted without hesitation. Jenkins's metamorphosis into a satyr, his attempted rape of the virginal young woman, becomes the defining event of her life. Alluding to the trauma, she confides to Paul de Géry, the Nabab's personal secretary: "If you knew what my youth was like, what premature experience withered my spirit, what confusion between the permissible and the forbidden, reason and madness there was in my little girl mind! Only art, celebrated and discussed, remained standing in all of that, and I took refuge in it" (2:668). The biting sarcasm with which Félicia responds to Jenkins's subsequent expressions of concern for her welfare is thus justified, and her cruel impersonations of the physician underscore his hypocrisy:

> And Felicia . . . transformed her anger into irony, imitated Jenkins, gesturing broadly, putting her hand on her heart, then, puffing out her cheeks, saying with a loud, breathy voice, full of dishonest gushing:
> "Let's be humane, let's be kind. . . . Charity without hope of reward . . . that's the important thing!" (2:569–70)

Guided by the reactions of the characters who know the "real" Jenkins—his wife, his stepson, Félicia—the reader takes the proper measure of the man who is esteemed as a miracle-worker thanks to his famous restorative tablets. Behind the mask worn at the bedside of his wealthy patients, Jenkins reveals himself as volatile, passionate, and brutal in his egotism. The description of his violation of a young girl's innocence lingers on his animalism: Félicia, unexpectedly subjected to "the brutal grasp of a faun's paw" and frightened by "this bestial attack" (2:566), screams for help, stopping her aggressor in his tracks. But for the reader, a seed of doubt has been planted. Jenkins is not superhuman but subhuman, whence the irony of "The Bethlehem Society."

An ostensibly philanthropic enterprise spawned by the physician with Jansoulet's financial support, Jenkins's establishment, with its "legendary name, as soft and warm as the straw of the miraculous stable" (2:585), proves to be a disaster rather than a miracle. Separating infants from their mothers and their wetnurses (their mother surrogates) as he had separated his stepson from his mother, Jenkins experiments with artificial nursing, in this case using goats in lieu of lactating women to feed the babies. Such experimentation with animals was in fact common in the nineteenth century, and although physicians continued throughout the century to insist on the superiority of "mother's milk," medical literature concerning artificial nursing by animals was abundant.[5] Although Jean-Louis Cabanès is no doubt correct when he says that the description of "The Bethlehem Society" "owes much to the polemic on the feeding of newborn infants," I do not believe that it has merely anecdotal value, at least insofar as the doctor's role is concerned.[6] In the first place, Jenkins's association with the goat—and by metaphor with the cloven-hoofed devil and with male lust (the billy goat being the male of the nanny goat)—had been prepared by the passage describing the attempted rape of Félicia. Moreover, if by the grandiose name of his enterprise Jenkins wished to identify himself as a modern-day Christ, its catastrophic results suggest that he is more akin to Herod in his infanticide. Jenkins's callous insistence on pursuing his plan despite the mounting death toll reveals that he is motivated not by humanitarian sentiment but rather by the egotistical desire for self-glorification. Making a mockery of his bombastic tirades about "the long martyrology of childhood" and "the mercenary trade of wetnursing" (2:506), the babies starve to death, becoming martyrs to his own very mercenary cause. When the student practitioner in charge of "Bethlehem" brings in wetnurses to save them, Jenkins reacts with rage: "Wetnurses at Bethlehem . . . are you crazy? Well then, why goats, and meadows to feed them, and my idea, and the brochures describing my idea? . . . What becomes of all that?" (2:587). Confronted with his student's explanation that the babies refuse to suckle when presented with the teats of a goat, Jenkins replies sharply: "Well then, let them go without, but may the principle of artificial suckling be respected" (2:587). Daudet evokes "The Massacre of the Innocents" in describing the results of Jenkins's "philanthropic" experiment. The allusion to the babies killed by Herod's order places "Bethlehem" in a properly ironic light.[7] But the concept of the sacrifice of innocence applies as well to his abusive encounter with the youthful Félicia, who reflects that, on that date, "her youth died" (2:681). Clearly this doctor is associated not with life but with death.

His victims are not universally innocent, however. The duc de Mora, a character modeled on the duc de Morny, profligate representative of the Imperial regime itself, begs the physician for some of his magical pills so that he might keep a *rendezvous d'amour* with a woman whom Jenkins rightly suspects is the now-libertine Félicia. Daudet uses this scene and the subsequent scene of the duke's death to depict both the physician's despair—he is after all truly in love with Félicia—and his lack of professional ethics. Yielding to the wishes of his famous client, he prescribes an overdose of the arsenic pills, enabling him to satisfy the demands of his amorous encounter but hastening his death. When other physicians—with French names, significantly—are summoned to the bedside of the moribund duke, Daudet is able simultaneously to expose the Parisian medical establishment's opinion of the foreign charlatan, thereby lending credibility to his unflattering portrait, and to extend his criticism to the French practitioner as well. While Jenkins, "obsequious and attentive in the presence of his 'illustrious colleagues,' as he called them through pursed lips," seeks to join in their deliberations, the Paris physicians exclude him, respond haughtily to his queries "just as Fagon—Louis XIV's Fagon—might speak to some empiric summoned to the royal bedside" (2:731). The allusion is not without its ironies, since it is they, not he, who have been called in as consultants, while Jenkins is what in modern parlance one would term the duke's "primary-care physician." Nevertheless, for the Paris confraternity, he is nothing more than a "cantharides dealer" (2:732) and should be dispatched by the police to the other side of the Channel, where he could peddle his murderous aphrodisiacs to his own people. Despite their arrogant condemnation of Jenkins's methods, their own medicine is not presented as more efficacious, and through his description of their deathbed conference, Daudet in fact establishes their resemblance to their Irish colleague. Like him, they are serene and hypocritical; like him, they are associated not with science but with magic: "Doctors no longer wear large wigs as in Molière's time, but they still put on the same grave demeanor as astrologers, priests of Isis, bristling with cabalistic formulae, nodding their heads wisely. The comic effect would be complete if they still wore the pointed hat of yore" (2:731). Here, the physician's historically positive associations with the occult, which can be traced back to the Druids and beyond, is turned on its head with the suggestion that doctors use pretentious, formulaic language reminiscent of occult incantations in order to camouflage their incompetence. And although Daudet emphasizes the comic aspects of this medical voodoo, the ensuing description of Mora's physicians as impassive witnesses to his death—and by extension to all of life's tragedies—evokes a more chilling reality: "Always the same cold, sinister expressions on their faces, genuine physiognomies of judges who have on their lips the terrible sentence on human destiny, the last word that courts of law pronounce unflinchingly but that physicians paraphrase and avoid, for it makes a mockery of their science" (2:732). If Daudet's Parisian physicians are figurative judges—first because they condemn Jenkins, second because they pronounce the Duke's death sentence—they are also emblematic of mortality itself, grave figures who wait patiently for the demise of a man already "enveloped in serenity . . . as in a shroud" (2:731). Seen in this light, their association with the occult is more troubling, for they belong to a malevolent realm. It would hardly be stretching the analogy too much to say that they are implicitly identified with the Jew, who was often regarded as a menacing, evil power by late-nineteenth-century anti-Semites, many of whom dabbled in the occult.[8] The connection between physicians and Jews is moreover suggested by reference to the Cabala. Jenkins, too, is specifically linked with the occult by Félicia, who refers to him as French society's "Cagliostro" (2:834), alluding to the eighteenth-century Italian adventurer who enjoyed great success in pre-Revolutionary Paris with his "elixir of long life" and his practice of the occult sciences (specifically his ability to summon up the dead). Nor is it coincidental that Cagliostro was a Freemason: in France, Masonic lodges drew their members from anticlerical freethinkers. Drumont moreover associates masonry with Judaism. Through her epithet, Félicia thus associates Jenkins not only with charlatanism but with the practice of the occult and Freemasonry, both of which were felt to be dangerous by the Catholic Church. Finally, by her bitter criticism of the physician and by her name, Félicia recalls Cagliostro's wife, the Roman beauty Lorenza Feliciani, who later denounced him to the Inquisition.

In ironic counterpoint to the apparently distinguished titles listed in Jenkins's initial description ("illustrious doctor . . . knight . . . founding president," etc.), the remarkable multiplication of derogatory epithets used to describe the physician through the rest of the novel serves to underline his hypocrisy, his incompetence, and his malevolence. In addition to "Cagliostro," "cantharides dealer," "the handsome Tartuffe" (2:569), one notes "this honey-tongued man" (2:697) and, finally, the frequent and ironic use of "apostle" and "loyal" (as in "his apostle's air" and "the good and loyal Jenkins" [2:499]). Through the pairing of abstract adjectives with concrete nouns ("his loyal hand" [2:497]; "his loyal chest" [2:590]), Daudet establishes his ironic intention. For Félicia, Jenkins's hands were not "loyal" but "offensive" (2:566). Behind the "smug obsequiousness" and the "paternal, Franklin-like smile" with which he masks his true nature in the presence of others, the real Jenkins is sinister and vicious, his "row of sparkling teeth" (2:482) evoking not the radiance of a good health and a kind nature, but the cannibalistic brutality with which he "devours" others, both those after whom he lusts and those who threaten his happiness. Thus, after determining that he must suppress his rival, the duc de Mora, he has the "pallor of a Castaing or a La Pommerais hatching sinister betrayals" (2:700), an allusion to two early-nineteenth-century physicians who poisoned their victims (2:1367). His diabolical laughter as he leaves the duke with a prescription for a fatal dose of his arsenic-based tablets is revealingly described as "the laughter of a wolf with widely spaced white teeth" (2:704). The discrepancy between the "real" and the "false" Jenkins is admirably expressed by Félicia when, responding to his seemingly solicitous concern for her welfare, she says sharply, "Oh! enough of your paternal concern, Jenkins . . . We know what's behind it. . . . I prefer the mastiff to the setter in you. I'm less afraid of it" (2:833–34). The hypocrisy that enables the "mastiff" Jenkins (a variant on "faun," "brute," and "wolf") to transform himself into a setter is his single "talent." To describe this ability, the animal metaphor is again pressed into service, but in another context. Before announcing to the waiting crowds that the duke is drawing his final breaths, Jenkins must rearrange his facial expression to conform to their expectations:

> Monkeys flattening their short noses on their wire mesh cages, upset by an unusual commotion and very attentive to what was happening, as if they were conducting an analytical study of the human grimace, certainly had a magnificent model in the Irish physician. His pain—a wonderfully strong, masculine pain—was superb. (2:739)

Through his mimicry, Jenkins is a flawless mirror of the hypocritical society to which he belongs. In fact, as the text subsequently makes clear, Mora's death is meaningful only to those who in losing his protection risk being deprived of their social or political status. The man designated by the text as "the most brilliant incarnation of the Empire" (2:737) is sincerely mourned by no one, and the dominant emotion among those interested parties who fear a change in their fortune is anger, not sadness. In "killing" the duke, the physician has precipitated the demise of a host of other characters as well, from the Nabab, who correctly fears that "this death was his death as well, his ruin, the end of everything" (2:737), to the well-named marquis de Monpavon ("mon pa[v]on" [my peacock]), a stereotypical aristocrat who, dressed in his elegant best, walks with dignity to the outskirts of Paris, enters a bathhouse where he is unknown, has his bath drawn, and opens his veins: "Two razor cuts through the magnificent starched shirt front and all of his phony majesty was deflated, reduced to this nameless horror, a pile of mud, blood, and flesh still caked with makeup but cadaverous now; here, unrecognizable, lies the man of appearances, the marquis Louis-Marie-Agénor de Monpavon" (2:819). Jean-Louis Cabanès has seen a resemblance between the deaths of Mora, Monpavon, and Jansoulet, all three scenes "inscribed in a kind of theatricality."[9] He insists on the quasi-organic nature of the ties that bind these three characters, pointing out that Mora and Monpavon, who represent "the already-dead" since they continue to live only as long as their bodies respond to the dangerous stimulants prescribed by Jenkins, drain the apoplectic parvenu Jansoulet of his vital energy and thus precipitate his demise. From this perspective, one might compare them to the vampires that so stimulated the psyche of the late-nineteenth century in Europe. For Cabanès, the novel is allegorical, and the "spectacular" becomes "the supreme image of the degeneration of the social body."[10] I should like to expand somewhat on these observations. Monpavon's death serves to metaphorize the demise of the Second Empire in three ways. In the first place, the physiological metaphor of bursting open, deflating, complements the theatrical to evoke the fundamental vacuity of a society built on appearance, a society without a heart. Monpavon, reflecting Second Empire society, "lived for appearances until the very end, his chest swelled with vanity" (2:818). But his death is also presented as a wreck, a collapse recalling Mora's "collapse" (2:733) and anticipating the "shipwreck" of Jansoulet's demise. It is, finally, associated with the aquatic, his blood and tissue oozing out into the bath water just as the dying Mora's love letters had been consigned to the latrine, "[which] diluted the tender color of their ink before letting them disappear in the sewer's hiccough, at the bottom of the foul bilge" (2:735). The corrupt Second Empire will come to a similarly ignominious end with the Prussian defeat of France in 1870, followed by the fratricidal bloodbath of the Commune.

The allegory is incomplete without the doctor. While it is certainly enlightening to see physiological degeneration as a symbol of societal decadence, to imply that the Empire, the aristocracy, and the bourgeoisie (personified respectively by the duc de Mora, the marquis Monpavon, and Bernard Jansoulet) self-destruct is inaccurate. Rather, all three fall prey to the machinations of the opportunistic foreigner, here represented by the Irish charlatan Jenkins. In this organicist interpretation, Jenkins shares characteristics not with the Prussian, the *known* enemy, but with the Jew, the mysterious Other who, in anti-Semitic thought, was infiltrating French society in the guise of Friend and Helper and who was all the more dangerous in that his true power was unrecognized. Second Empire anti-Semites were persuaded that the government of Napoléon III, favorable to Jewish capitalism, was sealing its own doom. The financial speculation that empowered such Jewish families as the Rothschilds, the Pereires, and others often led to misery for the "true" Frenchman who, temporarily energized by bank loans, would soon come to realize that he had exchanged long-term happiness for the pleasure of the moment, just as Mora had done in seeking the services of Jenkins.[11] Mora's Faustian pact with Jenkins is perhaps insufficient to make of the physician a figure of Satan, and Murray Sachs is correct to point out that Jenkins too is a sorry specimen, "enslaved to an uncontrollable passion for Félicia Ruys."[12] However it is worth noting that he himself was originally the unsuspecting victim of a usurer from whom he had clearly learned "the tricks of the trade." His defense against Félicia's accusation of hypocrisy is relevant: "Hypocrite, yes, I guess I am, but one isn't born a hypocrite. . . . One becomes hypocritical out of necessity, when faced with life's harsh realities. When you have a headwind and you want to move forward, you have to tack. I tacked" (2:835). The return of the nautical/maritime imagery to describe Jenkins's unscrupulous behavior is particularly appropriate, for the notion of tacking explains both his deviant path to success and the principle of his "swelling." A skillful sailor, the physician will set his sails in such a way as to take advantage of the wind, and his tacking, zigzag motion will move his sloop forward. In the end, however, he makes a tactical error. His acquiescence before the duke's request for more tablets is tantamount to letting a competitor steal his wind, or—Daudet introduces a new sporting metaphor—to letting someone else win the horserace: "All right, then, my dear duke, we're going to give you enough stamina to win the Derby's grand prize" (2:704). It follows that his own career would suffer as a result. After Mora's death, the French physician Bouchereau attacks Jenkins's nefarious therapies in print, and the charlatan's popularity plummets. "The Irishman had felt the effect of these violent squalls that make Parisian infatuations so dangerous" (2:805). Navigating the treacherous waters of Second Empire France is difficult indeed.

If Jenkins's trajectory is described in nautical terms, if he, unlike the guests at Jansoulet's home, and Jansoulet himself, is metaphorized as a navigator rather than as a ship or a mere passenger, the novel's metaphors make it clear that he has not come by his power in lawful ways.[13] Having fled Paris, he is not present at the première of his stepson's play, described in the novel's last chapter. From Maranne's perspective, this is unfortunate, since it is Jenkins who is the implicit target of his attack "contre les forbans, si nombreux à cette époque, qui tenaient le haut du pavé après en avoir battu les coins les plus obscurs pour détrousser les passants" [against scoundrels, so numerous during this period, who walked on the inside of the pavement after having scoured its darkest corners in order to rob passersby] (2:848). The reference to *forbans*, a noun that in its original sense designated pirates who undertook unauthorized sea voyages for personal profit, inscribes the passage in the network of nautical metaphors that abound in the novel. The audience, mistakenly assuming the allusion to be inspired by Jansoulet ("Of course, Maranne, in writing those fine lines, had somebody completely different from the Nabab on his mind" [2:848]), turns accusing eyes on the Nabab, and his deep humiliation brings about the cerebral hemorrhage that will cause his death, "one of the biggest and most cruelly unjust deeds that Paris had ever committed" (2:851). But the Parisian populace has failed to recognize the real villain, the foreign charlatan who offered them a "fatal cure." Instead, they have indicted "the good Nabab," who came to Paris not to make his fortune (as Jenkins had) but to share it with others. In this light, the benevolent Jansoulet appears as a sacrificial victim, the "bon enfant" ("good-natured young man," but literally "good child") destroyed by his naiveté, not goat but scapegoat, whereas the scheming Jenkins, whatever the pathos of his theatrical confession to Félicia in the penultimate chapter, is the personification of hypocrisy and the incarnation of malevolent egotism. Through his exploitation of archetypes, Daudet stages the eternal battle between Good and Evil, with Good personified as a Christ figure, shown in the arms of his mother, "crucified" by those he came to help, while Evil is incarnated in the character of the foreign physician, peddling his bogus cures to a sick society and ultimately contributing to its decline.

Subtle though it may be, the anti-Semitic subtext of this combative novel is hard to dismiss. In Daudet's allegory, Second Empire France is defeated not by Prussian invaders but by an insidious foreign presence within its boundaries. Just as the Imperial government had encouraged the Pereires and other Jewish bankers and financiers to inject large sums of money into the French economy, so also does Mora, the Empire's in-carnation, entreat Jenkins to supply him with his "miraculous cure." And, just as ultimately the Empire succumbs to the Enemy, in part a victim of those very politics of expansion made possible by capitalistic investment (and for which the "bloat" mentioned earlier was a metaphor), so also does Mora succumb to a profligate lifestyle in which he was able to indulge thanks to the bursts of energy provided by "Jenkins capsules." The physician is a poisoner, his effect on France as deleterious as on the babies of its microcosmic double, "The Bethlehem Society."

Critical reaction to *Le Nabab* was mixed. In general, critics applauded Daudet's powers of observation and criticized the novel's organization, lamenting what were considered to be "sentimental" digressions. Zola, dissatisfied with some of the character portrayals, nevertheless consid-ered that the novel was a sterling example of the tradition he termed "le roman procès-verbal" ("the novel of indictment"), and this judgment seems to have been widely shared. Seizing upon the subtitle, "Mœurs parisiennes" ("Parisian Manners"), several of Daudet's contemporaries pointed to the historical interest of *Le Nabab*, seeing in it a powerful and faithful social analysis. Beyond this, the reviewers' major interpretive activity appears to have been limited to their attempts to identify the historical figures on whom Daudet's characters were modeled, a practice against which the author railed in an "Author's Statement" that prefaces the thirty-seventh and all subsequent editions of his immensely successful novel. By popular consensus, the duc de Mora was the fictional counterpart of Napoléon III's dissolute half-brother, the duc de Morny, Jansoulet was inspired by the wealthy François Bravay, and Jenkins himself was a composite of several contemporary physicians. Persuaded that there was nothing more to say about a work that an ambivalent twentieth-century scholar has referred to both as a "vast canvas" and a "sprawling novel," the critics thus consigned this text to the waters of Lethe.[14] The centenary of its publication passed unnoticed.

As an example of late-nineteenth-century antimedical fiction, *Le Nabab* is of vital interest, not only because it represents the physician as an immoral and hypocritical charlatan but because it represents him as Other. Although to this day there is no consensus among critics as to whether or not Alphonse Daudet was an anti-Semite, the fact that he was a friend of Edouard Drumont and that he used his influence to persuade the publisher Marpon and Flammarion to accept *La France juive* suggests that he was at least somewhat sympathetic to the views expressed therein.[15] Moreover, a close examination of *Le Nabab* reveals an anti-Semitic bias that, however subtle and however "typical" of the era, merits our attention. Jenkins, the foreigner, may well have been linked in his creator's mind with the most maligned Other of the Second Empire. The fact that he exhibits characteristics attributed to the Jew by contemporary anti-Semitic writings and that he is associated with "The Bethlehem Society" would seem to justify this interpretation.

7

HYDROTHERAPY AND MEDICAL BLOAT
IN MAUPASSANT'S *MONT-ORIOL*

ℊ

"The great defect in *Mont-Oriol* is, above all else, the absence of any irony or detachment." So wrote Edward Sullivan in 1954 in his pioneering study, *Maupassant the Novelist.*[1] The brief chapter devoted to Maupassant's third novel in Sullivan's monograph reflects the critic's lack of esteem for what he termed "the weakest" of Maupassant's novels. In *Mont-Oriol*, according to Sullivan, Maupassant's intended representation of "the sublime comedy" between doctor and patient is undermined by the overly sentimental love story involving Christiane Andermatt and Paul Brétigny. Sullivan's summary dismissal stands in sharp counterpoint to André Vial's favorable judgment, rendered the same year in his *Maupassant et l'art du roman.* For Vial, the triumph of one physician (Dr. Latonne) and the defeat of another (Dr. Bonnefille) are closely related to the sentimental and economic themes: "The overlapping is so complete and so cleverly carried out that every page of the novel . . . could be examined from this perspective."[2] Maupassant critics have, for the most part, failed to pick up the gauntlet cast down by Vial, and until very recently, Sullivan's harsh judgment has held sway, causing scholars to repeat the same familiar refrain: *Mont-Oriol* is composed of two rather poorly integrated thematic threads, the sentimental and the economic, against which the "ponderous mockery of medical science" appears as mere backdrop.[3] Even as perceptive a critic as Louis Forestier, in his excellent Pléiade edition of Maupassant's novels, subscribes to this viewpoint: "The plot that connects the protagonists unfolds against a backdrop of medical pantomime" (1435). If this judgment is correct, then Henri Mitterand's discovery of preparatory notes that bear witness to Zola's unrealized plans to write a novel about thermalism presents us with a paradox.[4] Zola intended to focus his novel on the exploitation of the ill, an interest which, in Forestier's view, "is only secondary in Maupassant's work" (1440). But then why did Zola abandon his project when he heard of Maupassant's novel? I do not wish to question *Mont-Oriol*'s obvious focus on financial speculation. However, I am persuaded that the novel is considerably more complex than it appears to be, and that only a reading attentive to the novel's medical details can reveal this complexity. Not only are the sentimental and the economic dramas that unfold in *Mont-Oriol* illuminated by its use of clinical discourse, but there is in fact a third drama, the medical. When we position the protagonist of this drama, Dr. Latonne, beside Andermatt and Brétigny, startling similarities among the three characters are revealed, both on the literal and the figurative levels. As we shall see, the text finds its unity and meaning in the metaphor of the pathological body, vulnerable to penetration by the Other.

The mimetic accuracy of Maupassant's account of the development of a spa village has been well established. Maupassant had firsthand knowledge of thermal stations, and his fictional village, Enval, was modeled after Châtelguyon, where, in 1883, 1885, and 1886, he had sought relief from the increasingly alarming symptoms of syphilis with which he, like his mentor Gustave Flaubert and his contemporaries Jules Goncourt and Alphonse Daudet, was afflicted. The expansion of thermalism in France, facilitated by the increasing network of railroads laid during the Second Empire and the concomitant development of tourism, was especially dramatic after the Franco-Prussian War of 1870, when it came to be regarded as unpatriotic to frequent the previously popular German spas, of which the best-known was Baden-Baden.[5] Medical professionals used their influence to persuade patients of the efficacy of hydrotherapy and thus contributed to the development of French spas, a phenomenon from which they benefited materially. Whether through the blossoming of the pharmaceutical industry, the sale of mineralized waters, or the popularity of spa treatments, the penetration of capitalistic interests into the once unsullied "medical corps" is well documented.

Consider, then, Maupassant's representation of the Prime Mover in this corrupting activity, William Andermatt. Andermatt, a stereotypical Jewish banker, has taken his Christian wife Christiane (like Nature, Maupassant abhors a vacuum, above all an onomastic vacuum) to Enval in search of a cure for infertility. During the course of her stay in the spa village, Christiane meets her brother's friend, Paul Brétigny, has an affair with him, and is "cured" of her condition, although her pregnancy has the unintended effect of driving her lover away. Co-extensive with this sentimental drama is the economic one: the dynamiting of a boulder on a neighboring property owned by the peasant Oriol reveals a mineralized spring; Andermatt, an avid speculator, persuades the old peasant to sell him his property, and on this newly acquired land, he builds a rival spa, successfully driving Enval out of business. The novel's closure is provided by the simultaneous birth of Christiane's daughter and the new thermal station, Mont-Oriol.

Among the scholars who have written about *Mont-Oriol*, few have failed to note the curious duality of the passages describing its Auvergne setting. Philippe Bonnefis, locating this duality in a distinction between the rugged province of rocks and ruins and the "Virgilian" province of sweet-smelling effluvia, believes that Maupassant created Auvergne in his own image. Trevor Harris, among others, believes that *Mont-Oriol* depicts a struggle between male and female that is figured by Maupassant's representation of fire and water, sun and moon. Claudine Giachetti sees in "Enval" the feminine, nocturnal regime of Christiane and in "Mont-Oriol" the masculine, diurnal regime of Andermatt. Pierre Danger, finally, contrasts the phallic fountains of the thermal station with the "dead volcanoes" of the Auvergne landscape to conclude that in *Mont-Oriol*, the "dominant theme is repression," the thermal station providing the reassuring image of a contained libido. What emerges from all of these analyses is a clear identification of the land with the body, a sexualization of the landscape that is typical of Maupassant's vision and is not limited to this novel.[6]

But if for Maupassant the land, with its valleys and mountains, crevasses and springs, is a corporeal reality, for the doctor destined to triumph over this physiological space, the body is also a land. Thus while the ultimately hapless Dr. Bonnefille conducts only a cursory examination of Christiane Andermatt before writing out a prescription, the more astute Dr. Latonne practices organographism, using a three-colored pen to map out the position of Christiane's organs on a white robe she wears for the examination. Engaged by Andermatt, Latonne uses his pen to transform the female body into a geographical space: "After a quarter of an hour of this work, she looked like a map indicating continents, seas, capes, rivers, kingdoms, and cities, and bearing names of all these earthly divisions, since the doctor wrote, on each demarcating line, two or three Latin words, comprehensible to him alone" (490). This scriptural mystification, which corresponds to the illegible handwriting of Bonnefille's prescription, theoretically affords the physician the means of dominating the female patient entrusted to his care. When we remember that cartography was one of the most important tools of colonialism (for it was only when a new colony could be properly mapped that it could be subjugated), we are able to see Latonne's "mapping" of Christiane's body as an act of appropriation. However, in order to proceed to the next step in the process, which involves copying his observations into his notebook, he must first decipher his own scribblings "as an Egyptologist deciphers hieroglyphics" (490). Since it is the doctor, facetiously identified both as cartographer and Egyptologist, who has created this female map, he alone can understand her. Lest the misguided reader be tempted to interpret this metaphor as a profound reflection on the mysterious nature of the creature whose sexuality Freud would later dub "the dark continent," Maupassant takes care to insist on the physician's resemblance to an "actor on vacation" (487), a comparison that recalls Alphonse Daudet's theatrical Jenkins. But whereas Jenkins had been portrayed as malevolent, Latonne is merely comical. Christiane's role as amused spectator leaves little doubt as to the stance the reader is expected to take, and the physician's brusque departure, which he judges "in very good taste and likely to awe the patient" (490), contributes to the impression of *performance*, besides calling to mind those sexual/textual strategies of rupture about which

Charles Stivale has written extensively.[7] Latonne's transformation of the female body into a map bears all the marks of a magic act, an appropriate spectacle for a thermal station, as springs have been associated since antiquity with the supernatural. (To this day, we wish not only on stars but on coins thrown into fountains.)

Like the medical practitioner, whom he has hired to cure his wife's infertility, the banker is a magician, transforming women into land and ultimately into money. The dowry system provides Andermatt with a basis for his magic, while Christiane's profligate brother Gontran and (eventually) Brétigny become his props. Their successful courtship of Oriol's daughters ensures that Andermatt will be able to acquire all of the property he needs for his commercial venture. The fact that Andermatt establishes the relationship between women and land through writing adds another link to the chain of allusions that binds him to Latonne: "A detailed map of Mount Oriol had been spread out on the table, and one by one the pieces of land given to Louise were marked with a cross" (664). The physician had mapped the feminine; the banker feminizes the map. As was the case with Latonne, Andermatt's scriptural conquest is effected in two steps, the second consisting of the transfer of the agreement to notarized papers.

In the mind of Paul Brétigny, the equation women = land is somewhat different. Sensually attracted to the Auvergne landscape as to a woman, this androgynous male describes to Christiane his relationship with the earth, and his narration is in itself a seduction:

> As for me, Madame, I feel like I'm wide open, and everything enters me, passes through me, makes me cry or clench my teeth. For example, when I look at that slope over there, that great green fold in the earth, that crowd of trees climbing the mountain, I have the whole forest in my eyes; it penetrates me, invades me, courses through my veins, and I feel like I'm eating it, like it's filling my stomach; I become the forest myself! (533)

In this mini-allegory of copulation, Brétigny presents his visual relationship with the forest as alternately passive and active. Penetrated and impregnated by a personified nature to which he is then assimilated,

Maupassant's updated version of the Greek god Pan will in turn penetrate Christiane, first verbally, then carnally. From this point forward, Christiane herself will be assimilated to the earth, initially as a plant, when Brétigny de-Christianizes her name and baptizes her "Liane," "because she wrapped herself around him to hug him, the way a vine twists around a tree" (577), then as earth itself, when in a theatrical gesture of passionate love he falls to the ground and embraces her dusty shadow. Such histrionics further identify the lover with the doctor/actor Latonne, and the fact that Brétigny, not Latonne, will "heal" Christiane of her supposed infertility solidifies the connection. Christiane's arresting statement of submission to him ("I belong to you body and soul. From now on, do with me what you will" [567]), is strikingly similar to that of the madman to his doctor in "Lettre d'un fou": "My dear doctor, I'm putting myself into your hands. Do with me what you will."[8] Indeed, the male-female relationship in *Mont-Oriol* appears to be modeled on that of doctor-patient, but if this is the case, then there is some irony in the fact that Christiane, so skeptical where the medical profession is concerned, allows herself to be seduced by the clichés of Brétigny's romantic discourse and submits herself to him with confidence and docility.

This brings me to the next point of convergence between doctor, banker, and lover: all three become agents of a phallic penetration of the Other. In all three cases, this penetration is mediated and indirect. It is, of course, easy to imagine the ways in which medical science penetrates and violates the human body. Maupassant's whimsical transliteration of Dr. Bonnefille's illegible prescription in the novel's first chapter serves as an excellent opening salvo in his attack on the medical profession, for it enumerates the ways in which medicines actually cause suffering:

It looked like: "Considering that M. X. is afflicted with a chronic, incurable and fatal illness;

He will take— 1° Sulfate of quinine, which will make him deaf and will cause memory loss;

2° Bromide of potassium, which will destroy his stomach, weaken all his faculties, cause an outbreak of pimples over his whole body, and make his breath foul;

3° Iodine of potassium also, which, drying up all his glands, including those of the brain, will leave him in a short time as impotent as he is imbecilic;

4° Salicylate of soda, the therapeutic effects of which have not yet been proven, but which seems to lead to a sudden, devastating death in those treated with this remedy." (487)

Despite the clearly comic tone of this passage, even twentieth-century readers can appreciate the grim reality of the attack. And nineteenth-century Frenchmen were no doubt even more painfully aware of the accuracy of Maupassant's seemingly lighthearted expansion of the old saw about the remedy being worse than the disease. Cathartics, emetics, and other harsh medicines forced down their throats, often with debilitating side effects, were regarded more as instruments of torture than as potentially therapeutic agents. Thus the levity of this passage masks a serious criticism of medical practice by someone who was writing from experience. To this description of medical invasion corresponds Dr. Latonne's demonstration of the Baraduc probe, strategically placed in the opening chapter of part 2. This time, the role of spectator is assigned to Paul Brétigny. The dyspeptic patient, Riquier, gasps for breath and gags as a rubber tube, "which divided into three at about the midpoint of its length" (595), is pushed down his throat by Latonne while a bath boy attaches one of the other ends to a water faucet and drops the third into a glass container. Once the "rubber beast" has sufficiently penetrated Riquier's writhing, suffering body, the tap is opened and the patient's stomach swells; soon afterward, the contents of the stomach empty themselves into the glass container, where they are scrutinized by Latonne. The physician angrily admonishes his patient: "Never again will you be able to eat peas . . . or salad! Oh! Salad! You're not digesting it at all. No more strawberries either! If I've told you once, I've told you ten times: no strawberries!" (595). Latonne's admonitions are just as angrily countered by Riquier, who accuses him of paying inadequate attention to the hotel menu. Brétigny watches silently, but there is an obvious analogy to be drawn between this medical infiltration of the body and the resultant swelling of the stomach and Brétigny's sexual penetration of Christiane and her subsequent pregnancy. Similarly, just as Latonne fails to take into account his own responsibility for his patient's diet, Brétigny's disgust with his pregnant mistress, expressed later in the same chapter, bears witness to his blatant disregard for causality, his utter refusal to acknowledge his own role as pathogen in what he considers to be her illness.

In the episode of the Baraduc probe, which accurately records one of the more barbaric treatments of nineteenth-century medicine (a treatment, incidentally, that Maupassant had undergone himself), the three-colored pen of the organographism scene has been replaced by the more invasive tripartite tube, the tube in turn compared to a "thin snake with a double tail" (595). Latonne's phallic penetration of his patient's body, mediated both by this medical instrument and by the bathboy, finds a counterpart in Andermatt's imperialistic penetration of the peasant's social and geographical space that is also effected through intermediaries. Andermatt needs the cooperation of others in order to carry out his plan of territorial expansion. Without the scientific community, specifically the geologist, Aubry-Pasteur, who excavates Oriol's land, and the physicians who attest to the water's therapeutic qualities, Andermatt's commercial venture is not possible. Moreover, his penetration and commercial exploitation of Oriol's property is equally inconceivable without the old poacher Clovis, who becomes a living advertisement by allowing himself to be "cured" of his rheumatism each year in exchange for monetary payment (a clever reversal of the usual flow of monies between doctor and patient). Andermatt is equally beholden to Gontran and Brétigny who, by obtaining the hands of Oriol's daughters in marriage, bring him needed land. This proliferation of phallic "instruments" is well represented by the flag poles lining the entrance to the new spa, from which "enormous banners unfurled in the blue sky with serpentine undulations" (592).

Like the invasive activities of Andermatt and Latonne, Brétigny's sexual penetration of Christiane, carefully prepared by a verbal seduction, is in a sense mediated, for were it not for the warm baths prescribed by Dr. Latonne and the seductive beauty of Auvergne, which act as stimuli to Christiane's sensual awakening, her transgression would be implausible. As was the case with Andermatt, who, with the five or six million francs he had at the time of his marriage, "had sown enough to harvest ten or twelve" (488), Brétigny's successes are expressed in agricultural terms. Christiane, the earth-woman, "surrounded and penetrated" by Brétigny's affection, becomes like him sensitive to the charms of Auvergne itself or, more specifically, to that part of Auvergne known as la Limagne:

> And the charm of . . . this blue Limagne . . . its extinct craters on the mountainside . . . the coolness of the its shady groves, the faint sound of the streams running over pebbles, all of this penetrated the young woman's heart and body, penetrated and softened them just as a soft, warm rain on a still-virgin soil brings to blossom flowers whose seed has already been planted. (545)

A slight variation on a well-known literary topos saves this passage from banality. Christiane is penetrated, impregnated by the charm of a land of extinct volcanoes, a land associated with a spent virility. Incidentally, Maupassant took some liberties with geography here, since it is the south of Auvergne, not la Limagne in the north, that is known for its volcanic landscape. When, later in the novel, Christiane's pregnancy is expressed in similar terms ("Deep within her, [Paul] had sown his own life" [613]), we have confirmation of her identification with the rich, fertile earth; in addition, because Paul Brétigny has been substituted for Maupassant's version of la Limagne as the agent of penetration, we are prepared for his waning desire and for the reversal of roles that takes place in part 2 when Brétigny, falling under the spell of Charlotte Oriol, will again be the penetrated object: "He had let the seed germinate in his heart, the little seed of tenderness that they sow in us so quickly, and that grows so large" (661).

Brétigny's oscillation between penetrator and penetrated, seducer and seduced, also characterizes both banker and doctor. Andermatt's initial credulity in the face of Clovis's bogus "cure" is the result of a carefully orchestrated plan on the part of the Oriol father and son who, looking for the means by which they might "enflame the banker's ardor until he can't stand it any longer" (522), first decide to embellish the spring ("They would clean up the field and the spring itself . . . would make it pretty" [523]), then strike the deal with the rheumatic old poacher.

Initially seduced by the hope of a miraculous cure, Andermatt soon realizes that Clovis's recovery and subsequent relapse are pure farce, and he becomes an active player in the comedy, putting Clovis on the permanent payroll with the understanding that his "cure" will necessitate continued treatment.

Dr. Latonne, who at the outset appears to have some professional scruples—declaring haughtily that he never hesitates "between my personal gain and my conscience" (564), an ambiguous statement that will ironically prove true (one can almost feel Maupassant's jab in the ribs)—is eventually seduced by the increasingly powerful Andermatt. The latter's promise to name him "physician-inspector" of the new thermal station completes the seduction, and Latonne, abandoning his scruples, subscribes wholeheartedly to the charade of Clovis's cure. As representative of his professional class, Latonne's dual role as seduced and seducer is emblematic. In order to attract patients to his thermal station, Andermatt needs to engage the physician to help with advertising: "C'est par les médecins que nous devons conquérir les malades" [It's through their physicians that we must conquer the sick] (584). "Conquérir" (to conquer): the word is well-chosen, not only because it rhymes with "guérir" (to cure), but because it *isn't* "guérir." Andermatt's strategy depends not upon *cure* but upon *conquest*. But before conquering the ill, Andermatt must conquer the physicians. His careful seduction, predicated on the expectation that the medical practitioners in turn will seduce their patients, reveals his cynicism with regard to the physicians: "I don't mean to imply that they could be corrupted. . . . But where's the man who couldn't be won over, if you knew how to go about it? There are also women you can't purchase; these women, you have to seduce" (584). Besides what it reveals about him, Andermatt's tendency to view his project in erotic terms is congruous with his plan, for he proposes to the Parisian medical corps the pleasure of possession. In exchange for their patients, he offers the physicians not only the possibility of purchasing mobile "Swiss" chalets at a low price but also, gratis, the property on which the chalets are located. Once again, land and people are deemed interchangeable. Physicians too fall prey to the seductive force of Auvergne.

As seducers, banker, lover, and doctor are all sensitive to the persuasive potential of language. Hence, for Andermatt, the naming of the new station and its springs is of utmost importance. Brétigny's seduction of Christiane is largely effected through language, as we have seen. Finally, Latonne's collaboration in the advertising scheme and his cynical promise that the weather reports from Mont-Oriol will be superior to those of neighboring stations betrays an implicit understanding that desire must be created by language and that truth is irrelevant.

Alternately seduced and seducers, passive and active, *Mont-Oriol*'s three male protagonists are also linked by their androgyny, which is evoked either explicitly or implicitly. Brétigny, we are told, "had to an excessive degree a truly feminine temperament . . . with a man's superior intelligence" (537). Andermatt's virility is implicitly called into question by his wife's infidelity. Latonne's femininity, finally, is encoded in his name. Besides being phonetically identical to that of the Roman goddess Latone (in Latin *Latona*), who suffers a difficult parturition,[9] Latonne (*l'atone*) suggests lack of muscle tone, thus the antithesis of the muscularity and virility characteristic of the spa workers in that other important clinical scene, the demonstration of Mont-Oriol's *Institut médical de gymnastique automotrice.*

This leads us to another point of resemblance among the three male protagonists, for if the organographism scene had identified the physician with the magician, if the stomach purification episode had featured the physician as torturer, the scene in the exercise room, a masterpiece of medical parody, presents him as an enemy of nature. Latonne's passionate defense of such artificial exercises as "dry swimming" and "seated walking," his blind theorizing about the value of "this completely muscular labor" (597) in which the mind plays no part, ignores the obvious: the employees who turn the cranks of the exercise apparatus and force artificial movement on the patients strapped to them are lean and muscular, whereas the patients remain obese and flaccid. This scene features the corpulent engineer Aubry-Pasteur, who is strapped in a sitting position to a walking machine. Once again, Maupassant has maliciously cast Brétigny as spectator, implicitly suggesting parallels between the physician's denial of nature and Brétigny's. In this chapter alone, the narrative will focus successively on such other displays of artifice as a two-act vaudeville comedy and an ill-timed fireworks display, to end with a lengthy meditation on the superiority of nonprocreative sexuality. Here, it is the idealistic Paul Brétigny, repulsed by the reality of biological reproduction, who is associated with the unnatural: "What really exalted him in his tenderness was that flight of two hearts toward an inaccessible ideal, that entwining of two immaterial souls, all the unrealizable and contrived qualities that poets put into their descriptions of passion" (613). In his recent study of Maupassant, Pierre Danger has asserted—and I concur—that Brétigny's love for women is a matter of *impulse* rather than *desire*, a primitive instinct reflected moreover in his appearance, "which had something brutal and unfinished about it" (540).[10] The reader is not fooled by his lyrical meditation on ideal love. Christiane's nickname, Liane, was inspired not by the immaterial entwining of two souls but by a more carnal reality. Brétigny's repugnance for the pregnant woman stems from his view of the fetus as a pathogenic occupant that sullies and deforms its host body, transforming it from a goddess into "the animal that reproduces its species" (613). Despite his romanticizing discourse, Brétigny is himself the real animal; without him, the fetus would not exist. Thus he is ultimately the culprit in Christiane's "sickness," as Christiane herself realizes when she reflects that her lover "had penetrated to the depths of her flesh" (613). Her metonymic reduction of her lover to his reproductive organ allows us to see in a properly ironic light the principle upon which Latonne's organometric medicine is based: "I maintain that a large number of our illnesses stem exclusively from the excessive development of an organ that encroaches upon its neighbor, impedes its functions, and in no time manages to destroy the body's general harmony" (596). Reduced to a pathological swelling that recalls Flaubert's cynical formula for eros, Brétigny's "love" for Christiane has indeed destroyed the general harmony of her body. The medical theories expounded in the novel's opening chapter are essential to an understanding of this part's action, just as the apparently superfluous descriptive passages that provide the opening frame in so many of Maupassant's short stories prove to be intimately related to the plot of the embedded tale. The same is true in part 2 of *Mont-Oriol*, where the ease with which Brétigny transfers his attentions to Charlotte Oriol is prefigured by Latonne's extemporizing on the merits of artificial exercise, in which the body, rather than the mind, is engaged. For Brétigny, as for Latonne's patients, courage, mental energy, and moral effort have been replaced by pure physical movement. Love is reduced to coitus, "this completely muscular labor" (597).

Latonne's defense of his gymnastic program, his decision to substitute for willpower "a foreign and purely mechanical force" (596), also brings Andermatt to mind. For what is Maupassant's Jewish banker if not a purely mechanical foreign force? Like Latonne and Brétigny, Andermatt is associated with artifice, both through the metaphor of the theater and through a skill that is more mechanical than human: "Andermatt, in fact, evoked the idea of a strange human machine constructed with the sole purpose of mentally calculating, moving around, and manipulating money" (516–17).[11]

After the magician man (the physician) and the human animal (Paul Brétigny), we find ourselves face to face with the mechanical man. Interestingly, this view of Andermatt as a human adding machine presents us with a paradox. The text makes quite explicit that Christiane has denied her husband access to her for a full eleven months prior to her daughter's birth. Now, while in Rabelais, pregnancies can last eleven months, this is not the norm in Maupassant's work. Given the acuity of Andermatt's calculations, it is impossible to believe that he cannot subtract nine from eleven, that is, that he doesn't realize the impossibility of his paternity. On the contrary, Andermatt appears as a willing accomplice to his wife's infidelity, implicitly engaging Brétigny as associate in his biological project just as he has explicitly engaged Clovis and the Parisian physicians in his economic venture. His hasty suppression of the incriminating cause of Aubry-Pasteur's death, a measure he considers essential to the success of his thermal station, thus corresponds to his taking possession of Christiane's daughter.[12] Similarly, Brétigny's refusal to acknowledge his responsibility for the condition of his mistress parallels the clearly feigned ignorance of Andermatt, who is no more mystified about his wife's fertility than about Clovis's magical "cure."

Even the casual reader cannot fail to notice the almost vertiginous repetition of allusions to corpulence in *Mont-Oriol*. The fact that there are more than twenty-five mentions of stomachs, and forty-four instances of the word *gros* (fat) and its derivatives, bears testimony to the importance of the grotesque body in *Mont-Oriol*. Were we to add such related terms as "immense," "gigantic," "enormous," "huge," "monstrous," and so forth, many of which refer to the vast body of Auvergne, the picture would be even more compelling. From the ironically named Paille women, "stout everywhere, in the front and in the back" (509) to "the fat Monsieur Aubry-Pasteur," who walks "with his legs spread apart and his arms held out from his body" (597)—not forgetting the casino director, "whose soft, flabby stomach bounced about beneath his shirt" (496), or the duc de Ramas-Aldavarra, who is afflicted with "a monstrous obesity" (617)—what we might term the "pathological body" is ubiquitous in *Mont-Oriol*. Further, most of the curists believe themselves to be victims of digestive difficulties, and dietary concerns—forgive the pun—nourish conversations at the dinner table. The three male protagonists are also gross, each in his own way. Andermatt uses his stomach as a weapon of aggression, indeed, as a phallus: "Andermatt cut through the crowd, as he knew so well how to do, rolling his round little stomach among the others" (602). Latonne, too, described as "an important personage," is associated with corpulence by another homonym of his name, *la tonne* (the ton). (Philippe Bonnefis is right on the mark when he says of Latonne's patronym that it is "in itself an allegory.") Brétigny, finally, with his Herculean build, is responsible for Christiane's swollen stomach, and the accuracy of Dr. Latonne's organometric lesson is retrospectively revealed: "A swelling of the stomach is sufficient to make you think you have a heart ailment" (489). Christiane's broken heart will result directly from her pregnancy, a "swelling" caused by the incorporation of the Other represented by Paul Brétigny.

The metaphorical *ventre* (stomach) is equally ubiquitous. Here the example that comes immediately to mind is that of Oriol father and son who, having filled with gunpowder "le *ventre* vidé de l'énorme rocher" [the hollowed-out cavity of the enormous boulder] (498), which is shading their vineyard, expose a mineralized spring that will make

Andermatt's fortune. The death of a small dog who is *éventré* (eviscerated) by the explosion is incidental, although it has considerable prophetic value as a metaphor for Christiane, as critics have noted. But *roquet* (nasty little lapdog) also suggests *Riquier*, the patient who undergoes the painful purge of his stomach. Each of these sequences of penetration-swelling-explosion/expulsion corresponds to one of the novel's main thematic threads.

On the one hand, then, we have hypertrophy, the abnormal growth of an organ, a subject which has a patently metaphoric value in this novel, whether we think of the organ as physiological (Brétigny's swollen member, Christiane's swollen belly), sociocultural (the growing importance of the Jewish financier), or professional (the grossly inflated power enjoyed by the physician during this period). On the other hand, we witness the body's invasion, whether medical, venereal, or economic, by species foreign to it. Claudine Giachetti's parenthetical comment that in this novel, "si proche de la comédie" [so close to comedy], "mariage et capitalisme ont un but commun, celui de *la multiplication des espèces*" [marriage and capitalism have a common goal, the propagation of the species/of cash], is richly insightful.[13] However, biological reproduction and capitalistic enterprise do not begin to account for all of the species that multiply in the world of *Mont-Oriol*. The proliferation of patients in part 1 or of physicians and foreigners in part 2, the almost Balzacian descriptions of Andermatt, Gontran, Brétigny, and others as social species or of Doctors Bonnefille, Latonne, and their colleagues as medical species, the repeated references to *breeds* of people, and the numerous allusions to the carriage of Mont-Oriol as Noah's Ark suggest that this novel is pregnant with a meaning that, among all of Maupassant's critics, only Trevor Harris has come close to discerning.

To appreciate this meaning, we must consider the linguistic hegemony exercised by the medical profession in late-nineteenth-century France. Following the Franco-Prussian war, as we have noted, it became commonplace to see France's humiliating defeat in medical terms, the inevitable failure of the sick, weak nation to resist invasion by a powerful, healthy opponent. Maupassant's originality in *Mont-Oriol* is to have recounted this drama on three closely related levels: the sexual, the economic, and the medical. Beneath the novel's ostensible subject—the rise of a thermal station, village of Hope and Life, from the ashes of a "sick" province of ruins and extinct volcanoes figured as "monstrous pustules"—there lies a profoundly xenophobic subtext, or what Harris calls, perhaps more charitably, a "brief flirtation with a nationalist discourse."[14] Under the solitary influence of the Jewish capitalist, Andermatt, the primitive and impoverished province of Auvergne, the very heart of France, is invaded not only by the Parisian medical corps but by foreign doctors and curists. Claudine Giachetti has argued persuasively that *Mont-Oriol* records a conquest of space and may thus be paired with Maupassant's second novel, *Bel-Ami*. The association is more fruitful than even Professor Giachetti suspects, for if in the former novel it is the true Frenchman, Duroy, the country boy, who gradually dispossesses the Jew, Walter, first of his wife and daughter, then of his urban space, in *Mont-Oriol*, Andermatt, the Jew, evens the score by dispossessing the French peasant of the very land with which he is identified. At the same time, he dispossesses him of his daughters, through the intermediary of Gontran and Brétigny. I make a distinction between Jew and Frenchman because Maupassant himself does so by his onomastic choices. Interestingly, although he uses names that are encoded as Jewish for Andermatt's associates (Abraham Lévy, Simon Zidler), he does not do so in the case of Walter and Andermatt. Besides evoking the Prussian soldier, Walter Schnaffs, the name *Walter* incorporates *alter*, l'autre ("the Other"), to which it adds the Germanic "W";[15] likewise, Andermatt incorporates the German word for *autre*, *ander*, in addition to evoking an actual toponym, the Swiss-German village of the same name. Moreover, his first name, William, identifies him with that other historic enemy of the French, the Englishman. This reduction of the Jew to a generic Other, the Foreigner, is highly significant. If, in *Bel-Ami*, the protagonist's role as an "African hunter" had related his conquest to the colonial adventure in which the newspaper industry was heavily involved, the drama of *Mont-Oriol* suggests rather a foreign assault on France led by the banker, with the doctor and the lover as collaborators. The fact that the name of Brétigny also derives from a toponym and is associated with a treaty that abandoned a large slice of territory to England during the Hundred Years' War supports this interpretation.

Reproduced in dim outline here, foreign incursion onto French soil, besides evoking sexual penetration, an association Maupassant had made as early as "Boule de suif," is rendered metaphorically as a medical intervention. Seen in this light, the various clinically inspired scenes that feature Latonne, from the organ mapping and the physical penetration of the body to the torture of forced movement, all forms of medical aggression, can be identified with the invasion, occupation, and torture of the political and social body of France.

Mont-Oriol's serialized publication in the newspaper *Gil Blas* took place between December 1886 and February 1887. The definitive version of Maupassant's most famous fantastic tale, "Le Horla," was published three months after the novel's last installment. The two narratives, although superficially different, in fact bear witness to a similar fear of the Other. Transported by a Brazilian sailing ship in "Le Horla," the mysterious Other insinuates himself into the home and the very being of the narrator, and this insinuation is experienced as an illness that is, moreover, aggravated by the observation of a hypnotic experiment performed by a doctor with a German surname.[16] Indeed, on a structural level, the physician doubles the Horla, since both put their subjects to sleep, rob them of their willpower.[17]

In *Mont-Oriol*, the Other, personified above all by Andermatt, is portrayed as a conquering foreigner who collaborates with the doctor and the lover to penetrate the sanctity of the Body/Country/Self.[18] These images, separate throughout the first part of the novel, gradually coalesce in part 2 with the creation of two theoretically distinct medical species, represented by Drs. Black and Mazelli, each of whom incorporates the three faces of the Other. The mercenary motives of Black's religious fervor, his association with the English enemy through his name and his appearance (he resembles a bulldog), and his role in provoking Christiane's labor identify him symbolically with Latonne, Andermatt, and Brétigny. As for Mazelli, an unscrupulous Italian physician whose success owes as much to his cynicism regarding the efficacy of medical treatments as to his personal charm, he imports foreign therapies into

France, substituting pleasure for pain, massage for *lavage*, curaçao for mineral water, and he uses his medical skills ("he feels, he sniffs, he probes" [668]) not to diagnose illness but to test the vulnerability of nubile young women. Literally combining the roles of doctor, lover, and foreign capitalist, Mazelli becomes the incarnation of the opportunistic pirate or *écumeur* (sea-rover), a term by which Andermatt is also designated (670). Again one is reminded of Daudet's Jenkins, the *forban* (pirate). With the admission of such species as this, the integrity of the Ark is in serious jeopardy. The fact that immigration into France began in earnest during the 1880s, causing considerable anguish among Frenchmen already concerned about national identity, is surely not coincidental. *Mont-Oriol*, haunted by a fear of the Other, engages and entertains the reader with an ostensibly simple story of love and abandonment and a corresponding tale of capitalism triumphant. An analysis of the novel's medical dimension reveals beneath the playful parody a disquieting xenophobia that is inseparable from the fear and hatred of the medical practitioner. Furthermore, the fact that the novel's physicians are in league with the Jewish banker Andermatt, whose successes can be attributed not only to his business acumen and his aggression but also to his ability to exploit "Christians," hints at an anti-Semitic subtext as well.[19] It is perhaps not mere coincidence that Edouard Drumont's *La France juive* was published just months before *Mont-Oriol*.

8

MEDICAL MENACE IN LÉON DAUDET'S
LES MORTICOLES

ɡ

At the beginning of a lengthy meditation on the medical profession, Montaigne writes about his kidney stones, a condition he believes he has inherited from his father, and then suggests that his skepticism regarding the efficacy of medical treatment is also hereditary: "I hope that physicians will forgive my frankness, because, by the same fatal infusion and insinuation, I have received my hatred and contempt for their teachings: this antipathy that I have for their art is hereditary."[1] Three centuries and many medical discoveries later, when medicine considered itself a science rather than an art, and when "heredity" had become the buzz word of a whole generation of physicians and writers, another son, one Léon Daudet, agonized over the physical ills that his father may have transmitted to him. However, lacking the self-knowledge that Montaigne so painstakingly acquired through his writing, Daudet seems to have been less lucid in identifying the source of his contempt for the medical practitioner.

It was in 1894, just three years before Alphonse Daudet would die the painful death of syphilis, that Léon published his justly famous invective against the Parisian medical profession, *Les Morticoles*. Denigrated as a "pamphlet" by scholars who objected to the rancorous tone and polemical structure, the novel was, by the author's admission, a medical "anti-thesis." Léon Daudet, having undertaken medical studies at the age of seventeen in hopes of understanding his father's illness and perhaps even of finding a cure for it, had completed his course work but failed the competitive examination for an internship in Paris, not through ignorance or lack of zeal but because he had managed to offend an influential member of the Paris medical faculty, Dr. Albert Robin. This, at any rate, is Daudet's analysis of the situation.[2] Like Flaubert, who explained in a letter to George Sand that he was writing *Bouvard et Pécuchet* in order to "spit up the venom that is choking me, that is, to tell a few truths, purge myself, and then be more Olympian,"[3] Daudet conceived of the literary work in general and this work in particular as a therapeutic purge. For a novel inspired by hatred of the medical profession, the metaphor was certainly appropriate.[4]

Daudet came by this hatred naturally, for although it was his father who had encouraged him to pursue medical studies in the first place rather than follow his natural inclinations to become a writer, the elder Daudet had included in his fictional accounts of life in Second Empire society some extraordinarily unflattering portraits of the physician, as the example of *Le Nabab* illustrates dramatically.

Ironically, perhaps, whereas the elder Daudet's novel had few admirers among nineteenth-century critics, Léon Daudet's *Les Morticoles*, "of which the literary worthlessness is obvious" according to one modern critic,[5] received rather more favorable publicity at the time of its appearance although, understandably, most medical periodicals did not deign to review it, and it was virtually ignored for the first eighty years of the twentieth century.[6] Like *Le Nabab*, *Les Morticoles* sold stunningly well. Like *Le Nabab*, it was seen as a denunciation of the ideological foundation of its era (in this case, the early Third Republic), and it fascinated critics who sought, usually with little difficulty, to strip the physician-characters of their fictional disguises. In contrast to Alphonse Daudet, who, when faced with this same obsession, attempted to underplay the resemblance between his characters and historical personages, the intrepid Léon Daudet counted upon readers' acuity in identifying his real-life sources, for it was upon this recognition that his novel's *succès de scandale* depended. Nevertheless, in order to avoid a lawsuit, he insisted that his fictional physicians were all composites, and it was not until 1940, with the publication of *Quand vivait mon père*, that he provided a "key" to his portraits.

What is most intriguing about *Les Morticoles*, published some seventeen years after *Le Nabab* and strikingly different in tone and ostensible subject, is the degree to which, at a more fundamental level, it resembles the elder Daudet's novel. An analysis of Léon Daudet's first-person narrative will allow us to illuminate the principles upon which this resemblance is based.

"Comment sont vos matières et en général celles de vos camarades?" [Describe your feces and, in general, those of your friends.] (5). This request, addressed by a physician, Dr. Crudanet, to Félix Canelon, the seventeen-year-old protagonist of *Les Morticoles*, sets the tone for the dialogues to follow, a tone that Richard Terdiman would no doubt characterize as "intensely counter-discursive" by virtue of the fact that it includes "a corrosive irony concerning the here-and-now."[7] A bold satirist in the lineage of Rabelais and Swift, Léon Daudet establishes from the outset both the physician's coprophilia, thinly disguised by the scientific euphemism "matières," and his preoccupation with the material world. The novel is set in the fictional "Morticole country," where a hapless Félix and his shipmates are imprisoned by the natives when their ship, the *Courrier*, sails off course. Accosted by a Morticole vessel bearing a skull on its flag (the conventional pirate banner), the worried sailors offer little resistance when the barbaric Morticoles board their ship, force them to throw all their provisions overboard and to exchange their clothing for hygienic regulation uniforms, then limit them to a diet of tasteless biscuits during a thirty-three-day "quarantine" at sea.[8] Once they are properly "sanitized," they are permitted to disembark. The country they discover is dominated at every level—judicial, legislative, administrative—by physicians, and the entire population is divided into two classes: doctors and patients. Readers are introduced *seriatim* to both as they follow the hero first to l'Hôpital Typhus, where he is admitted as a patient and undergoes a surgical procedure necessitated by medical mistreatment (part 1), then to medical school where he completes his course work but fails the most important exam of all, the "foot-licking" (part 2), and finally through a succession of menial positions with the most influential members of the medical community (part 3). Félix's stay in the land of the Morticoles is a brutal introduction to a wholly materialistic society. When he finally escapes, Christian ethics intact, at the end of the novel, it is only because he is able to bribe Crudanet into securing a vessel for himself and the other two survivors from the *Courrier,* Trub and Sanot. Narrated at a great temporal remove from the action (for the 105-year-old Félix had waited until he could tell his story "without venom"), the adventures of Daudet's protagonist function metaphorically to expose the foibles of the Godless practitioners of medicine.

In recent years, *Les Morticoles* has attracted the attention of two medical historians who, despite different perspectives, come to surprisingly similar conclusions. Elisabeth Roudinesco, in her monumental history of French psychoanalysis, sees in the vitriolic novel, particularly in those passages that deal with hypnotism and hysteria, the proof of "a veritable delirium" in which Léon Daudet subconsciously substitutes Charcot for Alphonse Daudet as hated father figure, source of all the ailments that he did not dare to attribute to his biological father. It is worth noting that the Daudet family was for a time very close to the Charcots, and that Charcot had hoped in vain that Léon would marry his daughter, Jeanne. Instead, the young man had elected to marry Victor Hugo's granddaughter (also named Jeanne), who had previously been married to Charcot's son, an action that did not endear him to the master of la Salpêtrière and that may well have contributed to his difficulties in medical school. Roudinesco considers that the novel's main interest lies in its use of certain rhetorical devices that would, during the following century, characterize "the spectacular phrasing of the anti-Semitic pamphlet."[9] The medical historian Toby Gelfand, for his part, contends that the novel "aspired to be a kind of medical version of Edouard Drumont's *La France juive* (1886) with doctors instead of Jews as scapegoats for the ills of the modern world."[10] But the novel was not "merely" antimedical. Gelfand concurs with those of Daudet's contemporaries who saw that *Les Morticoles* was more far-reaching than it at first appeared. Daudet had exploited medical language "to fuel a polemic whose target, modern society, is much bigger than medicine."[11] How did this come about? Why was the medical idiom particularly appropriate to this task? How did doctors come to be villains, the target of so many attacks inspired by *fin-de-siècle* angst? In order to answer these questions, we must consider, first, the context in which *Les Morticoles* was written.

Published in 1894, just before the Dreyfus Affair divided the country and in the midst of a movement of conservative religious nationalism that saw in the Third Republic's secular spirit a danger to public morality, *Les Morticoles* was dedicated to Edmond de Goncourt, friend of the Daudet family and a well-known anti-Semite. In a curious way, Daudet's novel seemed a response to *Madame Gervaisais*, with "la Morticolie" replacing Rome, and with doctors, hospitals, ovarectomies, and the "Celebration of Matter" being substituted respectively for priests, churches, confession, and religious festivals. Since the Goncourt brothers had dedicated *their* novel to Léon Daudet, it is reasonable to assume that, in returning the compliment, the latter wished to express gratitude to the elder novelist and to suggest that their fictional targets were not incompatible. Indeed, both novelists fulminated against materialism, which, whether it took the form of gaudy pietistic objects and vulgar religious practices in *Madame Gervaisais* or scientific and economic pragmatism in *Les Morticoles*, they considered inimical to spirituality. The reading of *Madame Gervaisais* from a certain "oppositional" perspective that would place it among those influential pre-texts inspiring *Les Morticoles* is thus to some extent validated by the inscriptions. Nevertheless, while we can certainly illuminate Daudet's novel by juxtaposing it with *Madame Gervaisais*, we can show even more clearly how it flows from Alphonse Daudet's *Le Nabab* (1877) and Maupassant's *Mont-Oriol* (1886), both of which, as we have seen, betrayed a deep mistrust of the medical professional who becomes the incarnation of the generic Other, associated simultaneously with the invading foreigner and with the unscrupulous, opportunistic Jew. With *Les Morticoles*, however, the focus sharpens. Discreet allusions give way to violent invective, a subtle cynicism to an almost hallucinatory paranoia in which the physician is blamed for all of the world's evils.

As might be expected, the filiation with *Le Nabab* is particularly strong. As if to nudge his reader to make the connection, Léon Daudet sets his first scene aboard a ship. No longer imbued with metaphorical importance, the vessel serves instead as an allegory, when a seafaring society that goes astray is delivered into the hands of a country governed by doctors. The criticism of the physician, which in *Le Nabab*'s third-person narration had been shared approximately equally by the omniscient narrator and the character Félicia Ruys, is here assumed by a first-person narrator, Félix Canelon, *Félix* being the masculine form of *Félicia*. The doctor's legendary association with death, progressively revealed through plot in the father's novel, is established immediately and without concession to subtlety in that of the son, first by its title and second by the sinister Morticole vessel with its pirate banner. Medical incompetence gives way to medical malice, literary theater to operating theater and the charade of Charcot's Tuesday clinic. Finally, the image of the city as corrupt and profoundly ill is transformed by Léon Daudet to that of the city as "a huge, sprawling cadaver" (105), its sewers constructed on the model of "these vessels of the human body that [physicians] spend their lives studying" (105). While in *Le Nabab* the physician Jenkins was portrayed as a parasite, nourishing himself at the expense of a sick society and sapping it of its strength, the physicians of *Les Morticoles* are more akin to microbes. Having circulated on society's body and infected it with a deadly virus, they have destroyed all hope of a cure. Their victim, society itself, has been reduced to the status of a corpse lying at their feet.

Thus while physical descriptions of the vampiric Jenkins insisted on his radiant health, the physicians of la Morticolie are defined by their morbidity, and Crudanet's affirmation that the entire country is divided into the healthy, who are doctors, and the infirm, who are patients ("Except for us, everyone is sick" [19]), is belied by repeated suggestions that the real degenerates are the doctors themselves. The pathologization of the physician carried out by Léon Daudet assumes several forms. Sometimes it is expressed in physical stigmata, as in the description of the surgeon Crudanet, whose face is "scarred by smallpox" (23). More often, it is encoded onomastically. Through an analysis of patronymics, one becomes aware that Daudet's antipathy toward the medical professional is nothing more than a disguise for his anti-Semitism, a prejudice that would be revealed by his strongly anti-Dreyfusard stance in 1894–95. In the first place, the physicians are associated with racial impurity, Tabard being an anagram of *bâtard* (bastard), Tismet de l'ancre containing *sémite* as well as being an imperfect anagram of *métis de race* (mixed breed), Crudanet being a homonym of *cru damné* (cursed vintage). In addition, they are stigmatized in ways that are strikingly similar to those used by late-nineteenth-century anti-Semites: they are identified with filth (Cudane evoking *cul d'âne* [monkey's arse], Cloaquol evoking *cloaque* [cesspool]); with bodily excretions (Foutange containing a form of the verb *foutre* [to copulate], Vomédan suggesting *vomir* [to vomit], Purin-Calcaret evoking urine); and with evil and death (Malasvon and Florimal containing *mal* [evil], Cercueillet encompassing *cercueil* [coffin]). Finally, their lack of moral probity is called into question: Tartègre is tainted by a name that weds the beginning of *tare* (flaw) with the ending of *intègre* (honest) to evoke an irremediably blemished integrity; Avigdeuse contains *avide* (greedy), suggesting the impure motives that lie at the heart of la Morticolie's iatocracy.

Jenkins had worn an elaborate mask that enabled him to win the confidence of his patients; the sinister nature of the physicians in *Les Morticoles* is revealed in their appearance, and the shrill, polemical tone of Léon Daudet's defamatory treatment of the medical profession is apparent in the semantically loaded language that he uses in their description. Crudanet and his cohort have "small, distrusting eyes," Tabard is "a small, dark-complexioned man with a cold glimmer in his eye" (22), Cloaquol "a ruddy gnome with a white goatee and grey hair invading his weasel face" (80), Foutange "analogous to a parrot, his nose forming a curve above a rather small mouth" (165). The caricaturized portraits betray Daudet's phantasm through the prevalence of stereotypically Semitic features. Whether or not the physicians who inspired the individual characters were Jews is irrelevant: for Daudet, all doctors are Jews. Hence Boustibras, inspired by the Jewish physician Bernheim, becomes emblematic of the whole profession, being "one of those little Jews who infest Morticole country and of whom Wabenheim is the most illustrious representative" (167).

Besides being inscribed in their names, such characteristics as the physicians' lack of hygiene and their avarice are also revealed through plot. The surgeon Tabard, said to have been modeled at least in part on Péan, who performed surgical operations in street clothes, is nicknamed "the king of dung" because of his poor hygiene.[12] "With his dusty jacket, and his shirt sleeves . . . drenched in blood" (23), he growls at Félix, accusing him of neglecting to wash his feet, then gives his ankle a violent twist, causing a sprain, which is later brutally transformed into "a magnificent dislocation of the lower astragalus, with a double fracture of the astragalus and probable tearing of one or two ligaments" (68) by the "Rasta" assigned to him. There is potent irony here: in addition to suggesting that physicians—and their surrogates, suspicious foreigners—themselves cause illness in order to render the patient "more interesting," Daudet takes aim at the medical profession's preoccupation with cleanliness by implying that practitioners have become the apostles of hygiene without themselves observing even the most elementary of its dictates. In a subsequent chapter, during the examination Daudet refers to as the "foot-licking" and which he renders literally, Félix will be so overwhelmed with disgust at the sight and smell of Tabard's filthy feet that he will be unable to perform the ritual licking:

> I thought about . . . my poor mouth, which I was going to drag across this bitumen. . . . I lowered my head. Then, accompanying the color, but even stronger, an atrocious stench rose up, composed of all the black ingredients of a witch's caldron. It penetrated my nostrils, reached my throat, my stomach, filled my soul, and suddenly, without being able to stop them, I vomited the contents of the previous evening's meal and the morning's breakfast in a resounding cataract on those infernal feet. (251)

The graphic materialism of this repulsive description should not distract the reader from its serious subtext, which reveals many anti-Semitic prejudices. Allusions to stench ("atrocious stench"), blackness ("bitumen," "black"), witchcraft ("witch's caldron"), and especially to the infernal realm ("infernal feet") identifies the filthy physician with the Jew whose foot, according to Sander Gilman, was believed to have "analogies with the hidden sign of difference attributed to the cloven-footed devil of the middle ages."[13] Moreover, if Tabard's feet are "diabolical" in their filth, Boridan's feet, to which Félix successfully pays lingual homage before reaching Tabard, bear a more classic resemblance to the Jewish foot, which, in the "fantasy of the thought collective," is crooked and flat.[14] The little toe of Boridan's foot has a "bizarre form," and "the sole is just a joke" (249).

It has been pointed out that Félix is captured by the Morticoles at the age of seventeen, the very age at which Léon Daudet began his medical studies. The resemblance does not end here, of course, since Félix, like Léon, will fail his exams. Clearly, Daudet was convinced that his failure to win an internship in Paris was occasioned by his inability—perhaps his refusal—to humble himself before influential faculty members in order to win their approval. Here again, onomastics are revealing, for with the addition of a single grapheme, the letters of *Boridan* can be rearranged to spell "Dr. A. Robin," said to have been Daudet's nemesis. Félix Canelon's nausea reflects Daudet's, and his retching becomes the physiological equivalent of the literary activity that produced *Les Morticoles.* The narrator's physical revulsion for the physician is matched by a moral indignation caused by the practitioner's indifference to suffering and his crass materialism. Insensitive to his patient's pre-operative terror, the surgeon Malasvon has "an expressionless face" (71); Tripard contemplates his victim "with a malicious look on his face" (148); Wabandheim, "the scientific jewel" of "the Jewish race" (255), "is coarse, especially with women," speaking to them "harshly and curtly" (258). Noticeably absent from the professional ethos of these physicians are humanitarian goals; clinical experimentation leads not to the relief of suffering but to knowledge ("Were you born yesterday? Do you really think that medicine exists to cure people? Grave mistake! Its only goal is to establish facts" [33]); monetary ends justify all means. When Félix tells the interns he meets at l'Hôpital Typhus of the capture of his ship and the subsequent quarantine of its passengers by Crudanet, they laugh incredulously and ask, "How come your captain didn't grease his palm?!" (28). Mocking the naiveté of Félix, "a traveler from primitive countries where . . . people still genuflect in front of crucifixes" (30), they proclaim that, for them, "gold is the true God" (32). Patients are valuable only insofar as they are able to enrich the medical professionals: in dying, the poor leave "their meat" (32), enabling the physicians to perform autopsies and thus contribute to their own glorification and well-being;

4 Honoré Daumier, "To Operate or Not to Operate: Medicine Has to Bring in Money," illustration for *La Némésis médicale illustrée*, Paris, 1840. The nineteenth-century proverb according to which the physician will get his money one way or the other is wittily rendered by Daumier, whose crassly materialistic physician establishes fees both for his services and for the *patient*'s suffering.

the rich leave their fortunes, allowing the doctors to build "laboratories, which are our churches" (32): "Thanks to gold, we dominate those inferior scholars of accessory forms of knowledge, geologists, zoologists, mineralogists, botanists, physicists, chemists, histologists, embryologists, etc." (32). The medical doctors' hubris (also suggested by onomastics, since the name of their hospital, *typhus*, is linked etymologically with pride) is evident here, as is their sense of rivalry with other branches of science, a sentiment that can be verified historically. Nevertheless, the emphasis is on their avarice. As might be expected, Wabandheim, "the Jew with such hard eyes" (186), becomes the personification of greed: "Money, money, money! Such was his love of silver that he had in his eyes its glint, its immobility, its hardness" (259). For him, as for most of his colleagues, science is simply "the means of dominating and winning all the honors" (257). Morality is meaningless: the cross of the Legion of Honor is purchased, plagiarism is rampant, and the physician conspires with the pharmacist to the economic advantage of both. Wabanheim's inherent evil is biologically determined. When, on his deathbed, leeches are applied, they draw black blood. Félix has a sudden illumination: "I understood in a flash that all the cruelty of the Morticoles is based upon an immense misunderstanding. They're like those savages who eat venomous roots and become eternally ferocious and bloodthirsty. *Their* root is science" (273). Daudet's counter-discursive strategy—he uses the language of scientific materialism against itself—may not be subtle, but it is effective. For the Morticoles (read: physicians, Jews, and anticlerical, atheistic materialists of every ilk), the Christian Félix Canelon and his compatriots are associated with the primitive, uncivilized past. In taxing the Morticoles themselves with a savagery that rests on "an immense misunderstanding" and in equating science with a poisonous root, Daudet raises his voice against the secular culture of Third Republic France, daring to suggest that it is as empty of meaning as the pretentious language of its deified medical corps. Whether "silent like slabs or flowing like blood and pus" (83), the Morticoles are great pretenders who exploit science for their own materialistic ends. Pressing the case for a return to tradition that he interprets as a renewal of Christian values, Daudet distorts the major scientific theories of his day, providing a reductio ad absurdum of the ideas of Darwin, Bernard, Pasteur, and others, and mocking the nascent science of statistics, "that marvelous science by which white becomes black, red yellow, and which has an answer to every argument" (111). Darwin's evolutionary theories are grotesquely summarized by a fourteen-year-old boy whose Morticole education has taught him "that we come from animals, which come from plants, which come from stones, which are in space and form the universe and the stars" (42). Félix marvels at the docility of the Morticole citizens, who accept so readily the indoctrination of their leaders: "Certes, les Morticoles ont savamment organisé les esprits pour les dominer, les asservir. Celui qui se croit issu d'un caillou n'a plus qu'à se laisser rouler" [Of course, the Morticoles had cleverly formed the minds of their citizens in order to dominate and enslave them. He who thinks he comes from a pebble might as well let himself be rolled around/cheated] (42). The horrible weight of heredity is an article of faith for the Morticoles, one to which even the "good" doctor Charmide subscribes:

> Morticole illnesses are truly like people. As human parasites are parallel to humans, they have their sons who prey on their sons, their grandchildren who prey on their grandchildren, and so on. . . . You must learn, Canelon, that the son of a madman is a madman, the son of a cardiac sufferer is going to be a cardiac sufferer, the son of someone afflicted with tuberculosis is going to have tuberculosis. (89)

Whereas the virtuous Dr. Charmide chooses to characterize illness as a person, the evil Morticoles, who represent all but one of the other doctors encountered in this novel, reify the ill, reducing them to their morbid conditions. Thus the sick child Alfred is "vertebral decay," while Félix is identified on one occasion as a "thigh ulcer," a "club foot" on another. The despair to which such impersonal treatment leads is matched by the bleak outlook of those who subscribe to the philosophy of hereditary determinism preached by the Morticoles, whence the necessity of a "school for suicide" (108) where the desperate learn how to "depart neatly from the world" (110) without pain or anguish. Besides solidifying the link between the physician and death, this fantasy recalls both the Maupassant story "L'Endormeuse," published a decade earlier, and the lure of suicide experienced by two characters in *Le Nabab*.

Indeed, were it not for the fact that Félix and his compatriot Trub manage to escape at the novel's end, suicide would seem to be the only exit from the infernal realms of la Morticolie, a country that knows neither justice nor religion, a country ruled by doctors who have lost the capacity to feel emotion, who exploit such scientific inventions as anesthesia and antiseptics not to relieve pain and to increase survival rates but to attempt ever bolder surgical interventions, most of them fatal. Daudet rails against the violence done to the human body in surgery: "Everything that breaches the body's sacred dams is the work of the devil. Surgery has its pretexts just as war does, but it's no more justified. To prolong a frail existence is horrible. Let the blood stay where it is!" (64–65). The image of surgery as warfare and (by extension) the surgeon as warrior supplants the notion of the physician as secular priest, sacrificing his patients on the operating table, "the altar of torture" (72). Thus it represents an intensification of the polemic, for it identifies the physician with the Enemy, the Other who penetrates the body of the Self. Connected to this image is that of the physician as rapist, an image that informs the lengthy description of the activities of the surgeon Sorniude, whose name is an anagram of *soin rude* (harsh care). Sorniude specializes in ovarectomies and makes mistresses of his newly sterilized patients. In Daudet's allusion to a controversy that was raging at the time regarding the morality of this gynecological procedure, he attributes evil motives to the physician who victimizes women for his own pleasure, tempting them with the promise of nonprocreative sexual intercourse so that he and his lecherous colleagues might enjoy them with impunity. The portrait of Dr. Sorniude recalls that of the lascivious Dr. Jenkins and anticipates that of Zola's Dr. Gaude in *Fécondité* (1899), a "castrator of women" who takes his newly sterile patients as his mistresses.

With his misogynistic portrait of Morticole women who thrive on brutality, Daudet wishes to suggest a "natural" complementarity between the sadistic physician and the masochistic female patient. In the world of la Morticolie, women collaborate with physicians. Nowhere is this clearer than in the passage describing Charcot's Tuesday séances.

Daudet presents Charcot's hysterics as actresses and the Tuesday public lessons as theater. A brief dialogue between Rosalie, Charcot's principal "patient," and Tripard, his underling, illustrates the point:

> "Hello, Tripard! Hi, everybody! I'm not late?"
>
> "No, you're on time. What's new?"
>
> "I'll tell you what's new: you can inform your boss that I will no longer be his model for less than three louis. C'mon, young people, don't you think it's reasonable to ask forty francs for a hysterical attack? They make me act lethargic, cataleptic, they make me sleepwalk. This stuff is exhausting." (148)

Rosalie's talent is extraordinary; on command ("C'mon, give us an attack" [149]) she thrashes about, moaning, trembling, rolling her eyes: "Gigade laughed till his sides hurt. 'It'd be impossible to do a better simulation! The damned she-ass!'" The point is hard to miss: the father of neurology is an impostor. The defense of hypnotism that Daudet puts into Gigade's mouth builds to a burlesque conclusion that is self-explanatory:

> Hypnotism is the finest conquest of modern medicine. It illuminates everything, jurisprudence, history, daily life. It diminishes responsibility. It serves to explain philosophy, painting, religion, music, and literature. It allows us to meddle in everything. We owe our omnipotence to it. We suggested to the public that we be placed on the throne, in place of kings, and on the altar, in place of priests. (152)

The hyperbolic claims for hypnotism that were common in the late-nineteenth century are parodied in this *apologia*. Like chloroform, hypnotism is in the final analysis a tool of domination, and Charcot, a metaphoric "surgeon" who penetrates the mind rather than the body, is its principal practitioner. The idea that an entire society has fallen under the spell of the medical profession lends a sense of urgency to Daudet's impassioned outcry.

Léon Daudet's physicians are ardent defenders of surgical experimentation, euthanasia, obligatory education for all, vivisection, and capital punishment. Their creed can be summed up in two words, *evolution* and *microbes*: "Those two concepts answered all questions, explained the universe, and replaced God" (178). Their books have no other subject than science, their schools no other courses. Their disdain for religion is surpassed only by their disdain for artistic endeavor of all sorts. Enter Dr. Ligottin.

The novel's last chapter, devoted to a guided visit of a psychiatric hospital in the company of a physician whose name promises an archaic punishment, provides what may well be the principal explanation for Daudet's sharp antagonism vis-à-vis the physician. Explaining that his wife, crazed by "unhealthy reading" (331), had to be committed to the institution, Ligottin allows Félix to accompany him on his rounds, all the while fulminating against various categories of dreamers and melancholics.[15] In Ligottin's opinion, which echoes opinions expressed by Plato in *The Republic*, the most dangerous are the poets: "I despise poets! They pervert humanity. I've already succeeded in getting rid of most of them, but I intend to get a law passed which will keep under surveillance anyone who strings irregular sentences together, sentences that echo each other in a sonorous way. This indicates a pathological defect of the ear" (332). The physician thunders against the evils of art, bringing to mind both the physicians of *Madame Gervaisais* and *Le Nabab*'s supercilious Jenkins, who was indifferent to Félicia's talents as a sculptress and openly disdainful of his son's literary endeavors. Ligottin's pathologization of the artist—poets are "grotesque graphomaniacs," the sculptor is a "statuo-maniac," and so forth—reflects a long-standing animosity between physician and artist. The violence with which Ligottin excoriates all forms of artistic production, from music, which is "an artifice that excites the nervous system and causes a profound disturbance in the organism" (338), to painting, which, since the invention of photography, is "as useless as music" (339), mirrors that of Daudet's attack on doctors, making of this chapter a *mise-en-abyme* of the entire novel. Léon Daudet imprisons his physicians in the fictional space of a lugubrious land, heaping reproaches on them and presenting them as pathological specimens: inhuman, insensitive, unscrupulous materialists who threaten Christian values. Attentive students of the history of medicine can identify Charcot, Bernheim, Péan, Germain

Sée, Bourneville, Brouardel, Ricord, Féré and others among the doctors targeted by Daudet's acerbic pen. The fictional doctor Ligottin shackles and imprisons the artist, subjecting him to humiliating and painful treatments, reducing his art to a collection of symptoms. Students of literature and the arts have little difficulty in identifying Rodin ("that poor moron [who excites people] to debauchery by his representations of nude men and women in obscene postures" [339]); Van Gogh ("He faithfully transcribes on his canvas the disorder of his brain" [340]); Verlaine, "[who compares] a violin to a heavy heart"; Rimbaud, "[who] claimed that letters of the alphabet were colored" (341); and others. The profound ideological rift between art and science that lies at the heart of this angry novel is thus exposed. That this cleavage becomes for Daudet emblematic of another can be gleaned from the following passage, which describes a madman, one of Ligottin's patients: " 'He repeats the sentences of Jesus Christ, that other madman, the father of so many dangerous superstitions,' shouted Ligottin. 'Now there's someone I'm sorry I wasn't able to lock up!' " (343). In his *Vie de Jésus*, published in 1863, Ernest Renan had presented Christ as an extraordinary man, but a mere man just the same, one who may well have suffered delusions of grandeur. For different reasons, Renan's unorthodox version of religious history drew criticism from Jews and Christians alike, seriously damaging his academic career. Thirty years later, Léon Daudet renews the polemic, fanning the dying coals of outrage by attributing to the medical profession the opinion that Christ was not only "merely human" but was quite obviously insane as well.[16] To inflame hostility against the medical practitioner even further, he suggests that the hegemony that medicine enjoys in Third Republic France derives directly from its blasphemous denigration of Christianity. *Les Morticoles* concludes with a prayer: "God, you are the source of all goodness and love. Without you, 'conscience' is nothing but a word, man just a heap of dirt and blood. May the Morticoles' example . . . be useful to everyone. . . . Glory to you, for you alone are glorious! Woe betide this evil city where your name has been forgotten!" (358–59). Read in the light of Léon Daudet's later writings, the dichotomous oppositions that divide this novel and pit doctors against patients, the present against the past, materialism against spiritualism, and science against religion can be seen as a foil for Daudet's deep hostility toward Jews.

While Léon Daudet never did contract the syphilis that killed his father, he was not lucky enough to escape the contagion of an equally virulent moral disease of his era, the disease of anti-Semitism. Did his father share with him the offending opinions that made him susceptible to this disease? While, as we have seen, the elder Daudet's anti-Semitism remains a subject of some debate, it is well known that racial biases are acquired at an early age, and the evidence suggests that prejudice against Jews may indeed have been handed down from father to son. Further, my analysis of *Le Nabab* and *Les Morticoles*, while inconclusive, suggests the possibility of a filiation. Whatever the case, the venomous attack on the medical profession that was published under the title *Les Morticoles* took the form of an ardent plea for a return to Catholic orthodoxy that emphasized its author's sympathies with such conservative nationalists as Paul Bourget, Maurice Barrès, and Barbey d'Aurevilly. In the closing decade of the nineteenth century, the struggle against medical imperialism coalesces with what Malcolm Scott terms a "mystical backlash" to produce an almost paranoid vision of the medical practitioner not as "un ennemi de la mort" ("an enemy of death"), to borrow the title of Eugène Le Roy's novel, but as an enemy of Christianity.[17]

CONCLUSION

9

In his impressive article on *Les Morticoles*, Toby Gelfand asserts that "a cogent antimedical polemic presupposes a society in which medicine has established its strength to a level where it can serve as a credible target."[1] He distinguishes between the buffoonery of Molière's incompetent doctors and "the more malevolent literary view of medicine" that characterizes late-nineteenth-century antimedical literature.[2] While it is true that all of the works examined in this study do not present an equally "malevolent view," while a certain playfulness in the antimedical portraits can be found as late as 1886 with Maupassant's *Mont-Oriol*, and while Léon Daudet's bitter tone is by no means typical, attention to the subtext of even the most "light hearted" of these works reveals them to be part of a vast effort to discredit the medical practitioner. In Molière's time, the medical profession, "inefficacious, full of lofty theories, embodied in pretentious idiots stupidly rigged out and spouting bad Latin," lent itself readily to caricature.[3] The physician did not need to be discredited, since public opinion of his abilities was low indeed. Whence the hearty laughter provoked—for example—by the burlesque conferral of a medical degree in *Le Malade imaginaire*.[4] The nineteenth-century fictional attacks on medical incompetence, while occasionally of "moliéresque" inspiration, are considerably more complex and far-reaching, since the target is a more formidable one. Moreover, the danger represented by the physicians in the works we have examined extends well beyond the risk to the individual patient: the medical profession is actually seen as a menace to society itself. From the first work analyzed in this study (*Madame Bovary* 1857) to the last (*Les Morticoles* 1894), there is both an easily perceptible continuity and an unmistakable evolution. The continuity lies in the view that conventional medicine is not only powerless to cure the ill but actually contributes to their demise. The evolution can be found in the increasingly grim portrayals both of the physicians themselves and of the nefarious social consequences of their actions. Whereas the first two novels studied here feature mere incompetents who fail to heal their patients despite their best efforts (*Madame Bovary*, *Madame Gervaisais*), the later works present cynical practitioners interested more in their own economic well-being than in their patients' health (*Mont-Oriol*, *Le Nabab*) and medical doctors who consciously inflict harm on those who entrust themselves to their care (*Les Morticoles*). Flaubert's witless health officer and foolish pharmacist seem relatively benign compared to Alphonse Daudet's scheming Dr. Jenkins or Léon Daudet's sadistic *Morticoles*.

Although it would be simplistic to argue, on the basis of a small sample, that there was a generalized deterioration in the relationship between the literati and the medical profession in the second half of the nineteenth century, the numerous bleak portrayals of physicians and scientists in fiction published after the installation of the Third Republic hint that additional research may confirm this hypothesis. Barbey d'Aurévilly's "Le Bonheur dans le crime" (1874) depicts a physician-narrator, Dr. Torty, who is more spy than clinical observer and who by his silence becomes an accomplice to a murder.[5] Louise Michel's *Les Microbes humains* (1886) features a physician-torturer, Dr. Gaël, who performs a vivisection on a pregnant woman, forcing her to describe her pain as he operates. She dies in surgery. Villiers de l'Isle-Adam's sinister Dr. Bonhomet, who stones swans in order to hear their dying song, parades his insensitivity and his bourgeois materialism through the five tales of *Tribulet Bonhomet*, published in 1887. Although he is presented with some compassion, Maupassant's Pierre of *Pierre et Jean* (1888) also inflicts pain—upon a woman, his own mother. The physician's sadistic impulse is explicit. André Couvreur's *Le Mal nécessaire* (1899) conflates stereotypes of the Jew and the physician to produce an unscrupulous, ambitious Jewish surgeon who takes advantage of a young patient's fainting spell to rape her. From murderer's accomplice to murderer, sadist, and rapist, these fictional practitioners bear witness on the part of their creators to a highly contemptuous attitude toward medicine. Even when a physician is presented in a positive light, as is the young Dr. Jean Stival in Paul Adam's *La Force du mal* (1896), he is shown to be an anomaly, struggling more successfully against the "evil" of illness than against the other evil to which the novel's title alludes: professional corruption.[6]

At this point, a parenthesis needs to be opened, for it is important to note that the apparent disaffection for medicine that is reflected in much of the literature of the period is part of a wider phenomenon, namely, the reaction against science and technology in general that characterizes the closing decades of the nineteenth century. By this time, the very eighteenth-century infatuation with rational explanations and the concomitant prestige of French science that had peaked very early in the century had given way to disillusionment and a decline in French scientific activity, this despite the stunning achievements of many French scientists, among whom Claude Bernard, Louis Pasteur, Marcellin Berthelot, and Marie Curie hold pride of place. Many reasons have been advanced for the public resistance to science. The well-publicized disputes among the scientists themselves (on the subject of contagion, for example) certainly did nothing to increase confidence in scientific endeavor. Moreover, as Theodore Zeldin argues, the scientists' apparent reluctance or inability to communicate with the layman meant that they were at the mercy of their interpreters—popularizers, philosophers (Comte, Renan, Taine), and moralists, and in spite of the enthusiasm of many of their commentators, this did not always work to their advantage, particularly among those who held fast to traditional beliefs and feared the displacement of religion by science. Too often, scientific progress seemed to fly in the face of "old wisdom and hoary certainties," to borrow an expression from Eugen Weber.[7] The antipathy toward the medical practitioner must be understood in this context.

Besides this general dissatisfaction with science and its principal spokesperson, the medical practitioner, the period provides evidence of considerable exasperation with regard to the widespread use of clinical discourse. The inflated rhetoric of an Homais, Huysmans's impudent exploitation of medical language to describe the banalities of daily life, the grandiloquent formulae of the spa physicians in *Mont-Oriol*, the cynical discourse of atheistic medicine in *Les Morticoles*—these and the other examples of literature's counter-discursive strategies analyzed in the preceding chapters signal the parodic dimension of these texts. Here, too, one could add other examples at will. Paul Bonnetain's *Charlot s'amuse* (1883), a work that earned for its author the sobriquet "Bonnemain" ("Goodhand"), offers a particularly irreverent parody, presenting a reductio ad absurdum of the hyperbolic clinical discourse on onanism. Huysmans's *À rebours* ridicules the provincial physician's incomprehensible muttering while effectively reducing the celebrated Parisian specialist to a stubborn silence when des Esseintes questions his prescription. Flaubert's *Bouvard et Pécuchet* mocks the bourgeois infatuation with medical discourse as exemplified in the *Dictionnaire des science médicales*, a reference work that becomes for a time the bible of his two naive copyists.

Finally, in an era that witnessed an ideological cleavage between those who welcomed society's secularization and those who longed for a spiritual revival, medicine is attacked on philosophical grounds. Paul Bourget's *Le Disciple* (1889) depicts in all its horror the dangers of an amoral faith in positivistic science. The novel's philosopher-scientist, Adrien Sixte—who was probably modeled after the physician Jules Soury rather than Hippolyte Taine, as was once believed—is held accountable for his disciple's callous experimentation with the emotions of a nobleman's daughter, an experimentation that leads to her death and ultimately to his own.[8] Stepping over into the twentieth century, Huysmans's *Les Foules de Lourdes* (1906) continues the trend by showing the power of faith in its triumph over medical science, mocking the medical skepticism displayed in Lourdes's "miracle registry office."[9] These novels, each in its own way, constitute a questioning—in some cases an indictment—of scientific inquiry and discourse. In this context, Eugène Le Roy's *L'Ennemi de la mort* (1906), with its saintly physician Daniel Charbonnière, bears all the marks of a rebuttal. Nor is it by chance that Le Roy's physician, who struggles against superstition and ignorance, appears as a hybrid composed of Balzac's Benassis and Zola's Pascal Rougon. It is as if Le Roy had elected to carry on the battle of a fallen comrade, Emile Zola. For, as we have seen, among the authors we have studied, only Zola—who, with his presentation of the physician as secular saint (*Le Docteur Pascal* 1893) and his generally docile incorporation of medical discourse in his novels (for example, the discourse relating to childbirth in *Fécondité* 1899)—sounds a discordant note in this symphony of cynicism, and even he at times displays ambivalence with regard to the practice of medicine. The irony, as I have already discussed, is that the writers are able to take advantage of the immense popularity of medicine by using medical themes, language, and characters in their fiction, and simultaneously to undercut the authority of the medical profession in subtle or—as the century progresses—less subtle ways.

The question of *why* physicians and their discourse would be represented in such an unfavorable light is more difficult to answer. I have already pointed to the professional rivalry that pitted doctors against writers. But what was the source of this rivalry? In the first place, the increasing affluence of the physician that accompanied professionalization did much to damage the doctor's image in the eyes of the literati. Although for the greater part of the century the image of the modest country doctor making his rounds in horse and carriage prevailed and inspired little envy, and although in fact the vast majority of the physicians who ran for public office in the early Third Republic—in other words, those who were most "visible"—originally came not from the wealthy classes of society but rather from the lower middle and middle classes,[10] improved professional conditions in the last decades of the century and the stunningly prominent role played by doctors in public life conspired to create the image of political power and social privilege. Writers, even when they themselves came from the ranks of the bourgeoisie, had nothing but contempt for the crass materialism of the upwardly mobile middle class, and as physicians were associated increasingly with the Third Republic's ruling elite, the writers' antipathy was extended to them. Moreover, as I have suggested, the fact that the growing hegemony of medicine was founded, not upon therapeutic advances but upon the seemingly unrestrained political and social influence that resulted from professionalization, was a source of considerable consternation to the writers. James Burke has pointed out that as medicine became more scientific, physicians turned their attention "from bedside to hospital to laboratory," thus relegating the patient to the margins of their practice, so to speak.[11] And if this move provided the setting for dramatic advances in the understanding of diseases (for example, in the single period between 1879 and 1884, the causative organisms for gonorrhea, streptococcus, diphtheria, leprosy, tuberculosis, cholera, malaria, typhoid, and tetanus were identified), the cures for these diseases were still to be developed. Thus, whereas physicians reaped the benefits of such scientific discoveries, the patient did not. In his brilliant study of nineteenth-century Anglo-American medicine, S. E. D. Shortt argues that the public's increased faith in medical science created an atmosphere in which physicians were able to put into circulation a rhetoric of science, thereby securing "a vehicle for their professional recognition": they alone were able to name, describe, and explain.[12] "That therapeutics remained circumscribed and theoretical assumptions little different from previous decades," explains Shortt, "was largely irrelevant to this transformation." By the end of the nineteenth century, "Physicians had become the personification of omniscient science."[13]

The situation was similar in France, as Robert Nye has shown, and if the imperialistic spread of a clinical rhetoric was a source of annoyance for nineteenth-century writers, it would be disingenuous to deny that their cynicism was tainted by jealousy. Writers, in short, envied the freedom of expression enjoyed by physicians. During the Second Empire, state censorship contributed to the writers' frustration, and the Goncourts were no doubt speaking for the majority of the literati when they lamented in 1866 that "in literary life we're being stifled by what we can't say or write."[14] But even after the fall of Napoléon III, when governmental control of the arts was relaxed, fear of critical reaction and the pecuniary need to "please the public" led authors to censor their own works. They did not do so with a willing heart. Zola in particular appears to have been irritated by the double standard that permitted medical doctors to describe pathological realities in all their lurid detail while novelists had to resort to euphemism and symbol. One of Zola's newspaper articles provides convincing evidence of this irritation. Zola recounts therein the tale of three elegant women attending a trial and taking perverse delight in the narration, by a physician, of a triple crime of theft, murder, and arson. The description of the state of the cadaver thrills them to the quick. And, Zola comments,

> Oh! What a picture! And how the finely gloved hands of the young women would have applauded if the gravity of the place didn't prevent them from doing so. How interesting this cadaver was! Try to describe one in a book and you'll see how the women will grimace. I wrote about a drowning victim in a novel, a corpse that was hardly uglier than Dr. Alias's cadaver: all of the proper women, I've been told, threw my book into the fire.[15]

Even within the context of "that putrid literature" that naturalism was thought to be, it was clear that Zola did not enjoy the expressive liberties of his medical peers. This is not to imply that writers envied physicians their descriptive abilities or talent for rhetoric. Witness the Goncourts' disparaging comments about Charles Robin, or this, from Flaubert's correspondence: "There is no style more verbose or more vacuous than that of physicians. What windbags! And to think they look down their noses at lawyers!"[16] On the contrary, the doctors' vapid discourse was considered to be all the more reprehensible given the superior tools (lexical, thematic) with which they had to work and the intensity of the clinical experience, described as follows in a rare moment of modesty by the Goncourts:

> Leaving Dr. Magne's office, where Edmond has just had his eyes examined, we think about the practice of medicine: with what immense pride this constant struggle against God must fill the physician, and how gripping this chess game against death must be! To follow the progress of an unknown illness, to save someone: compared to that, how insignificant everything else is! And, compared to this life that the physician touches from every conceivable angle, what a dead thing literature is![17]

Six years later, when it became clear that the medical profession was powerless to save Jules from the disease that was killing him, the Goncourts' respect for medicine was to be replaced by disdain.

Another source of jealousy can be located in the perception that physicians abused professional privilege to enjoy a distinctly sexual intimacy with female patients. The very act of examining a woman's body for signs of disease was believed to bring scopic and tactile pleasures to the medical doctor. Thus, even when he was innocent of unethical behavior, the physician's relationship with female patients was unavoidably erotic in nature. Michelet, who used his private diary to record the results of his "scientific investigation" of his wife's body, was especially sensitive to this aspect of the physician's role and wished, in Vivian Kogan's words, "not only to imitate doctors, but also to replace them."[18] Portrayals of the physician as a lecher (as, for example, in Alphonse Daudet's *Le Nabab* and André Couvreur's *Le Mal nécessaire*) offer evidence of this preoccupation.

Yet another aggravation may have been the propensity of the medical profession to regard genius as pathological and creative writers as inherently ill, whether or not they manifested physical symptoms.[19] Inspired perhaps by Césare Lombroso's 1884 work (translated into French as *L'Homme de génie* in 1889 and endorsed by the French physiologist Charles Richet), French medical doctors became fascinated by the links between neurosis and genius. The number of medical theses devoted to writers, artists, and historical figures in the late-nineteenth and early-twentieth centuries was imposing. Every one of the authors in this sample was the object of numerous medical case studies.[20] Generally speaking, these (often) postmortem treatises took the authors' biographies and correspondence as their basis. Thus, for example, scholars combed the memoirs of Maupassant's servant, François Tassart, in order to arrive at a diagnosis of his master's ailment. Attributed variously to leuco-encephalitis, systemic progressive delirium, hereditary neuro-arthritic degeneration, and Basedow's Syndrome, Maupassant's symptoms were not accurately diagnosed until long after the syphilis virus had been discovered and the three stages of syphilis were properly understood. Nevertheless, the fascination with his illness and the publication of works

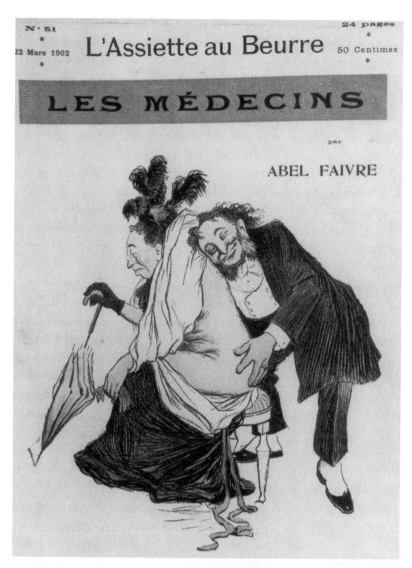

5   The suggestion that physicians are lechers is represented in Abel Faivre's "Doctors," in which a doctor is shown listening to the heart of a female patient by putting his ear to her back (the stethoscope was invented in 1816 by René Théophile Hyacinthe Laënnec and was in wide use by the end of the nineteenth century). An anti-Semitic subtext is also present. Cover of *L'Assiette au beurre,* 22 March 1902.

purporting to diagnose it by Drs. Normandy, Ladame, Pillet, and others continued unabated well into the twentieth century, with the result that for a long time biographies and medical theses far outnumbered critical works devoted to the fiction. Flaubert's health problems, ascribed at different times to epilepsy, hysteria, apoplexy, and venereal infection, were the subject of publications by Drs. Félix Regnault and Edouard Allain, among others. Occasionally, physicians and literary critics who adopted a "biographical" approach relied for their information on the fictional production. In this perspective, the literary work, regarded as a product of the unconscious, was reduced to a set of symptoms, and the physician moved comfortably back and forth between text and author, unaware of the circularity of his arguments. Zola's work, with its emphasis on the lower bodily functions, earned for its author the diagnosis of neuropath (Dr. Toulouse) and degenerate (Dr. Magnan). Regardless of the form it took, this interpretive activity on the part of the medical professional, a kind of intellectual "parasitism" (the physicians actually fed off the writers' illnesses in order to earn their medical credentials), might be regarded as the counterpart of the writers' own parasiting of clinical discourse in the composition of their works, except for one important difference: the physicians maintained their position of power even in the midst of their parasitic activity. Writers, in other words, were generally in a position of abject servility with regard to physicians, all the more so because they were often under medical care. The fact that they frequently sought treatment for physical maladies for which there was at the time no known cure did not alter the hierarchical relationship that existed between physician and patient.

Faced with the medical tendency to objectify them in their published studies, to apply clinical methods and experience to an analysis of their conditions, the writers responded in two ways. In the first place, they offered tit for tat, pathologizing the physician as the physician had pathologized them. Maupassant's "Le Rosier de Madame Husson" and Léon Daudet's *Les Morticoles*, as we have seen, offer a particularly good example of this process. But in what appears to be a logical extension of the well-known Romantic topos of suffering as muse, they also valorized illness. Outside of France, one finds examples of this phenomenon in Dostoevsky, Nietzsche, and Thomas Mann.[21] Within France, this strategic maneuver is exemplified by Baudelaire, Rimbaud, the Goncourts, and most of the Decadent writers. Influenced by the theories on emotional disorders of Dr. Moreau de Tours, the Goncourts were persuaded that their nervous constitution was both the source and the result of their literary genius. Their perception that illness is propitious for creativity and that health is "plebeian and contemptible" is frequently evoked in the *Journal*, sometimes with humor, as the following example illustrates:

> When Flaubert had boils last year, Michelet said to one of his friends: "I hope he won't seek medical attention, or he'll lose his talent!"
>
> Maybe this is an important idea. Once Napoléon was cured of scabies, he stopped winning battles.[22]

The notion that skin eruptions signal power is not unrelated to the widely accepted belief that the man infected with the pox is strengthened and therefore superior to his uninfected peer. Part bravado, part wishful thinking, the contention has the effect of marginalizing the physician, whose cure is ultimately regarded as detrimental to genius. "Good health and no more talent, what a dream!" The ironic formula for happiness proposed by Huysmans's character Cyprien Tibaille conforms perfectly to this paradigm. In fact, the work of Huysmans is rife with similarly subversive strategies, and he can be said to epitomize the tradition whereby, as Barbara Spackman puts it, "decadent writers place themselves on the side of pathology and valorize physiological ills and alteration as the origin of psychic alterity."[23] From a place that Spackman describes as "the island of normalcy," critics directed their attack on the literary Decadence, a particularly satisfying target that has been dubbed "pathological" through and through, from its subjects and its form to its style.

Having adumbrated the sources for the tensions that existed between writers and medical practitioners in the late-nineteenth century, I turn now to an examination of the curious logic whereby the later authors in my sample came to identify the physician with the Jew. In order to contextualize this peculiar phenomenon, I should like to point out that the beginning- and end-dates of my study, 1857 and 1894, correspond not only to the publication of its first and last works (*Madame Bovary* and *Les Morticoles*) but also to the publication of Dr. Bénédict Augustin Morel's *Traité des dégénérescences physiques, intellectuelles et morales de l'espèce humaine* (1857), a treatise that was to unleash a whole host of similar "meditations" on physical and societal degeneration; and to the arrest on charges of treason, in 1894, of the Jewish army officer Alfred Dreyfus. The period also witnessed a number of other important historical episodes, among which I shall not altogether arbitrarily single out two. The first of these is the cluster of events that occurred in 1870–71, notably France's stinging defeat in the Franco-Prussian War of 1870, the establishment of the Third Republic that same year, and the *guerre à outrance* ("all-out war") and fratricidal bloodbath of the Commune in 1871. The second is the reinstitution, in 1884, of a law permitting divorce for the first time since 1816. The new law, the "loi Naquet," took its name from the Jewish physician who had spearheaded the movement to reinstate divorce. Both the events of 1870–71 and the divorce legislation of 1884 entailed great soul-searching, elicited extended commentaries in the press, and inspired an abundant fictional production. The fear of a weakened France that emerged after France's loss to Germany in the Franco-Prussian War haunted politicians and pundits alike; the fear of a weakened family that followed the legalization of divorce was likewise regarded as simply another symptom in the alarming deterioration of the French nation. The fact that a physician—and a Jewish physician at that—had been responsible for the reinstatement of divorce did not go unnoticed, as Alphonse Daudet's comment, set down in the notes he took for the first draft of *Rose et Ninette*, a slim novel about divorce, suggests: "No, divorce is not a solution. It's the end of marriage that the Jew is bringing us with this legislation, but we've got to look for something else."[24] Nor was it coincidental that the same year (1884) saw the publication of Huysmans's *À Rebours*, which diagnosed the terminal decay of society. The appearance just two years later of Krafft-Ebings's *Psychopathia Sexualis*, an astonishing compendium of what were then perceived as aberrant sexual practices thought to reflect societal degradation; and, the same year, of Drumont's shrill attack on French Jewry, *La France juive*, was hardly coincidental. These jeremiads, and others of a similar nature, sought to identify the party responsible for the deplorable state of the French nation. Drumont was categorical: the villain was the Jew. We know from Marc Angenot's studies of the social discourses of the year 1889 that Drumont's hatred of Jews was in fact typical of his era—an era in which, according to Eugen Weber, anti-Semitism was "as French as croissants."[25] As Angenot shows, the *doxa* assumed many disguises: behind every lament about modern corruption (the materialistic exploitation of the poor by the banking community, the spread of pornography, rampant anticlericalism, the decline of the family, etc.), a Jew is being surreptitiously targeted (Rothschild, Catulle Mendès, Eugène Mayer, Naquet). How does one account for this growing anti-Semitism? Is it simply a variant on a more generalized xenophobia? And where does the physician come in?

In the first place, it is noteworthy that Jewish physicians in France were not especially numerous, partly as a result of a quota system that kept their numbers low in medical schools. Nevertheless, some very prominent physicians were Jewish (besides Naquet, there was Bernheim of l'école de Nancy, Germain Sée of Paris's General Hospital). Moreover, as Michael Nevins points out, the situation was in the process of transformation. Western Europe witnessed the increasing domination of Jews in the medical profession during the late-nineteenth century, and, by 1890, the celebrated medical faculty of Vienna University was 50 percent Jewish.[26] Back in France, a large percentage of the physicians who entered government in the early years of the Third Republic were freethinkers (44 percent of the group of eighty studied by Jack Ellis, the only ones for whom good information is available),[27] and of these, 24.5 percent were Freemasons, a group that has been historically associated with the Jews.[28] Thus, although only 1 percent of the physician-legislators described themselves as "devout Jews" (as opposed to 13 percent "devout Catholics"), the perception was that Jewish physicians were dominating the political landscape. This collapse of the distinction between "Jew" and "freethinker" resulted in an erroneous assumption that was not without ironies of its own, among which the fact that many physicians of this era were themselves anti-Semites, xenophobics, and eugenicists. For example, both Charcot and Soury professed a biomedical anti-Semitism, attributing to the Jew a hereditary taint that resulted in a weakened constitution, an effeminate character, and a tendency to neurasthenia and hysteria.[29]

Pointing to Drumont's contention (1886) that there were more than 500,000 Jews in France, Robert Byrnes rightly observes that "in anti-Semitism, fiction is almost always of greater importance than fact."[30] Statistics dealing with the growth in the French Jewish population during the nineteenth century vary, but most historians concur that the French Semitic community was among the smallest in Europe, numbering approximately 45,000 at the beginning of the century, and less than twice that number at the century's close. According to Byrnes, the demographic growth was most dramatic after the Franco-Prussian War, increasing from close to 50,000 in 1872 to 80,000 in 1900. Moreover, migration from Alsace-Lorraine to Paris, which had been taking place ever since civic equality was granted to Jews in 1791, was accelerated after 1870, when a large number of Jews fled German rule. Michael Graetz sets at 8,000 the number of Jews living in Paris in 1841. By 1880, the number had increased fivefold, to 40,000.

It is easy to see how this demographic shift (i.e., the growth in the population of Parisian Jews), together with the increased immigration that took place in *fin-de-siècle* France and the sense of humiliation and betrayal that followed the defeat of 1870 would provide a fertile breeding ground for xenophobia. When one considers that, at the same time, a bleak diagnosis that carried the stamp of medical approval was circulating, a diagnosis according to which France was terminally ill, victim of a declining population, rampant immorality, flourishing crime, an increase in physical and social pathologies from alcoholism and suicide to prostitution and syphilis—in short, when one understands that the literate population found it impossible to peruse a newspaper without finding therein a sample of what has been dubbed the "discourse of degeneration"—one is in a better position to understand the angst of the period and the need to find a scapegoat for France's problems. It has been said that all prejudices obey the same logic. Thus, the rhetoric of anti-Semitism had much in common with that of antifeminism and with a more generalized xenophobia. And since physicians, like Jews and foreigners and women, were thought to be profiting from and even contributing to the nation's decline, they too became targets of a rhetoric of hatred. In particular, they were held responsible for the secularization of the French state and thus—with Jews and foreigners and women—were seen as enemies of traditional morality, the Catholic Church, and "the old France." Now, while it would be a mistake to deny that many physicians were freethinkers and that they were indeed motivated by an anticlerical zeal, the humanitarian purposes of their stance, largely dismissed by those blinded by prejudice, must be underscored. Physicians were partisans of reforms that they were convinced would *strengthen* the nation. To give but two examples, the physicians carried out a tireless campaign to wrest control of hospitals and schools from religious orders and in so doing to institute a program of compulsory vaccination to which the Church was opposed. In truth, French citizens were indeed weaker than their Prussian counterparts, most of whom had been vaccinated against cholera and were thus able to withstand the epidemic of the mid-1880s. Similarly, the 1882 decree that set up drill battalions for military and gymnastic exercises that were scheduled at times previously devoted to catechism classes was motivated by a desire to make French youth more physically fit. As might be expected, however, conservatives were dismayed by these secular gestures.[31]

And so it was that Jews and doctors alike came to be seen in nationalist circles as representatives of the secular Republic, enemies of the France of yore, co-conspirators who cut France free from her traditional moorings and then applauded the drift. This is not difficult to understand. Yet the leap from the idea of physicians and Jews as accomplices to the notion of the physician *qua* Jew, in the absence of statistical evidence that there were in fact large numbers of Jewish physicians in France, is more difficult to fathom. How can we square this seeming contradiction?

It seems reasonable to assume that the medico-Semitic identification did not arise in a vacuum. Indeed, the association has a long history, and Jewish physicians have for centuries enjoyed an illustrious reputation, as an anecdote recounted by the sixteenth-century physician Juan Huarte de San Juan illustrates. According to Huarte's account, the French king Francis I, suffering from a "tedious sickness" and having exhausted the remedies of the court physicians with no noticeable improvement, sent to Spain for a Jewish physician.[32] A Jew freshly converted to Christianity was dispatched. When Francis learned of the conversion, he refused treatment and sent to Constantinople for a practicing Jew, "who recovered him only with Asses-milk." Whether or not it is apocryphal, the anecdote bears witness to a prejudice still widely held, that is, that Jewish physicians are more efficacious than their non-Jewish counterparts. Michael Nevins, pointing to Rudolf Virchow's claim in 1894 that Jews had a hereditary talent for medicine, explains the Jew's impressive record in the field of medicine as follows: "The Bible and the Talmud are replete with medical advice, talmudic discourse promotes a kind of intense analysis that is well suited to science, and the traditional Jewish zest for learning has served Jews particularly well in medical studies."[33] There can be little doubt that this positive face of the stereotype of the Jewish physician has persisted through the ages. However, late-nineteenth-century French writers appear to have infused the stereotype with a new, negative meaning. It is in the figure of the Jewish physician, portrayed as an archetypal villain, that xenophobia meets anti-science. A whole cluster of perceived similarities, numerous enough to explode the distinction between physicians and Jews, contributes to the notion that the two groups are co-conspirators. Just what are these similarities?

To answer this question, we necessarily enter the domain of speculation. The popularity in the nineteenth century of the myth of the wandering Jew may have played its part. Perhaps rootlessness and vagrancy, associated with the Jew, caused him to be associated with itinerant healers who were to be found throughout the century but who were particularly ubiquitous during the pre-1850 period. In his study of illegal healers in the department of the Bas-Rhin in the early decades of the century, Matthew Ramsey points out that the various categories of migrants were barely distinguishable. Ramsey quotes from an agricultural report that lumps together "beggars, especially vagrant Jews, Bohemians, and quack doctors," all of whom were considered to be "infesting the countryside."[34] Perhaps the lumping together of these apparently disparate groups stemmed from the observation that physicians, like Jews, appeared to dominate the press. It was true that one of the most influential newspaper editors, Arthur Meyer, was Jewish, and true also that medical professionals — from physicians and illegal healers to pharmacists — were exploiting mass journalism in order to advertise their services and remedies and preach the secular religion of hygiene. *Le Pays, Le National, Le Siècle,* and *La Patrie* were, as Jacques Léonard asserts, among the newspapers that featured regular columns by scientists.[35]

The perception that physicians and Jews were drawn together by greed may also account for the identification. Since well before the dawn of finance capitalism, Jews had been viewed as usurers and materialists, profiting from the misfortune of others. Although it hardly seems necessary to illustrate this banal association, the following quotation from the Goncourts' *Journal* underscores the mechanism by which Jews and physicians came to be identified: "Jews produce nothing, not even a grain of wheat. They're always agents, middlemen, go-betweens. In Alsace, you can't even sell a cow without seeing a Jew rise up from the pavement between the cow and the peasant to make money on the deal."[36] Similarly, the medical practitioner was perceived as an unscrupulous opportunist because he produced nothing "tangible." Yet one paid a price for the service he provided, whether or not it produced the desired result, the restoration of good health. Nor did it matter that earlier in the century physicians were ill-paid, especially in the provinces. For in addition to taking money without promising to deliver the desired product, they were seen as materialists of another stripe, since they were interested in the material body rather than the immaterial soul. Moreover, it was also believed that they benefited from the misfortune — specifically, the illness — of others. Maupassant's representation of the physician as relic peddler in "La Relique" provides a revealing example of the "greed" that enables the medical doctor to "sell" a worthless commodity in exchange for the satisfaction of his own very material needs.

A further cause of the collapse of distinctions between Jews and physicians may have been that both groups were organizing. Nineteenth-century France witnessed the establishment of the Alliance Israélite Universelle in 1886, just two years after the formation of the Union générale des syndicats médicaux de France hospitaliers (1884). The Jewish alliance, organized not to promote Jewish nationalism but to unite for the emancipation of Jews everywhere, was met with suspicion. Was it linked in the public imagination with the medical union, established not in order to exploit the ill but rather to protect their interests and those of the profession? The hypothesis seems reasonable. Finally, what Natalie Isser refers to as the "persistent stereotype of the Jew as the foreigner" added another element to the comparison: in a manner similar to the Jew's "invasion" of the "body" of the French nation, the physician violated the integrity of the human body with his poking and probing.[37]

Like a boomerang, the organic model of social and political analysis so favored by the medical profession veered back toward those who had launched it. To understand this phenomenon, we must be aware of the paradigm's corollary, expressed in 1858 by the "Pope of German medicine," Rudolf Virchow. The founder of cell pathology, Virchow defined disease as "life under altered conditions" and organisms as "societ[ies] of living cells, tiny well-ordered state[s]." The complementarity of the two notions can be expressed as follows: if nations are bodies, bodies are also nations. Thus, the notion of a sick society implied a society that contained diseased "cells." The widespread acceptance of this double metaphor had enormous implications for late-nineteenth-century France. Just as physicians spoke of microorganisms that invaded the body, infected the cells, and caused illness, just as they spoke of therapies designed to rid the body of these impurities, so did political theorists begin to speak of France in the same terms. The nation was in decline. Following the twin disasters of 1870–71, she was "sick." What was causing the malady? The Prussian takeover of Alsace-Lorraine, the influx of immigrants (especially Italians) at the *fin de siècle*, the growing prominence of the Jewish community: these phenomena contributed to the impression that France's decadence was caused by the presence within her borders of foreigners, "germs," metaphorical microorganisms that were weakening her, destroying her purity. The xenophobic discourse of nationalism was thus expressed in the language of clinical medicine. Furthermore, the Lamarckian and Darwinian ideas in cir-culation added another element to the diagnosis. Society's decadence, like the body's, could also be attributed to heredity. Subscribing to a genetic fatalism, the medical profession saw the race as increasingly flawed. The list of so-called "hereditary diseases" — alcoholism, epilepsy, syphilis, and so forth—grew each year. As Jacques Léonard explains, a four-pronged plan was executed. Doctors were expected to intervene (1) by persuading men to choose their wives wisely; (2) by sponsoring legislation requiring prenuptial certificates and permitting divorce; (3) by encouraging the indigent—especially those afflicted with alcoholism or tuberculosis—to practice birth control; and (4) by establishing eugenic measures designed to produce a superior race.[38] The eugenic measures, known euphemistically as "ethnic hygiene," betrayed the influence of Nietzsche in Germany and Toussenel, Gobineau, and Drumont in France, and smacked of a specific variety of xenophobia, anti-Semitism, for the Jew was seen as particularly susceptible to hereditary diseases.

One especially illustrative fictional example of this medical perspec-tive is Louise Michel's *Les Microbes humains*, evoked earlier. In her preface, Michel describes her 1886 novel as "a glance at the human microbes that are teeming in the rot of our *fin de siècle*."[39] Michel's metaphorical use of *microbes*, a word coined only eight years earlier in the wake of Pasteur's groundbreaking discoveries of microorganisms, to indicate her disdain for her contemporaries, was all the more important in that one of the "microbes" whose virulence her novel exposes is the physician himself. The ruthless Dr. Gaël, a "fanatical scientist" whose eugenic ambitions are meant to reflect those of a certain segment of his professional class, spares no sacrifice in the name of scientific inquiry: "If it had been in the interest of science to exterminate the whole world, he would have tried it without the least remorse."[40] Inhuman in his cruelty, Michel's physician is described as a beast of prey, his patients as prey. But it is in his social Darwinism, his belief in a "superior" race he considers it his duty to develop, that Dr. Gaël has relevance here. In the 1890s, this fictional physician had real-life counterparts in such doctors as Jules Soury and Maurice de Fleury, whose biomedical anti-Semitism, perhaps inspired by Charcot's belief in inherited pathological tendencies among Jews, was to provide the foundation for a rhetoric of intolerance that would grow to immense—indeed uncontrollable—proportions in the early-twentieth century. It is not my intention here to invoke the horrors of the Holocaust, for to do so would be to adopt a teleological perspective and to wander too far from my original subject. Rather, I should like to point to the supreme irony in the fact that with the identification of the physician and the Jew, the physician became both subject and object of his own discourse.[41] Although to be fair, I should specify that not all members of the medical profession promoted eugenic reforms, it was the profession at large that was responsible for providing a medical matrix for the analysis of social problems; thus, all were tarred with the same brush in the writers' counter-discursive strategy. Medical discourse was up-ended, doctors were portrayed as microbes infecting society, foreigners invading the national body and contributing to its demise. Nor were physicians pure of an eugenic agenda absolved from guilt. On the contrary, those who used the inventions of medical science to attempt to prolong the lives of the physically weak or the "genetically defective" were charged with intervening unwisely to sabotage the natural law of selection.[42] We are not far from the thesis of an Ivan Illich.

In his work of anti-Semitic propaganda, *Les Juifs, rois de l'époque* (1847), Toussenel had characterized Jews as vultures, since "infection attracts them instead of repulsing them." Physicians, drawn to the side of the diseased and dying, are likewise identified as predators, as we have seen. The historically positive face of the association between Jews and medicine is ignored, and Drumont goes so far as to speculate that the credit traditionally given to Jews for progress in medical science is pure myth:

> For centuries they monopolized the medical profession, which made espionage easy for them, since they were able to gain entrance anywhere, and not for one moment did they suspect that blood circulated through the body. . . . To claim that Jews have rendered any service whatsoever to science is to mock the naiveté of the young Christians with whose instruction Ferry has entrusted us. . . . It's to the Aryan that we owe every discovery, both large and small. . . . The Semite has only exploited what genius or work had

already conquered. The true emblem of the Jew is the nasty bird
that cynically moves into the nest built by others.[43]

Despite its purely subjective nature (Drumont does not allow himself to
be confused by facts), this demeaning and inaccurate assessment of the
role of the Jewish scientist confirms our hypothesis regarding the association between a professional class (physicians) and an ethnic minority
(French Jewry). The double notion of surreptitious foreign invasion
("espionage") and occupation (the image of the "nasty bird" that usurps
the place of another) evokes once again the image of the menacing,
misunderstood, unwanted Other. Like the Jew for many nineteenth-
century Frenchmen, the physician was that Other, as Maupassant's *Mont-
Oriol* makes abundantly clear.

In the conceptual move from devouring vulture to invisible microbe,
the image of the parasite serves as transition.[44] Whereas the vulture
stalks the dying and feeds on the dead, parasites derive sustenance from
the living, engaging in a shameless exploitation that weakens their *host*
while strengthening and enriching *them*. The mechanisms behind the
stereotypical analogy that links the physician and the Jew should by now
be sufficiently clear. Similarly, the resemblance between the parasite and
the microbe—the latter a microscopic enemy that attacks and invades
the body, then thrives and multiplies in this corporeal milieu, thereby
contributing to its demise—is self-evident.

It is thus above all by means of the vocabulary of pathology that
late-nineteenth-century writers hoist the physician with his own petard.
Whether discussing epidemiology or genealogy, doctors put into circulation a language of contamination and decay, contagion and demise,
thereby distributing routine doses of *angst* while simultaneously contributing to their own greater wealth and glory. What better way for
literati to even the score than to accuse *them* of pathogenicity, tax *them*
with contamination, target *them* as viruses to be cured? Long before it
was sanctioned by the dictionary, the notion of iatrogenesis had been
born in the literary imagination.

Because medical practitioners had lectured tirelessly about the importance of personal and social hygiene, they were associated with filth
and contamination (*Les Morticoles*). Because they had praised the virtues

of temperance, they were characterized as gluttonous ("Le Rosier de Madame Husson"). Because they had criticized religious practices and mocked superstition, they were portrayed as collaborators of religion (*Madame Gervaisais*), relic peddlers ("La Relique"), and magicians (*Mont-Oriol, Le Nabab*). Because they had warned of the "immigrant menace," they were identified with the foreigner (*Le Nabab, Mont-Oriol, Les Morticoles*). Because they had underlined the relationship between a healthy populace and a strong and productive nation, they saw sickness extolled as a spur to creativity and good health derided as a source of sterility (*En ménage*). Because they had insisted on self-discipline, they were presented as police inspectors (*L'Assommoir*). Because the source of their formidable power was the remarkable dissemination of their discourse, they witnessed the distortion and inflation of that very discourse by writers who parodied it, emasculated it, and rendered it ridiculous by putting it into the mouths of their least credible characters (*Madame Bovary*) or by pressing it into service to describe the most quotidian of activities (*En ménage*). Because they pathologized the writers, they were pathologized in turn. It seems fair, then, to question the sincerity of the positivist refrain that realists and naturalists sing in impressive unison, the scientific mantra they intone, the medical altar before which they genuflect, the secular deities to whom they offer the ritual sacrifice of "clinical" fiction.

It also seems fair to draw a parallel between the phenomena that we have observed in late-nineteenth-century French culture, and the culture—both French and American—of the twentieth century *fin de siècle*. If nineteenth-century French literature incorporated the discourses and methods of science, today such discourses, necessarily updated, have invaded literary criticism, philosophy, history. Mere opportunism? A bogus subservience? A ploy designed to conceal the vacuity of the ideas presented therein? Or is an element of parody present? Alan Sokol's 1997 exposé of the misappropriation of a scientific lexicon by twentieth-century French philosophers bears closer examination.[45] The same may be said of contemporary attitudes toward the medical profession, which, upon analysis, reveal themselves to be strikingly similar to those we have identified in the late-nineteenth century. The physician is no longer the primary spokesperson for science as he was then; nevertheless, he—and now we must add *or she*—remains the human link between the population at large and the scientific community. And despite the enormous strides made by medicine in the past century (many of them due to Jewish scientists, incidentally),[46] there is still a sizeable gap between practice and promise, diagnosis and cure.[47] As a result of this gap, and of such catastrophic medical errors as the distribution in France of blood contaminated with the AIDS virus, there is an enduring skepticism with regard to medicine and a mistrust of doctors. Even the most cursory review of newspaper and magazine headlines over the past decade bears witness to this mistrust. From *Newsweek*'s cover story, 5 April 1993: "America's Love-Hate Relationship with Its Physicians: Doctors under the Knife." From *The New York Times*, 22 March 1994: "Investigating a Medical Maze: Virus Transmission in Surgery"; 11 April 1994: "So It's Not What the Doctor Ordered: Herbs Are In," an article about France; 9 December 1997: "Doctors Urged to Admit Mistakes"; 23 December 1997: "Forget About Bedside Manners: Some Doctors Have No Manners"; 9 June 1998: "British Cast Spotlight on Misconduct in Scientific Research," an article about plagiarism and other "misconduct" in medical research; and finally, 11 January 1999: "Fever Pitch: Getting Doctors to Prescribe Is Big Business," an article suggesting an unhealthy collusion between the pharmaceutical industry and the medical profession.

Even more striking than the exasperation with medicine's limits and the desire to pull our less-than-omnipotent medical gods from their pedestals is the persistent association of physicians with Jews. Although as the twenty-first century dawns, statistics in the United States—particularly in the field of psychiatry—to some extent justify the assumption that Jewish representation in the medical profession is disproportionate to the number of Jews in American society, the association has much more to do with myth than reality, much more to do with the tired old stereotype of the secular, atheistic Jewish physician than with real numbers. Is it by chance that the primary targets of the so-called "Christian Right" are medical, that most of the controversies in which they are embroiled center on inventions and procedures that are clinical or surgical in nature? If the nineteenth century debated the morality of anesthesia (especially during childbirth), wetnursing, hysterectomies, and hypnotism, in the twentieth the issues have been contraception, abortion, artificial insemination, euthanasia, and cloning. These are the battlegrounds on which the war has been or will be waged, and the old religion versus science opposition still holds true, providing one defines "religion" as Christianity and "science" as Jewish. It is not by chance that conspiracy theories involving Freemasons "are a staple of the books and pamphlets published by militant antiabortion groups" or that hate mail received by the Brookline Preterm Clinic in Massachusetts "usually centered on killing Jew doctors."[48] There are, to be sure, conservative alliances of Jews and Christians, and orthodox Jews hold many of the same views as Christian fundamentalists. Moreover, the religious right is composed of many earnest, deeply concerned Christians who have no anti-Semitic agenda. Indeed, many evangelical Christians are Zionists.[49] Nevertheless, the presence of an ill-concealed anti-Semitic rhetoric in documents produced by the movement's more radical and militant faction invites comparison with the literature produced by conservative nationalists of the late-nineteenth century in France.[50] In modern-day France, the xenophobic nature of Le Pen's Front national is widely acknowledged.

One could of course protest that anti-Semitism is but one aspect of a complex phenomenon, and indeed, to insist that the fear and hatred of the Other assumes many forms would be to belabor the obvious. Nor is it surprising to note that our biases against those who differ from us center on a pathologization of the Other and a consequent fear of contamination. The ancient notion that evil causes (or is expressed in) illness is still widely held. Xenophobics, misogynists, and racists all tend to see the object of their hatred as tainted in some way, physically stigmatized, a phenomenon illustrated in the late-twentieth-century's homophobic assumption that AIDS is a "punishment" for the "sin" of homosexuality. What is interesting is that, to express our intolerance, we continue to have recourse to a clinical perspective. Indeed, as Mireille Rosello has shown in a recent essay, the AIDS epidemic and the anti-immigration movements have together been responsible for renewing the popularity, in our time, of the great paradigms of health and sovereignty:

> Nations and bodies are obsessed by their skin, their membrane, their limits, whether they are seen as filters, as permeable, or as hermetic. And there's always the astonishing back-and-forth movement that keeps shuffling the ethical deck of cards: the foreigner is a virus for some, the virus is a foreigner for others, and we're all hostages to our metaphors or our translations.[51]

The idea that we are all hostages to our metaphors brings me to a final point. Considering our preoccupation with personal and national boundaries, considering the Western tendency—commented upon by Jacques Derrida, among others—to construct binary pairs (health/sickness, good/evil, intelligence/stupidity, altruism/egotism, benevolence/malevolence, cleanliness/filth), there is immense irony in the phenomenon that I have identified in late-nineteenth-century French literature, namely the pathologization not of the patient but of the doctor, the stigmatization and vilification of a professional class traditionally associated with the positive poles of the binary opposite pairs. To present members of a professional class dedicated to eradicating illness and encouraging social and civic hygiene as sick, evil, stupid, egotistical, malevolent, and filthy; to mock and distort the language that was the source of that professional class's power, and to do so with discretion and wit, was the ultimate act of revenge in an epoch dominated, on other fronts, by the retaliatory spirit.

NOTES

ℸ

Introduction

1 Illich, *Medical Nemesis*, 11.

2 Illich, *Medical Nemesis*, 18.

3 Illich, *Medical Nemesis*, 26.

4 Canby, review of *The Apple Doesn't Fall*.

5 T. Bernard, *Sous toutes réserves*, 546–48.

6 T. Bernard, *Sous toutes réserves*, 548.

7 Shaw, *The Doctor's Dilemma*, v.

8 Danous, *Le Corps souffrant*, 185.

9 Sainte-Beuve, *Portraits contemporains*, 1:495–557.

10 See Foucault, *Naissance de la clinique*. For an excellent summary of the principal medical advances of nineteenth-century France, see also Furst, "Realism and Hypertrophy."

11 The new attitude toward the patient is articulated in disturbing terms in Charles Bell Keatley's *The Student's and Junior Practitioner's Guide to the Medical Profession* (London 1885). Outlining the rich resources of the teaching hospital, Keatley writes: "The clinical material is simply overflowing . . . and there is any amount of opportunity for men to work clinically at dresserships and clerkships, if they will only come and finger the material for themselves. It is a perfect paradise for every kind of tumour known, and the accidents are numerous" (quoted by Waddington, *The Medical Profession*, 223–24). Although the example comes from England, a similar shift in attitude took place in France.

12 Although, as Yvonne Knibiehler and Catherine Fouquet note in *La Femme et les médecins*, nuns practiced medicine throughout much of the nineteenth century, sometimes with the complicity of the government, laws—which they ignored with impunity—were passed to limit their jurisdiction. Moreover, physicians deplored

their insistence on the pathogenic influence of sin and their promotion of pilgrimages, processions, novenas, prayers to "mediator-saints," etc., and, as Jacques Léonard points out, "large battalions of nuns were in the front ranks of the medical corps' illegal rivals" (*La Médecine* 70).

13 See Ramsey, "Medical Power and Popular Medicine."

14 Physicians had run for public office in earlier periods as well, and Bianchon's sarcastic comment in Balzac's *La Muse du département*, "Only doctors without patients can get themselves named deputies" (Balzac, *La Comédie humaine*, 4:702), represents a typical attitude toward the phenomenon. During the Third Republic, when the practice reached stunning proportions, the writers' cynicism escalated. See Maupassant's "Un coup d'état," in *Contes et nouvelles*, 1:1004; and "Va t'asseoir!" in *Chroniques*, 1:274–80. My article "Doctoring History" analyzes the representation of the medico-politician. On the rise of the physician in politics, see Ellis, *The Physician-legislators*.

15 Lhermite, *Un sceptique s'il vous plaît*, 28.

16 I use the masculine pronoun deliberately. Although the Paris medical faculty graduated its first French woman in 1875, medicine was by and large a masculine profession throughout the nineteenth century, and according to Knibiehler and Fouquet, there was much literature in the medical press of the second half of the nineteenth century that decried the accession of women to the profession.

17 Indeed, as Vivian Kogan points out in "Michelet Plays Doctor," the comparison of the state with the human body goes all the way back to Plato.

18 See Nye, *Crime, Madness and Politics.* ·

19 See J. Léonard, *La France médicale.*

20 See Hunter, *Doctors' Stories*. Gillian Beer, in "Plot and the analogy with science," also shows how scientists drew on literary sources in support of their arguments.

21 Goldstein, "The Uses of Male Hysteria."

22 From Jules Michelet (1858), quoted by J. Léonard, *La Médecine*, 260. For more on Michelet's somewhat complex relationship to medicine, see Kogan, "Michelet Plays Doctor."

23 Quoted by J. Léonard, *La France médicale*, 251.

24 This self-importance is somewhat diminished by 1927, when the physician Maurice de Fleury writes: "With the opportunities that we would have to do evil—it's a profession that lends itself to everything—let's be proud that we don't have more ugly incidents" (*Le Médecin* 15).

25 Rideout, "The Medical Practitioner," 7.

26 See Furst, "Realism and Hypertrophy," for a more nuanced reading of fictional representations of medical practitioners.

27 See Foucault, *L'Archéologie du savoir* and *L'Ordre du discours.*

28 See Terdiman, *Discourse/Counter-Discourse.*

29   Chambers, *The Writing of Melancholy*, xi, 2.

30   Cabanès, *Le Corps et la maladie*.

31   See Rothfield, *Vital Signs*.

32   Rothfield, *Vital Signs*, xiv.

33   Rothfield, *Vital Signs*, xvi.

34   See Mitchell, "From Heart to Spleen."

35   Among other nineteenth-century French novelists who represent foreign doctors (licensed or otherwise) in an unflattering manner are Balzac (*L'Envers de l'histoire contemporaine*), Edmond About (*Le Cas de Monsieur Guérin*), and Zola (*Germinal*).

36   Sandras, "Sous le scalpel." Sandras's summary conclusion, "The image of the good doctor is still timely and that of the crook is really not new" (41–42), suggests that this study may be the modern counterpart of Rideout's (quoted in Guillaume's *Le rôle social du médecin*).

37   Isser, *Antisemitism during the French Second Empire*, 39.

38   Guillaume, *Le rôle social du médecin*, 38, 39.

39   *Les Rougon-Macquart*, 5:1593 (quoted by Mitterand).

40   Pick, *Faces of Degeneration*, 78.

41   Falconer, "The Human Comedy," 568.

42   Balzac, *La Cousine Bette*, 435.

43   Balzac, *La Comédie humaine*, 3:784.

44   Borel, *Médecine et psychiatrie balzaciennes*, 23–25.

45   Cabanès, *Le Corps et la maladie dans les récits réalistes*, 96–109.

Madame Bovary's *Blind Beggar*

1   See Rothfield, "From Semiotic to Discursive Intertextuality" (later incorporated into his *Vital Signs*); and Riffaterre, "Flaubert's Presuppositions."

2   Rothfield, *Vital Signs*, 44.

3   See, in addition to Rothfield's study, Gray, "The Clinical View of Life"; Siler, "La Mort d'Emma Bovary"; Lukacher, "Flaubert's Pharmacy"; Michot-Dietrich, "Homais, Homeopathy, and *Madame Bovary*"; and Cabanès, *Le Corps et la maladie*.

4   Among these, the most relevant are by Aprile, "L'Aveugle et sa signification"; Babuts, "Flaubert: Meaning and Counter-meaning"; Engstrom, "Flaubert's Correspondence"; Sachs, "The Role of the Blind Beggar"; Stein, "*Madame Bovary* and Cupid Unmasked"; Wetherill, "*Madame Bovary*'s Blind Man"; M. Williams, "The Hound of Fate"; and Bell, "Un pauvre diable."

5   *Enlightenment, Romanticism and the Blind in France*, 206.

6   Exceptions among recent scholars are those who are preoccupied with the role of speech versus writing in the novel. Naomi Schor ascribes to the blind man the heuristic function of doubling Emma as a structural opposite of Homais ("For a

Restricted Thematics"); for Gerald Prince, the blind man "stubbornly keeps on relating his own story"; like the numerous other characters who tell "bad stories," he is punished by his creator, for whom the only "good story" is one that is written (*Narrative as Theme* 75).

7   For an analysis of the ways in which the opera doubles the novel, see Lukacher's article. Another provocative reading of the opera scene is to be found in Wing's *Limits of Narrative*.

8   See Victor Brombert, *The Novels of Flaubert*, 75. An earlier version of the novel had attributed to Lagardy a "geste obscène." Furthermore, a manuscript variant offers additional proof that the beggar was to be seen as a debased Lagardy, since Flaubert originally intended to have his travelers discuss the beggar's mimetic talents, after which Homais was to express the opinion that "if this man had been properly educated in his youth, he would today be wowing the Parisian theater-goers" (Pommier and Leleu, *Madame Bovary*, 581).

9   Eric Gans (*Madame Bovary*) also sees this scene as pivotal, but in his interpretation, the transformation is in Emma's newfound attachment to the artist (as opposed to the illusions of art).

10   The English version of the beggar's song is from Bair's translation of *Madame Bovary*.

11   See Riffaterre, "Flaubert's Presuppositions."

12   *Dictionnaire des sciences médicales*, s.v. "femme."

13   Quoted by Bart, "Louis Bouilhet, Flaubert's 'accoucheur,'" 187.

14   Flaubert, *Correspondance*, 2:579–80.

15   Bart, "Louis Bouilhet, Flaubert's 'accoucheur,'" 188.

16   See Hocken, *Practical Treatise on Ophthalmic Medicine*.

17   Larousse, *Grand Dictionnaire universel*, s.v. "blennorragie."

18   The appearance of the first scientific periodical devoted exclusively to these specialties, the *Annales des maladies de la peau et de la syphilis*, founded and edited by the famous syphilologist, Pierre-Louis-Alphée Cazenave, dates from 1843; other periodicals followed later in the century (e.g. *Journal des maladies cutanées et syphilitiques*, *Bulletin de la société française de dermatologie et de syphiligraphie*). See Crissey and Parish, *The Dermatology and Syphilology of the Nineteenth Century*, for a thorough treatment of the topic.

19   Zeldin, *France 1848–1945*, 2:867.

20   Zeldin, *France 1848–1945*, 2:867.

21   Flaubert, *Œuvres*, 2:1022.

22   Quoted in Douchin, *La Vie érotique de Flaubert*, 118.

23   Voltaire, *Candide*, 8. It may be of some relevance that Flaubert, whose admiration for Voltaire was boundless, claimed to have read *Candide* twenty times. *Madame Bovary* contains more references to Voltaire than to any other author (seven mentions).

24   Balzac, *Œuvres*, 3:51. For an excellent analysis of the centrality of this icon in Balzac's novel, see Pasco, "Image Structure."

25   The translation is from *Old Goriot*, tr. Marion Ayton Crawford, 29.

26   Sachs, in "The Role of the Blind Beggar," has warned against interpretations of the beggar's role that fail to take into account episodes subsequent to Emma's death. Indeed, his own reading, which emphasizes the divergent reactions of Emma and Homais to the beggar, is particularly insightful and provocative.

27   In *Vital Signs*, Rothfield cites as an example of Homais's incompetence in treating Emma his use of aromatic vinegar to revive her, a method that had been declared ineffective in an 1850 treatise on hysteria (36). Salomon-Bayet, in "Histoire des sciences," points out that Homais's eclectic pharmacopeia betrays an author who is "both skeptical and well-informed" (52). See also Laurence Porter, who asks provocative questions about Homais's role, in the preface to Porter and Gray, *Approaches to Teaching Flaubert's* Madame Bovary.

28   See McGrew, *Encyclopedia of Medical History*, s.v. "King's Touch."

29   See Bertherand, *Précis des maladies vénériennes*; and Hocken, *Practical Treatise on Ophthalmic Medicine*. Hocken states that mild gonorrhoeal conjunctivitis yields readily to an antiphlogistic treatment, but that the remedy is not effective for more severe forms of the illness.

30   Does the criticism go even further? One recent critic, Roger Huss, has suggested that as an archetypal *paterfamilias*, Homais may evoke Flaubert's father who, like the fictional pharmacist, "experienced failure in attempting to correct a club foot" ("Flaubert and Realism," 185). Since Sartre suggested in *L'Idiot de la famille* that Flaubert never forgave his father for deciding in his place that the medical profession was too rigorous for him, many critics have felt that Flaubert was obsessed with his father and that this obsession shaped his representation of the medical practitioners—legal and illegal—in *Madame Bovary*. See also Rothfield, *Vital Signs*, 42; Matlock, "Censoring the Realist Gaze," 52–53; and Reeves, "Theatres of Operation." Cabanès, who warns against oversimplifying the relationship between Flaubert and medicine (1:176–84), sees Homais as a representative of the hygiene movement, for which Flaubert had little respect.

31   My reading complements that of Rothfield, who sees in *Madame Bovary* a "disarticulated autobiography" (*Vital Signs* 41) and believes that Flaubert is incarnated not only in Larivière and Emma but also in Charles because of his own failed ambition to become a doctor.

32   See R. Williams, *The Horror of Life*; and Lasowski, *Syphilis*, for two different approaches to the syphilis-literature connection in nineteenth-century France.

33   Brombert, "The Tragedy of Dreams," 18.

34   Chambers, *The Writing of Melancholy*, 181.

35   Culler, *The Uses of Uncertainty*.

The Doctor and the Priest

1   See Baguley, *Naturalist Fiction.*

2   O'Donovan, "The Body and the Body Politic," 224.

3   Fumaroli, "Des carnets au roman," 97, 98.

4   See Fumaroli's preface to *Madame Gervaisais.*

5   The pathological nature of religious ecstasy had actually been discussed as early as 1813; see Bowman's *French Romanticism.*

6   Favrot, *De la catalepsie,* 64.

7   Favrot, *De la catalepsie,* 63.

8   "Mystical Pathography" 124–46.

9   See Watroba's "*Madame Gervaisais,* roman hystérique ou mystique?"; and Mathieu's "De la métaphore à l'allégorie."

10   In fact, the lines were not drawn quite so neatly as this, and the "vitalist" camp, sometimes called "l'école de Montpellier," included many physicians and scientists, among them the anatomist and physiologist Marie François-Xavier Bichat.

11   Reaction to Loudun in the nineteenth century was characterized by a similar divergence of opinion; see Bowman, *French Romanticism,* 106–21. Bowman's investigation reveals the increasing predominance of the medical perspective in the nineteenth century. On this topic, see also Wajeman, *Le Maître et l'hystérique.*

12   Aside from the fact that both heroines are designated by the novelistic titles as married women, the phonetic proximity of "Gervaisais" to "jersiais," a breed of cow, recalls the evocation of "bovine" in "Bovary."

13   For two excellent discussions of nineteenth-century discourses on women, see Russett, *Sexual Science;* and Jordanova, *Sexual Visions.*

14   O'Donovan makes the same observation about *Germinie Lacerteux,* in which he sees an "insidious subversion . . . of medicine and science [that] reveals a brutal dialectic at work, whereby literature annihilates the claims of its own models" (225).

15   Edmond and Jules de Goncourt, *Manette Salomon,* 311–12.

16   This hotel actually existed and was a favorite of visiting foreign clergy; see *Journal* 1:255.

17   One would like to credit the Goncourts with onomastic inventiveness in their choice of the physician's name, "Andral," suggesting androcentrism, a characteristic shared by both clergy and physicians in the patriarchal society of nineteenth-century Europe. However, there is a real-life referent in the person of Dr. Gabriel Andral ("Andral fils"), who was in fact Nephtalie de Courmont's physician (see *Journal* 3:749) and who also authored the entry for "phtisie" in the *Dictionnaire de médecine.* The Goncourts refer several times to this physician, in generally unflattering terms; see *Journal* 1:281.

18   Although forceps—invented by a London family of male midwives late in the sixteenth century but not widely used until the nineteenth century—saved the

lives of many women by making vaginal deliveries possible in cases where the newer and far more dangerous cesarean sections often spelled certain death for the mother, instrument deliveries were not without risks of their own. Whether babies were delivered by physicians themselves (as was usually the case with forceps deliveries) or by midwives under their supervision, the medical profession was deeply implicated.

19   See Showalter, *The Female Malady*, 125.

20   Madame Gervaisais's identity as an androgyne *and* a hysteric serves to link her to Emma Bovary, her fictional elder. On gender and representation, see Kelly, *Fictional Genders*. On the connection between androgyny and hysteria in the literary and medical discourse of the time, see Goldstein, "The Uses of Male Hysteria."

21   Hamon, *Expositions*, 60.

22   See Knibiehler and Fouquet, *La Femme et les médecins*, 83–84.

23   Mathieu, "De la métaphore à l'allégorie dans *Madame Gervaisais*," 305.

24   See McGrew, *Encyclopedia of Medical History*, s.v. "Bloodletting."

25   The last three syllables of Monterone's name evoke "erronné"; moreover, the name contains "moron."

26   See Brachet, *Traité pratique*.

27   See, for example, *Dictionnaire des sciences médicales*, s.v. "La Femme."

28   *Interpreters' Bible* 2:463.

29   This, at any rate, is the traditional interpretation of the painting, certainly the one with which the Goncourts would have been familiar. For a divergent interpretation, see Bendersky, "Remarks on Raphael's *Transfiguration*."

30   Interestingly, Charcot was also to criticize Raphael's masterpiece some twenty years later; however, whereas the Goncourts' criticism was directed especially at the representation of the Transfiguration, Charcot's attack was aimed at the figure of the demonic child in the foregrounded lower half: "It seems . . . that in this figure alone, Raphael allowed himself to accumulate improbabilities and contradictions" (Charcot and Richer, *Les Démoniaques dans l'art*, 30).

31   The description of the Jesuit's dramatic sermon recalls Napoleon's monologue in the Pope Pius VII–Napoleon confrontation imagined by Vigny in *Servitude et grandeur militaires*, the juxtaposition of *commediante* and *tragediante* echoing Pope Pius VII's laconic reaction to the Emperor's histrionics.

32   See *Sœur Philomène* 47; and *Germinie Lacerteux* 54.

33   *Sœur Philomène* 10.

34   General anesthesia was available from 1847 on, but only used in major surgery; local anesthetics were not used until after 1884. Lister introduced the antiseptic method in 1867.

35   See Reiser, "Responsibility for Personal Health."

36   The same point is made by Léon Daudet: "In young people with normal reactions,

dealing daily with pain and death is a stimulant for sensual pleasure" (quoted by Borsa and Michel, *La Vie quotidienne des hôpitaux*, 155).

37   Chateaubriand, *René*, 158. The intertextual allusion is relevant in view of the fact that Chateaubriand's *œuvre* was to become Jules's constant companion as he neared death.

38   *Journal* 2:202.

39   The separation of a mother and son by a representative of the Papacy in Rome evokes the Mortara Affair, an 1858 incident that caused quite a stir in France. In the Mortara Affair, a Jewish boy of six, baptized by a servant girl who thought he was in danger of death, is kidnapped by the Vatican and raised as a Catholic; see Isser, *Antisemitism*.

40   Tuberculosis was also believed to be an aphrodisiac: see Whorton, "Of Sappho and Syphilis."

41   *Renée Mauperin* 308

42   Thomas à Kempis, *The Imitation of Christ*, 169.

43   See Jean-Louis Cabanès, "Désymbolisation." Cabanès attributes the downfall of Madame Gervaisais to Christian iconography and claims that her intellectual regression "is illustrated by the fact that the heroine comes to personify Christ, whose mental image she creates with the help of one of Raphael's paintings" (39). In my opinion, the heroine can be perceived as a personification of Christ only in an ironic sense.

44   "Des carnets au roman" 98.

Miasmatic Effluvia

1   Zola, *Œuvres complètes*, 11:172–73.

2   See Goldstein, " 'Moral Contagion.' "

3   See Baguley, "Event and Structure"; Colette Becker, "La Condition ouvrière dans *L'Assommoir*"; and Sandy Petrey, "Le Discours du travail dans *L'Assommoir*," 65.

4   Slott, "Narrative Tension," 99.

5   See Newton, "La Grande Bouffe," 20; and "The Decline and Fall of Gervaise Macquart," 62.

6   Girard, "Notice," *L'Assommoir* (extraits), 24.

7   Dubois, L'Assommoir *de Zola*, 39–40.

8   Zola, *L'Assommoir* in *Les Rougon-Macquart*, 2:502.

9   Frey, *Aesthetics*, 135.

10   The nouns also recall the laundry itself, as Julia Przyboš points out in "The Aesthetics of Dirty Laundry." In Przyboš's convincing interpretation of the novel, Gervaise's slide is a fictional representation of the replacement of realism's aesthetic of the "respectable" with naturalism's "indecency."

11 Zola, *La Fortune des Rougon* in *Les Rougon-Macquart*, 1:148.

12 Quoted by Massis, *Comment Emile Zola composait ses romans*, 153.

13 Dubois, L'Assommoir *de Zola*, 122.

14 Allard, *Zola*, 88.

15 Fossangrives, *Hygiène*, 398, 432.

16 Fossangrives, *Hygiène*, 138.

17 Corbin, "Cris et chuchotements," 595.

18 Monin, *L'Alcoolisme*, 54.

19 Barrows, "After the Commune."

20 Goncourt, *Journal*, 2:569.

21 Larousse, *Grand Dictionnaire universel*, s.v. "Blanchissage."

22 Patissier, *Traité des maladies des artisans*, 254. Tardieu, in his *Dictionnaire d'hygiène publique*, is more cautious: "We don't believe that laundresses are exposed to contagious disease during the actual washing process; however, it's not impossible that in handling soiled linen and sorting it, they may pick up the germs of contagious infections" (1:157).

23 Arlidge, *The Hygiene, Diseases and Mortality of Occupations*, 118.

24 Poincaré, *Traité d'hygiène industrielle*.

25 *Dictionnaire des sciences médicales*; and Sir Thomas Oliver, *Occupations*.

26 Michelet, *La Femme*, 22.

27 On the Louvre, see Lethbridge's brilliant analysis, "A Visit to the Louvre: *L'Assommoir* revisited."

28 See Perrot, *Le Travail des apparences*, 169.

29 Cadet-Gassincourt, quoted by Patissier, *Traité des maladies des artisans*, 256. See also Ripa's *La Ronde des folles*, which attests to the frequency of the assimilation of the prostitute and the laundress (84).

30 See, for example, Huysmans, *Croquis parisiens*, in which the author says of laundresses that "they work only intermittently and their true profession is probably more lucrative than worthy" (375).

31 See Corbin, *Le Miasme et la jonquille*, 241.

32 "We've searched, we've opened all the wounds, lanced the blisters of this decomposing body, and we've presented it exactly as it is, without exaggeration. You didn't think the illness was so far advanced, you thought the body was less affected. When you look at it, you become afraid. Well! So much the better if it scares you. Be careful: *sublimism* is epidemic and highly contagious." (Poulot, *Le Sublime*, 6). Poulot's text offers an excellent example of the confusion between the physical and the moral that spawns the notion of "moral contagion" (see Goldstein, "The Uses of Male Hysteria").

33 Girard, "Notice," 14.

34 See Martineau, *Le Roman scientifique*; and Pick, *Faces of Degeneration*, 78.

35   Pick, *Faces of Degeneration*, 78. See also Garabad and Byron Eknoyan, "Medicine and the Case of Emile Zola," 111.

36   Lavielle, "Le Cycle des *Rougon-Macquart*," 27.

37   Kelly, "Experimenting on Women," 231.

38   Schor ("Sainte-Anne: Capitale du délire") discusses Zola's derogatory portrayal of the physician in the Sainte-Anne episode of *L'Assommoir*, pointing out that the clinician's "distancing glance" is implicitly contrasted to Gervaise's "compassionate glance" (105).

Counter-Discursive Strategies in En ménage

1   *Le Figaro*, 11 April 1881.

2   Salières, *Ecrivains contre médecins*, 233.

3   Maingon, *La Médecine dans l'œuvre de J-K Huysmans*, 37–38.

4   Gaillard, "Le Discours médical."

5   In addition to Maingon's work, see Veysset, *Huysmans et la médecine*.

6   Cressot, *La Phrase et le vocabulaire de J-K Huysmans*, 470.

7   Antosh, *Reality and Illusion*.

8   See Juin, preface to Huysmans, *En rade / Un dilemme / Croquis parisiens*. Along with Antosh, Baldick (*Life of J-K Huysmans*) takes a more enlightened view.

9   Exceptions are Borie, "À propos d'*En ménage*"; and Maingon's *La Médecine*, which contains a chapter devoted to the novel. On the subject of a more generalized neglect of Huysmans's work, see Pasco, *Novel Configurations*, 125; and Issacharoff, *J-K Huysmans devant la critique*. Fortunately, the situation has improved in the last decade.

10   Gallot, *Explication*.

11   The medical profession's preoccupation with the promiscuity favored by boarding-school conditions was well known. In *Le pénis et la démoralisation de l'Occident*, Aron and Kempf discuss nineteenth-century medical recommendations intended to curb masturbation, as for example the arrangement of dormitory beds so that the top third is on one side of a partition, the bottom two-thirds on the other, the removal of pockets from pants, the removal of doors from toilet stalls, etc.

12   Borie, "À propos d'*En ménage*," 95.

13   The juxtaposition of the concrete and the abstract that characterizes such expressions was a standard feature of scholastic style; Rabelais had mocked this style in *Pantagruel*, chapter 7, which describes the Librairie Saint-Victor.

14   *Les Sœurs Vatard* 160. On the relationship between the views expressed by this character and the art criticism of Huysmans himself, see Maingon, *L'Univers artistique de J-K Huysmans*, 25.

15   See Wohnlich-Despaigne, *Les Historiens français de la médecine au 19ᵉ siècle* for a list of these postmortem examinations.

16 Huysmans's belief in the doctrine of mystical substitution finds its ultimate expression in his famous hagiography, *Sainte Lydwine de Schiedam.*

17 See Omar and Hamilton, *Wallpapers.*

18 See Lethève, *La Vie quotidienne des artistes français au XIXe siècle.*

19 This "penetration" may be seen as salubrious or harmful. The wounding of André by Berthe is clearly of the latter variety, while Mélie's medical penetration of Cyprien by means of cathartics, emetics, etc. is painful but ultimately healthful.

20 There is considerable irony in the fact that Huysmans has succeeded in this "coup" with a novel that does not feature a single physician-character (the only physician to be mentioned, a "docteur amateur de vieux livres" whose desire for Blanche's copy of *Manon Lescaut* provides the pretext for a meeting between Blanche and André, is purely episodic, and his novelistic existence is limited to two brief mentions).

21 Lloyd believes that there may be an element of self-parody here; see his engaging *Huysmans* 74

22 The words are attributed to Huysmans himself (quoted—in translation—by Baldick 59).

23 Huysmans's preoccupation with bodily orifices is illustrated in a witty article by Pryzboš, "Concerning a Physiological Geometry."

24 Koos ("Medical Asides") sees a similar problematizing of medical discourse in *À rebours.*

Voices of Authority?

1 Vial, *Maupassant et l'art du roman,* 463.

2 See my article " 'Conte de Noël' and 'Nuit de Noël'."

3 See Moger, "Narrative Structure in Maupassant," 323; and Maupassant, *Sur l'eau,* 83.

4 For a definition of the term narrating instance, see Prince, *Dictionary of Narratology.*

5 This power, also attributed to "substitute relics" (e.g., pieces of cloth that have touched real relics), explains the flourishing relics trade at such pilgrimage sites as Lourdes and Lisieux. See *New Catholic Encyclopedia,* s.v. "Relics."

6 In fact, none of the accounts of the eleven thousand virgins who, led by Saint Ursula, were supposedly martyred by the Huns in Cologne in the fourth century, have convincing authority, according to modern theologians; see *An Encyclopedia of Religion.* Larousse's *Grand Dictionnaire universel* (s.v. "reliques") also makes light of this legend, according to which eleven thousand miracles were attributed to each of the heads of the eleven thousand virgins.

7 Stivale, "Guy de Maupassant and Narrative Strategies of Othering."

8 For a contrary view, see Apter, *Feminizing the Fetish,* 100. See also Danger's enlightening reading in *Pulsion et Désir* 64–65.

9 See Paris, "Maupassant et le contre-récit"; and Nef, "Noms et échange."

10   Harris, *Maupassant in the Hall of Mirrors*, 109.

11   Physicians of this era, particularly in the provinces, often dined at the homes of their patients or were paid for their services in comestibles. Parisian doctors, known for their gastronomy, were singled out by Brillat-Savarin and others. "Physicians are generally among the most refined lovers of food. There's scarcely ever a good meal without at least one physician at the table," declares Monselet (*Lettres gourmandes* 105). See also Aron, *Le Mangeur du XIXᵉ siècle*.

12   Preface to *Le Rosier de Madame Husson* 11.

13   This detail is referentially precise. Along with Salency, site of the crowning of the first *rosière* in the sixth century, Nanterre was in Maupassant's era the best known of the towns that continued to practice this medieval custom; see Larousse, *Grand dictionnaire universel*, s.v. "Rosière."

14   Cabanès, *Corps et maladie*, 2:449.

15   Cabanès has pointed out that corporeal "excess" is itself pathological in the nineteenth century: "Laxness in pleasures, laxness in character: these traits are associated in the imaginary of the period, and they give birth to a sort of fantastic vision of abnormally large bodies" (2:450). See also Lasowski (preface to *Le Rosier de Madame Husson*) and Buisine ("Paris—Lyon—Maupassant"), who have both noted the connection between the story's rhetorical and gastronomical "overflow."

16   See Nye, *Crime, Madness and Politics*; and Baguley, *Naturalist Fiction*.

17   Although I have concentrated in this study on texts with a clearly parodical dimension, the same erosion of confidence in the medical practitioner can also be detected in such serious stories as "Berthe" and "Madame Hermet" or in stories in which the physician is a character, rather than a narrator, as in the two versions of "Le Horla." On the representation of the physician in "Berthe," see Whyte, "Maupassant et le réflexe conditionné."

The Physician as Foreigner

1   *The Horror of Life*, 275.

2   Drumont, *La France juive*, 11. Drumont's condemnation of these tales stems not from their origin in the Semitic Near East but rather from the fact that they relate adventures of found treasures and include no moral dimension, no altruistic characters.

3   This association is reinforced by the supposed inspiration for the character, the Jewish banker Oppenheim, and by such stereotypically "Semitic" features as his "hooked nose" and "heavy eyelids" (2:547).

4   Sachs, *The Career of Alphonse Daudet*, 105.

5   See Fay-Sallois, *Les Nourrices*, 161–64.

6   Cabanès, *Le Corps et la maladie*, 2:564.

7 High mortality rates were of course not limited to the infant population that was subjected to such schemes as that of Jenkins. In *Sick Heroes*, Pasco cites statistics that support his thesis that wetnursing itself was extremely dangerous, both physically and psychologically.

8 See Silverman, "Anti-Semitism and Occultism in *fin-de-siècle* France."

9 Cabanès, *Le Corps et la maladie*, 2:564.

10 Cabanès, *Le Corps et la maladie*, 2:565.

11 See Isser, *Antisemitism*.

12 Sachs, *The Career of Alphonse Daudet*, 105.

13 When Jansoulet arrives at Jenkins's soirée, "a crowd of people rushed at the door; there was a scuffle such as one sees on the dock of a large sea port when a Felucca carrying gold enters port" (2:525).

14 Sachs, *The Career of Alphonse Daudet*, 104, 108.

15 Byrnes (*Antisemitism in Modern France*) points out that Daudet further helped Drumont by persuading a friend, Francis Magnard, to write a review of the book for the *Figaro*, thus beginning a controversy that drew attention to the book and prevented Marpon and Flammarion from withdrawing Drumont's two-volume work, which had until then attracted little notice. Balancing these indications that Alphonse Daudet may indeed have had an anti-Semitic bias are the judgments of Sachs (*The Career of Alphonse Daudet*) and Roger Williams (*The Horror of Life*). Williams cites in defense of his position the fact that Alphonse Daudet never joined the Anti-Semitic League and actually had a falling-out with Drumont the year of the publication of *La France juive*.

Hydrotherapy and Medical Bloat in Mont-Oriol

1 Sullivan, *Maupassant the Novelist*, 100.

2 Vial, *Maupassant et l'art du roman*, 360.

3 Sullivan, *Maupassant the Novelist*, 100.

4 Mitterand, "Un projet inédit d'Emile Zola en 1884–85."

5 See Wallon, *La Vie quotidienne dans les villes d'eaux*.

6 See Bonnefis, preface to *Mont-Oriol*; Harris, *Maupassant in the Hall of Mirrors*, 149; Giachetti, *Maupassant*, 140; and Danger, *Pulsion et désir*, 95. For other provocative commentaries on the novel, see Leuwers, preface to *Mont-Oriol*; Bancquart, preface to *Mont-Oriol*; and Besnard-Coursodon, *Etude thématique et structurale de l'œuvre de Maupassant*.

7 See Stivale, *The Art of Rupture*.

8 Maupassant, *Contes et Nouvelles*, 2:461. Christiane's words also solidify her onomastic identification with Christ, as they echo the words of Christ to his heavenly Father: "Father, into Thy hands I commend my spirit. Thy will be done."

9   Latona, the name the Romans gave to the Greek goddess Leto, a descendant of the Titans, was persecuted by Zeus's third wife, Hera, after she became pregnant by him. Along with her difficulties in finding a country that would allow her to deliver her twins, her nine-day labor is legendary.

10 Danger, *Pulsion et désir*, 540.

11 Like the other two, he is a performer: "And he smiled, looking as if he were chatting, changed his tone to indicate the woman's speech, waved his hand to represent the gentleman. . . . Three of the extras [Gontran's name for his stockholders] applauded" (582).

12 The engineer succumbs to a massive stroke, "in the middle of his treatment, in the middle of spa season" (674).

13 Giachetti, *Maupassant*, 136.

14 Harris, "Maupassant's *Mont Oriol*," 581.

15 See Harris, "Maupassant's *Mont-Oriol*, 588.

16 See Prince's brilliant analysis of the xenophobic aspects of Maupassant's fantastic tale in " 'Le Horla,' Sex, and Colonization."

17 See Besnard-Coursodon, "Une 'chaise basse en crêpe de Chine.' "

18 "Lover" should be understood generically here. In Maupassant's personal imaginary, the Other is often Woman, and the role reversal that takes place in the last chapter of *Mont-Oriol* is highly suggestive. Christiane regains possession of herself, whereas Brétigny is again dispossessed by Woman. As for the equation Jew equals foreigner, the literature is abundant: see Isser, *Antisemitism*; and Graetz, *The Jews in Nineteenth-Century France*. In addition, Zola's *Nana* offers eloquent literary proof of the association: the Jewish banker Steiner is referred to both as "that Prussian" and "filthy Jew" (*Les Rougon-Macquart*, 2:1454).

19 Among the characters who are enlisted (wittingly or not) in Andermatt's grand commercial venture are several who bear names that identify them with Christianity (e.g., Aubry-Pasteur, Clovis, and of course Christiane).

Medical Menace in Les Morticoles

1   Montaigne, *Essais*, 434.

2   See Léon Daudet, *Quand vivait mon père*, 86–87.

3   Letter to George Sand, 12 December 1841, quoted in the introduction to *Bouvard et Pécuchet*, *Œuvres*, 2:701.

4   Gelfand, in "Medical Nemesis, Paris, 1894" (158 n.2), points out that Daudet specified on a page inserted with the manuscript of the novel that he had written it "with anger, bile, and soot."

5   Roudinesco, *La Bataille de cent ans*, 1:61.

6   The only exception was *Union médicale*, which published what Gelfand terms "a contemptuous review" on 17 July 1894.

7   See Terdiman, *Discourse/Counter-Discourse*, 76.

8   The Morticoles are further associated with pirates by their name, which, besides its obvious evocation of death, may also suggest Maures (Moors), who were known for piracy. It should by now be obvious that the association of medicine with piracy was a leitmotif of antimedical literature.

9   Roudinesco, *La Bataille de cent ans*, 62.

10 Gelfand, "Medical Nemesis" 166.

11 Gelfand, "Medical Nemesis" 175–76.

12 Péan also inspired Malasvon, as Gelfand has noted.

13 Gilman, *The Jew's Body*, 39.

14 Gilman, *The Jew's Body*, 112.

15 The fear that reading could prove dangerous for women, a notion that ironically inspired both the creation of Madame Bovary (the character) and the subsequent trial of *Madame Bovary*, was in fact commonplace; see Matlock, *Scenes of Seduction*.

16 As Bowman reminds us in *Le Christ des barricades*, the topos of the *Christus insanit* was adopted in the nineteenth-century by Esquiros, among others, who believed that all prophets, in advance of their time, were treated as insane. Thus "Jesus gives value to madmen" (212).

17 Scott, *The Struggle for the Soul of the French Novel*, 967.

Conclusion

1   Gelfand, "Medical Nemesis," 155.

2   Gelfand, "Medical Nemesis," 156–67

3   Faure, *Histoire sociale de la médecine*, 9.

4   For a brief explanation of the historical significance of Molière's mockery, see R. Porter, *The Greatest Benefit to Mankind*, 226–27. Even as late as the eighteenth century, medical practice remained highly primitive; see Peschel, "Medicine and Literature."

5   For a discussion of Torty's role, see Respaut, "The Doctor's Discourse."

6   Although it is not within the scope of this study, popular literature may provide further examples of similarly unflattering portraits. The reader interested in investigating this path may wish to begin with Louis Noir's *Le Médecin juif* or Xavier de Montepin's *Le Médecin des folles*.

7   See Zeldin, *A History of French Passions*, 2:574–645; and Weber, *France Fin-de-siècle*, 76.

8   See Gelfand, "From Religious to Bio-Medical Anti-Semitism," 266.

9   "If tomorrow the Virgin resuscitated a dead man, the whole camp of Freethinkers would yell from the rooftops that the man had only been in a state of lethargy" (*Les Foules de Lourdes* 247). It is of course not by chance that both Bourget and Huysmans returned to the Catholic Church.

10   See Ellis, *The Physician-Legislators of France*.

11   Burke, *The Day the Universe Changed*, 237.

12   Shortt, "Physicians, Science and Status," 64–65.

13   Shortt, "Physicians, Science and Status," 68.

14   Goncourt, *Journal*, 2:54.

15   Zola, *Œuvres complètes*, 13:147. The allusion is presumably to the morgue scene in *Thérèse Raquin*.

16   Flaubert, *Correspondance*, 3:709.

17   Goncourt, *Journal*, 1:1036.

18   Kogan, "Michelet Plays Doctor," 11. Kogan quotes the following statement about physicians from volume 3 of Michelet's *Journal*: "Having the right to see what others can't see is the most precious jewel in their crown. Aside from the sensuality associated with this right, they believe they derive their power from it" (554).

19   See the *Dictionnaire des sciences médicales*, s.v. "Génie." Here, hypochondriacs are said to count many geniuses among them. "Genius is often an illness," argue the authors.

20   The Bibliothèque nationale de France houses a partial collection of these slim studies, many still uncataloged; a more complete collection can be found at the Bibliothèque de l'Ecole de Médecine.

21   The ideology that subtends this valorization is analyzed in Meyers, *Disease and the Novel*.

22   Goncourt, *Journal*, 1:1189. The words "plebeian and contemptible" belong to Roger Williams (*The Horror of Life* 109). Rather than "plebeian," avows Williams, Jules would likely have found health to be "bourgeois."

23   Spackman, *Decadent Genealogies*, vii–viii.

24   Quoted by Sachs, *The Career of Alphonse Daudet*, 158.

25   Weber, *France fin-de-siècle*, 130.

26   Nevins, *The Jewish Doctor*, 10.

27   Ellis, *The Physician-Legislators of France*, 98.

28   See Birnbaum, *Anti-Semitism in France*, 263; and Drumont, who states in *La France juive* that "one could do an interesting study on the Jewish origins of Freemasonry, on the alliance of Freemasons and Jews, the former taking the Christian's beliefs away from him, the latter taking away his money" (n. pag.).

29   Birnbaum, *Anti-Semitism in France*, 150.

30   Byrnes, *Antisemitism in Modern France*, 93.

31   See Weber, *France fin-de-siècle*, 216.

32   Quoted in Ruderman, *Jewish Thought*, 286.

33   Nevins, *The Jewish Doctor*, xii.

34   Ramsey, "Medical Power and Popular Medicine," 563.

35   J. Léonard, *La Médecine entre les savoirs et les pouvoirs*, 261.

36   Goncourt, *Journal*, 1:796.

37 Isser, *Antisemitism*, 10.

38 J. Léonard, *La Médecine*, 270.

39 Michel, *Les Microbes humains*, 1.

40 Michel, *Les Microbes humains*, 102.

41 As Gilman observes in *The Case of Sigmund Freud*, this is especially true in the case of Jewish physicians who, in an era of "racial science," associated their Jewishness with certain pathologies. Gilman distinguishes between today's acknowledgment of certain medical consequences of race and the older, biological view of race as marker of inferiority.

42 See Weber, *France fin de siècle*, 13.

43 Drumont, *La France juive*, 33–34.

44 I use the word "invisible" here in the sense of "invisible to the naked eye." With the advent of more sophisticated methods of microscopy, microorganisms did of course become visible to the scientist.

45 See Van Renterghem, "L'Américain Alan Sokol face aux 'imposteurs' de la pensée française," *Le Monde*, International Edition (4 October 1997): 13.

46 Ironically, it was a Jewish physician, the immunologist Paul Ehrlich, who found a cure for syphilis. Ehrlich won the Nobel Prize in 1908 for his discovery of Salvarsan (see Nevins, *The Jewish Doctor*, 121).

47 Abigail Zuger's article in *The New York Times* on 16 December 1997, entitled "New Way of Doctoring: By the Book," dealt with precisely this problem. According to the article, physicians tend to follow certain patterns in their patient care, regardless of what the latest research shows. "Old strategies grow obsolete and new ones appear daily. Would your doctor actually be able to sift through all that information to assemble the best, most up-to-date options for a person like you, and then organize your care accordingly? The simple but unnerving answer: probably not" (F1).

48 See Sara Rimer, "Gunshots and Sirens Pierce a Suburb's Quiet," *The New York Times* (31 December 1994).

49 A group that calls itself "Voices United for Israel" opposes overtures to the Palestinians that would result in the loss of territory for Israel. Interestingly, despite the fundamentalists' loyalty to Israel, based upon a literal reading of Genesis, the group has alienated mainstream Jews. See Goodstein, "Falwell to Mobilize Support for Israel," *The New York Times* (21 January 1998): A6.

50 Byrnes (*Antisemitism in Modern France*) discusses the connection between anti-Semitism and the conservative Christian movements of late-nineteenth-century France. For more on anti-Semitic elements in twentieth-century Christian Fundamentalism in the United States, see Martin, *With God on Our Side*.

51 Rosello, "Contamination et pureté," 4.

BIBLIOGRAPHY

¶

Allain, Edouard. *Le Mal de Flaubert.* Paris: M. Lac, 1928.

Allard, Jacques. *Zola: Le Chiffre du texte.* Grenoble: Presses Universitaires de Grenoble, 1978.

Ambrière, Madeleine. "Balzac homme de science(s): Savoir scientifique, discours scientifique et système balzacien dans *La Recherche de l'absolu.*" In *Balzac: L'Invention du roman.* Ed. Claude Duchet and Jacques Neefs. Paris: Belfond, 1982.

Angenot, Marc. *Ce que l'on dit des Juifs en 1889: Antisémitisme et discours social.* St. Denis: Presses Universitaires de Vincennes, 1989.

Antosh, Ruth. *Reality and Illusion in the Novels of J.-K. Huysmans.* Amsterdam: Rodopi, 1986.

Aprile, Max. "L'Aveugle et sa signification dans *Madame Bovary.*" *Revue d'Histoire Littéraire de la France* 76 (1976): 385–92.

Apter, Emily. *Feminizing the Fetish.* Ithaca: Cornell University Press, 1991.

Aries, Philippe, and Georges Duby, eds. *Histoire de la vie privée.* Paris: Seuil, 1987.

Arlidge, J. T. *The Hygiene, Diseases and Mortality of Occupations.* London: Percival, 1982.

Aron, Jean-Paul. *Le Mangeur du XIX* siècle. Paris: Laffont, 1973.

Aron, Jean Paul, and Roger Kempf. *Le Pénis et la démoralisation de l'Occident.* Paris: Grasset, 1978.

Babuts, Nicolae. "Flaubert: Meaning and Counter-Meaning." *Symposium* 40 (winter 1986–87): 247–58.

Baguley, David. "Event and Structure: The Plot of Zola's *L'Assommoir.*" *Publications of the Modern Language Association* 90 (1975): 823–33.

———. *Naturalist Fiction. The Entropic Vision.* Cambridge MA: Cambridge University Press, 1990.

Baldick, Robert. *Life of J.-K. Huysmans.* Oxford: Clarendon, 1955.

Balzac, Honoré de. *La Comédie Humaine.* Ed. Pierre-Georges Castex. Paris: Gallimard, Bibliothèque de la Pléiade, 1976–81.

———. *La Cousine Bette.* Paris: Gallimard, Folio classique, 1972.

————. *Old Goriot*. Trans. Marion Ayton Crawford. London: Penguin, 1986.

Bancquart, Marie-Claire. Preface to *Mont-Oriol*, by Guy de Maupassant. Paris: Gallimard, 1976.

Barrows, Susan. "After the Commune: Alcoholism, Temperance, and Literature in the Early Third Republic." In *Consciousness and Class Experience in Nineteenth-Century Europe*. Ed. John M. Merriman. New York: Holmes and Meier, 1979.

Bart, Benjamin. "Louis Bouilhet, Flaubert's 'accoucheur.'" *Symposium* 17, no. 3 (fall 1963): 183–201.

Becker, Colette. "La Condition ouvrière dans *L'Assommoir*: Un Inéluctable Enlisement." *Cahiers naturalistes* 52 (1978): 42–57.

Beer, Gillian. "Plot and the Analogy with Science in Later Nineteenth-Century Novelists." In *Comparative Criticism: A Yearbook*. Ed. Elinor Shaffer. Cambridge: Cambridge University Press, 1980.

Bell, Sheila. "Un Pauvre Diable: The Blind Beggar in *Madame Bovary*." In *Studies in French Fiction in Honor of Vivienne Mylne*. Ed. Robert Gibson. London: Grant & Cutler, 1988. 25–39.

Bendersky, Gordon. "Remarks on Raphael's *Transfiguration*." *Source* 14, no. 4 (summer 1995): 18–25.

Bernard, Claudie. "Monsieur Bovary." *French Forum* 10 (September 1985): 307–24.

Bernard, Tristan. *Sous toutes réserves*. Paris: Calmann-Lévy, 1994.

Bernheimer, Charles. "L'Exorbitant textuel: Castration et sublimation chez Huysmans." Trans. Michèle Vialet. *Romantisme* 45 (1984): 105–13.

————. *Figures of Ill Repute*. Cambridge: Harvard University Press, 1992.

Bertherand, A. *Précis des maladies vénériennes*. Paris: Baillière, 1852.

Besnard-Coursodon, Micheline. *Etude thématique et structurale de l'œuvre de Maupassant: Le Piège*. Paris: Nizet, 1972.

————. "Une 'chaise basse en crêpe de Chine': Sommeils maupassantiens." *Romantisme* 37 (1982): 41–52.

Birnbaum, Pierre. *Antisemitism in France*. Trans. Miriam Kochan. Oxford, U.K.: Blackwell, 1992.

Bonnefis, Philippe. Preface to *Mont-Oriol*, by Guy de Maupassant. Paris: Albin Michel, 1988.

Borel, Jacques. *Médecine et psychiatrie balzaciennes*. Paris: Corti, 1971.

Borie, Jean. "À propos d'*En ménage*." In *Huysmans*. Paris: Editions de l'Herne, 1985. 93–103.

Borsa, S., and C. R. Michel. *La Vie quotidienne des hôpitaux en France au XIXᵉ siècle*. Paris: Hachette, 1985.

Bowman, Frank Paul. *Le Christ des Barricades 1789–1848*. Paris: Editions du Cerf, 1987.

————. *French Romanticism: Intertextual and Interdisciplinary Readings*. Baltimore: Johns Hopkins University Press, 1990.

Brachet, J. L. *Traité pratique des convulsions des enfants*. Paris: Baillière, 1837.

Brillat-Savarin. *La Physiologie du goût.* Paris: E. Dentu, 1883.

Brombert, Victor. *The Novels of Flaubert.* Princeton: Princeton University Press, 1966.

———. "The Tragedy of Dreams." In *Modern Critical Interpretations: Madame Bovary.* Ed. Harold Bloom. New York: Chelsea House, 1988.

Brooks, Peter. "Constructions psychanalytiques et narratives," *Poétique* 65 (February 1985): 63–74.

Buisine, Alain. "Paris—Lyon—Maupassant." In *Maupassant miroir de la nouvelle.* Ed. Jacques Lecarme and Bruno Vercier. Saint Denis: Presses Universitaires de Vincennes, 1988.

Burke, James. *The Day the Universe Changed.* Boston: Little, Brown, 1985.

Byrnes, Robert F. *Antisemitism in Modern France.* New Brunswick NJ: Rutgers University Press, 1950.

Cabanès, Jean-Louis. *Le Corps et la maladie dans les récits réalistes (1850–1893).* Paris: Klincksieck, 1991.

———. "Désymbolisation, imitation et pathologie de la croyance." In *Littérature et Pathologie.* Ed. Max Milner. St. Denis: Presses Universitaires de Vincennes, 1989.

Canby, Vincent. "Trish Vradenburg's *The Apple Doesn't Fall.*" Performance review. *The New York Times,* 15 April 1996, C11.

Chambers, Ross. *The Writing of Melancholy.* Chicago: University of Chicago Press, 1993.

Charcot, J-M, and Paul Richer. *Les Démoniaques dans l'art.* Paris: Bourloton, 1887; reprint, Amsterdam: B. M. Israel, 1972.

Chateaubriand, François-René de. *René.* Paris: Garnier-Flammarion, 1964.

Clark, Linda. *Social Darwinism in France.* Tuscaloosa: University of Alabama Press, 1984.

Constable, Liz. "*Fin-de-siècle* Yellow Fevers: Women Writers, Decadence and Discourses of Degeneracy." *L'Esprit créateur* 37, no.3 (fall 1997): 25–36.

Corbin, Alain. "Cris et chuchotements." In *Histoire de la vie privée.* Ed. Philippe Ariès and Georges Duby. Vol.4. Paris: Seuil, 1987.

———. *Le Miasme et la jonquille.* Paris: Aubier Montaigne, 1982.

Coulont-Henderson, Françoise. "Sang, mort et morbidité dans *Madame Gervaisais* d'Edmond et Jules de Goncourt." *Nineteenth-Century French Studies* 14, nos.3–4 (spring–summer 1986): 295–302.

Couvreur, André. *Le Mal nécessaire.* Paris: Plon, 1899.

Cressot, Marcel. *La Phrase et le vocabulaire de J.-K. Huysmans.* Geneva: Slatkine Reprints, 1975.

Crissey, John, and Lawrence Parish. *The Dermatology and Syphilology of the Nineteenth Century.* New York: Praeger, 1981.

Csergo, Julia. *Liberté, Egalité, Propreté.* Paris: Albin Michel, 1988.

Culler, Jonathan. *The Uses of Uncertainty.* Ithaca: Cornell University Press, 1974.

Danger, Pierre. *Pulsion et désir dans les romans et nouvelles de Guy de Maupassant.* Paris: Nizet, 1993.

Danous, Gérard. *Le Corps souffrant.* Paris: Champ Vallon, 1994.

Daudet, Alphonse. *Le Nabab.* In *Œuvres II.* Ed. Roger Ripoll. Paris: Gallimard, Bibliothèque de la Pléiade, 1990.

Daudet, Léon. *Les Morticoles.* Paris: Editions Fasquelle, 1956.

———. *Quand vivait mon père.* Paris: Grasset, 1940.

Dictionnaire de médecine. Paris: Bechet Jeune, 1824.

Dictionnaire des sciences médicales. Paris: Panckoucke, 1821.

Dijkstra, Bram. *Idols of Perversity: Fantasies of Feminine Evil in Fin-de-siècle Culture.* New York: Oxford University Press, 1986.

Donaldson-Evans, Mary. "'Conte de Noël' and 'Nuit de Noël': Ironic Diptych in Maupassant's Work." *French Review* 54, no.1 (October 1980): 66–77.

———. "Doctoring History: Maupassant's 'Un coup d'état,'" *Nineteenth-Century French Studies* 16, nos.3–4 (spring–summer 1988): 351–60.

Douchin, Jacques-Louis. *La Vie érotique de Flaubert.* Paris: J-J Pauvert, 1984.

Drumont, Edouard. *La France juive.* Paris: Marpon et Flammarion, 1886.

Dubois, Jacques. *L'Assommoir de Zola: Société, discours, idéologie.* Paris: Larousse, 1973.

———. "Une Écriture à saturation. Les présupposées idéologiques dans l'incipit du *Nabab.*" *Études littéraires* 4 (December 1971): 297–310.

Dupuy, Aimé. "Le Docteur Jenkins dans *Le Nabab* d'Alphonse Daudet." *La Presse médicale* (5 December 1959): 2157–59.

Eknoyan, Garabed, and Byron A. Eknoyan. "Medicine and the Case of Emile Zola." In *The Body and the Text: Comparative Essays in Literature and Medicine.* Ed. Bruce Clarke and Wendell Aycock. Lubbock: Texas Tech University Press, 1990.

Ellis, Jack. *The Physician-Legislators of France: Medicine and Politics in the Early Third Republic, 1870–1914.* Cambridge: Cambridge University Press, 1990.

Engstrom, Alfred. "Flaubert's Correspondence and the Ironic and Symbolic Structure of *Madame Bovary.*" *Studies in Philology* (July 1949): 471–95.

Evans, Martha Noël. *Fits and Starts: A Genealogy of Hysteria in Modern France.* Ithaca: Cornell University Press, 1991.

Falconer, Graham. "The Human Comedy." In *Encyclopedia of the Novel.* Ed. Paul Schellinger. Vol. 1. Chicago: Fitzroy Dearborn, 1998.

Faure, Olivier. *Histoire sociale de la médecine (XVIIIe–XXe Siècles).* Paris: Anthropos, 1994.

———. *Les Français et leur médecine au XIXe siècle.* Paris: Belin, 1993.

Favrot, Alex. *De la catalepsie, de l'extase et de l'hystérie.* Paris: Rignoux, 1844.

Fay-Sallois, Fanny. *Les Nourrices à Paris au XIXe siècle.* Paris: Payot, 1980.

Felman, Shoshana. *La Folie et la chose littéraire.* Paris: Seuil, 1978.

Fern, Verigilus, ed. *An Encyclopedia of Religion.* New York: Philosophical Library, 1945.

Flaubert, Gustave. *Correspondance.* 4 vols. Ed. Jean Bruneau. Paris: Gallimard, Bibliothèque de la Pléiade, 1973–98.

———. *Madame Bovary.* Paris: Garnier-Flammarion, 1986.

———. *Madame Bovary.* Trans. Lowell Blair. Toronto: Bantam, 1988.

―――. *Œuvres complètes*. Ed. A. Thibaudet and R. Dumesnil. Paris: Gallimard, Bibliothèque de la Pléiade, 1952.

Fleury, Maurice de. *Le Médecin*. Paris: Hachette, 1927.

Forestier, Louis. Preface to *Le Rosier de Madame Husson*, by Guy de Maupassant. Paris: Gallimard, 1990.

Fossangrives, J. B. *Hygiène et assainissement des villes*. Paris: Baillières, 1874.

Foucault, Michel. *L'Archéologie du savoir*. Paris: Gallimard, 1969.

―――. *Naissance de la clinique: Une Archéologie du regard médical*. Paris: Presses Universitaires de France, 1963.

―――. *L'Ordre du discours*. Paris: Gallimard, 1971.

Frappier-Mazur, Lucienne. *L'Expression métaphorique dans La Comédie Humaine*. Paris: Klinksieck, 1976.

―――. "Sémiotique du corps malade dans *La Comédie Humaine*." In *Balzac: L'Invention du roman*. Ed. Claude Duchet and Jacques Neefs. Paris: Belfond, 1982.

Frey, John. *Aesthetics of the Rougon-Macquart*. Washington DC: Studia Humanitas, 1978.

Fumaroli, Marc. "Des carnets au roman: L'Ironie esthétique des Goncourt dans *Madame Gervaisais*." In *Romans d'Archives*. Ed. Raymonde Debray-Genette and Jacques Neefs. Lille: Presses Universitaires de Lille, 1987. 79–102.

―――. Preface to *Madame Gervaisais*, by Edmond and Jules de Goncourt. Paris: Gallimard, 1982.

Furst, Lilian R. *L'Assommoir: A Working Woman's Life*. Boston: Twayne, 1990.

―――. "Realism and Hypertrophy: A Study of Three Medico-Historical 'Cases.'" *Nineteenth-Century French Studies* 22, nos.1–2 (fall–winter 1993–94): 29–47.

Gaillard, Françoise. "Le Discours médical pris au piège du récit." *Etudes françaises* 19, no.2 (1983): 81–95.

Galerant, Dr. Germain. *Médecine de campagne: De la révolution à la Belle Epoque*. Paris: Plon, 1988.

Gallot, H. M. *Explication de J.-K. Huysmans*. Paris: Agence Parisienne de Distribution, 1955.

Gans, Eric. *Madame Bovary: The End of Romance*. New York: Twayne, 1989.

Gelfand, Toby. "Medical Nemesis, Paris, 1894: Léon Daudet's *Les Morticoles*." *Bulletin of the History of Medicine* 60 (1986): 155–76.

―――. "From Religious to Bio-medical Anti-Semitism: The Career of Jules Soury." In *French Medical Culture in the Nineteenth Century*. Ed. Ann La Berge and Mordechai Feingold. Amsterdam: Rodopi, 1994.

Giachetti, Claudine. *Maupassant: Espaces du roman*. Geneva: Droz, 1993.

Gilman, Sander.
The Case of Sigmund Freud: Medicine and Identity at the Fin-de-siècle. Baltimore: Johns Hopkins University Press, 1993.

―――. *The Jew's Body*. New York: Routledge, 1991.

———. *Smart Jews: The Construction of the Image of Jewish Superior Intelligence.* Lincoln: University of Nebraska Press, 1996.

Girard, Marcel. "Notice." *L'Assommoir* (extraits). Paris: Larousse, 1972.

Goldstein, Jan. *Console and Classify: The French Psychiatric Profession in the Nineteenth Century.* Cambridge: Cambridge University Press, 1987.

———. "'Moral Contagion': A Professional Ideology of Medicine and Psychiatry in Eighteenth- and Nineteenth-Century France." In *Professions and the French State.* Ed. Gerald L. Geison. Philadelphia: University of Pennsylvania Press, 1984. 181–222.

———. "The Uses of Male Hysteria: Medical and Literary Discourse in Nineteenth-Century France." *Representations* 34 (spring 1991): 134–65.

Goncourt, Edmond and Jules de. *Germinie Lacerteux.* Paris: Flammarion and Fasquelle, 1921.

———. *Journal.* 3 vols. Ed. Robert Ricatte. Paris: Fasquelle & Flammarion, 1956; reissued with a preface and chronology by Robert Kopp, Paris: Robert Laffont, 1989.

———. *Madame Gervaisais.* Ed. Marc Fumaroli. Paris: Gallimard, 1982.

———. *Manette Salomon.* Paris: Gallimard, Folio, 1996.

———. *Renée Mauperin.* Paris: Flammarion and Fasquelle, 1922.

———. *Sœur Philomène.* Ed. Pierre Dufief. Tusson: Du Lérot, 1996.

Graetz, Michael. *The Jews in Nineteenth-Century France: From the French Revolution to the Alliance Israélite Universelle.* Trans. Jane Marie Todd. Stanford CA: Stanford University Press, 1993.

Gray, Eugene. "The Clinical View of Life: Gustave Flaubert's *Madame Bovary.*" In *Medicine and Literature.* Ed. Enid Rhodes Peschel. New York: Neale Watson, 1980. 81–87.

Guillaume, Pierre. *Médecins, Église, et Foi: XIXᵉ–XXᵉ Siècles.* Paris: Aubier, 1990.

———. *Le Rôle social du médecin depuis deux siècles (1850–1945).* Paris: Association pour l'étude de l'histoire de la sécurité sociale, 1966.

Hamon, Philippe. *Expositions: Littérature et architecture au XIXᵉ siècle.* Paris: Corti, 1989.

———. *Texte et idéologie.* Paris: Presses Universitaires de France, 1984.

Harris, Trevor A. le V. *Maupassant in the Hall of Mirrors: Ironies of Repetition in the Work of Guy de Maupassant.* New York: St. Martins Press, 1990.

———. "Maupassant's *Mont-Oriol*: Narrative as Declining Noun," *Modern Language Review* 89, no.3 (July 1994): 581–94.

Harsin, Jill. "Syphilis, Wives, and Physicians: Medical Ethics and the Family in Late-Nineteenth-Century France." *French Historical Studies* 16, no.1 (spring 1989): 72–95.

Hocken, Edward. *Practical Treatise on Ophthalmic Medicine.* London: Samuel Highly, 1844.

Horrobin, David F. *Medical Hubris: A Reply to Ivan Illich.* Montreal: Eden Press, n.d.

Hunter, Kathryn Montgomery. *Doctors' Stories: The Narrative Structure of Medical Knowledge.* Princeton: Princeton University Press, 1991.

Huss, Roger. "Flaubert and Realism: Paternity, Authority and Sexual Difference." In *Spectacles of Realism: Body, Gender, Genre.* Ed. Margaret Cohen and Christopher Prendergast. Minneapolis: University of Minnesota Press, 1995.

Huysmans, Joris-Karl. *Croquis parisiens*. Paris: Union générale d'éditions, 1976.

———. *En ménage*. Paris: Fasquelle, 1955.

———. *Les Foules de Lourdes*. Paris: Plon, 1947.

———. "Sac au dos." In *Les Soirées de Médan*. 1880; Paris: Fasquelle, 1955.

———. *Sainte Lydie de Schiedam*. Paris: Stock, 1901.

———. *Les Sœurs Vatard*. Trans. James Babcock. Kentucky: University Press of Kentucky, 1973.

Ibsen, Henrik. *An Enemy of the People*. Chicago: Great Books Foundation, 1963.

Illich, Ivan. *Medical Nemesis*. London: Calder & Boyars, 1975.

Interpreters' Bible. New York: Abingdon Press, 1951.

Issacharoff, Michael. *J.-K. Huysmans devant la critique en France (1874–1960)*. Paris: Klinksieck, 1970.

Isser, Natalie. *Antisemitism During the French Second Empire*. New York: Peter Lang, 1991.

Jordanova, Ludmilla. *Sexual Visions: Images of Gender in Science and Medicine between the Eighteenth and Twentieth Centuries*. Madison: University of Wisconsin Press, 1989.

Juin, Albert. Preface to *En rade/Un dilemme/Croquis parisiens*, by J.-K. Huysmans. Paris: Union générale d'éditions, Collection 10/18, 1976.

Kelly, Dorothy. "Experimenting on Women: Zola's Theory and Practice of the Experimental Novel." In *Spectacles of Realism: Body, Gender, Genre*. Ed. Margaret Cohen and Christopher Prendergast. Minneapolis: University of Minnesota Press, 1995.

———. *Fictional Genders*. Lincoln: University of Nebraska Press, 1989.

Knibiehler, Yvonne, and Catherine Fouquet. *La Femme et les médecins*. Paris: Hachette, 1983.

Kogan, Vivian. "Michelet Plays Doctor." Paper delivered at the 19th annual Nineteenth-Century French Studies Colloquium, Lawrence, Kansas, 1993.

Koos, Leonard. "Medical Asides: Decadent Doctoring in *À rebours*." Paper delivered at the 23rd annual Nineteenth-Century French Studies Colloquium, Athens, Georgia, October 1997.

Kudlick, Catherine J. *Cholera in Post-Revolutionary Paris: A Cultural History*. Berkeley: University of California Press, 1996.

Lagree, Michel, and François Lebrun. *Pour l'histoire de la médecine*. Rennes: Presses Universitaires de Rennes, 1994.

Larousse, Pierre. *Grand Dictionnaire universel du XIXe siècle*. Paris: Larousse et Boyer, 1866–90.

Lasowski, Patrick. Preface to *Le Rosier de Madame Husson*, by Guy de Maupassant. Paris: Livre de Poche, 1984.

———. *Syphilis: Essai sur la littérature française du XIXe siècle*. Paris: Gallimard, 1982.

Latour, Bruno. *The Pasteurization of France*. Trans. Alan Sheridan and John Law. Cambridge MA: Harvard University Press, 1988.

Lavielle, Véronique. "Le Cycle des *Rougon-Macquart*, la science et l'imaginaire." *Cahiers naturalistes* 68 (1994): 23–27.

Lehrmann, Charles C. *The Jewish Element in French Literature*. Trans. George Klin. Rutherford PA: Fairleigh Dickinson University Press, 1971.

Léonard, Jacques. *La France médicale au XIXe siècle*. Paris: Gallimard/Julliard, 1978.

——. *La Médecine entre les savoirs et les pouvoirs*. Paris: Aubier Montaigne, 1981.

——. *La Vie quotidienne de médecin de province au XIXe siècle*. Paris: Hachette, 1977.

Léonard, Martine. "De la science comme cliché, ou comment penser la littérature." *Etudes françaises* 19, no.2 (fall 1983): 97–110.

Le Roy, Eugène. *L'Ennemi de la mort*. 1906; Paris: Calmann-Lévy, 1981.

Lethbridge, Robert. "A Visit to the Louvre: *L'Assommoir* Revisited." *The Modern Language Review* 87, no.1 (January 1992): 41–55.

Lethève, Jacques. *La Vie quotidienne des artistes français au XIXe siècle*. Paris: Hachette, 1968.

Leuwers, Daniel. Preface to *Mont-Oriol*, by Guy de Maupassant. Paris: Flammarion, 1990.

Lhermite, Albert. *Un Sceptique, s'il vous plaît*. Ed. Julia Przyboś. Paris: Corti, 1996.

Lloyd, Christopher, ed. *Epidemics and Sickness in French Literature and Culture*. Durham, U.K.: Durham University Press, 1995.

——. *J.-K. Huysmans and the Fin-de-siècle Novel*. Edinburgh: University of Edinburgh Press, 1990.

Lombroso, Césare. *L'homme de génie*. Paris: Alcan, 1889; translation of *L'uomo di genio in rapporto alla psichiatria, alla storia ed all'estetica*. Torino: Fratelli Bocca, 1888, 1894.

Lukacher, Maryline. "Flaubert's Pharmacy." *Nineteenth-Century French Studies* 14, nos.1–2 (fall–winter 1985–86): 37–50.

Maingon, Charles. *La Médecine dans l'œuvre de J.-K. Huysmans*. Paris: Nizet, 1994.

——. *L'Univers artistique de J.-K. Huysmans*. Paris: Nizet, 1977.

Maleuvre, Didier. "A Natural Death: Zola and Literature." *French Forum* 19.3 (1994): 309–28.

Martin, William. *With God on Our Side: The Rise of the Religious Right in America*. New York: Broadway Books, 1996.

Martineau, Henri. *Le Roman scientifique d'Emile Zola: La Médecine et les Rougon-Macquart*. Paris: J. B. Baillière, 1907.

Massis, Henri. *Comment Emile Zola composait ses romans*. Paris: Charpentier, 1906.

Mathieu, Martine. "De la métaphore à l'allégorie dans *Madame Gervaisais*: Ecriture de la transfiguration et pétrification de l'écriture." In *Les Frères Goncourt: Art et écriture*. Ed. Jean-Louis Cabanès. Bordeaux: Presses Universitaires de Bordeaux, 1997. 301–13.

Matlock, Jann. "Censoring the Realist Gaze." In *Spectacles of Realism: Body, Gender, Genre*. Ed. Margaret Cohen and Christopher Prendergast. Minneapolis: University of Minnesota Press, 1995.

——. *Scenes of Seduction: Prostitution, Hysteria, and Reading Difference in Nineteenth-Century France*. New York: Columbia University Press, 1994.

Maupassant, Guy de. *Chroniques*. Ed. Hubert Juin. Paris: Union Générale d'Editions, Collection 10/18, 1980.

————. *Contes et Nouvelles*. 2 vols. Ed. Louis Forestier. Paris: Gallimard, Bibliothèque de la Pléiade, 1974, 1979.

————. *Romans*. Ed. Louis Forestier. Paris: Gallimard, Bibliothèque de la Pléiade, 1987.

————. *Le Rosier de Madame Husson*. Ed. Louis Forestier. Paris: Gallimard, 1990.

————. *Sur l'eau*. Paris: Conard, 1947.

McGrew, Robert. *Encyclopedia of Medical History*. London: Macmillan, 1985.

Meyers, Jeffrey. *Disease and the Novel 1880–1960*. London: Macmillan, 1985.

Michel, Louise. *Les Microbes humains*. Paris: Dentu, 1886.

Michelet, Jules. *La Femme*. 2nd ed. Paris: Hachette, 1860.

————. *Le Prêtre, la Femme et la Famille*. Paris: Chamerot, 1861.

Michot-Dietrich, Hela. "Homais, Homeopathy, and Madame Bovary." *Stanford French Review* 11 (1987): 313–21.

Miguet-Ollagnier, Marie. "Idéologie du *Traité d'hygiène* d'Adrien Proust." *Colloque "Proust et la médecine"*. Paris: La Gazette du CHU, 1992

Mitchell, Robert. "From Heart to Spleen: The Lyrics of Pathology in Nineteenth-Century French Poetry." In *Medicine and Literature*. Ed. Enid Rhodes Peschel. New York: Watson, 1980. 153–59.

Mitterand, Henri. "Un Projet inédit d'Emile Zola en 1884–85: Le Roman des villes d'eaux." *Cahiers naturalistes* 4 (1958): 401–13.

Moger, Angela. "Narrative Structure in Maupassant: Frames of Desire." *PMLA* 100, no.3 (May 1985): 315–27.

Monin, Dr. Ernest. *L'Alcoolisme: Etude médico-sociale*. Paris: Octave Doin, 1917.

Monselet, Dr. Charles. *Lettres gourmandes*. Paris: Dentu, 1877.

Montaigne, Michel de. *Essais*. Ed. Pierre Michel. Paris: Gallimard, 1965.

Nef, Frédéric. "Noms et échange dans 'Le Rosier de Madame Husson.'" In *Exigences et perspectives de la sémiotique*. Ed. Herman Parret and Hans-George Ruprecht. Amsterdam: John Benjamins, 1985.

Nevins, Michael. *The Jewish Doctor. A Narrative History*. Northvale NJ: Jason Aronson, 1996.

New Catholic Encyclopedia. New York: McGraw-Hill, 1967.

Newton, Joy. "The Decline and Fall of Gervaise Macquart." *Essays in French Literature* 16 (1979): 62–79.

Newton, Joy, and Claude Schumacher. "La Grande Bouffe dans *L'Assommoir* et dans le cycle Gervaise." *L'Esprit créateur* 25, no.4 (1985): 17–29.

Nordau, Max. *Psycho-physiologie du génie et du talent*. Paris: F. Alcan, 1897.

Nye, Robert. *Crime, Madness and Politics in Modern France: The Medical Concept of National Decline*. Princeton: Princeton University Press, 1984.

O'Donovan, Patrick. "The Body and the Body Politic in the Novels of the Goncourts." In *Spectacles of Realism: Body, Gender, Genre*. Ed. Margaret Cohen and Christopher Prendergast. Minneapolis: University of Minnesota Press, 1995.

Oliver, Sir Thomas. *Occupations from the Social, Hygienic and Medical Points of View.* Cambridge: Cambridge University Press, 1916.

Omar, Charles, and Jean Hamilton. *Wallpapers: An International History.* New York: Harry N. Abrams, 1982.

Paris, Jean. "Maupassant et le contre-récit." In *Le Point aveugle.* Paris: Seuil, 1975.

Pasco, Allan. "Image Structure in *Le Père Goriot.*" *French Forum* 7 (1982): 224–34.

———. *Novel Configurations.* Birmingham AL: Summa Publications, 1987.

———. *Sick Heroes: French Society and Literature in the Romantic Age, 1750–1850.* Exeter, U.K.: University of Exeter Press, 1997.

Patissier, Philippe. *Traité des maladies des artisans.* Paris: Baillière, 1822.

Paulson, William. *Enlightenment, Romanticism and the Blind in France.* Princeton: Princeton University Press, 1987.

Perrot, Philippe. *Le Travail des apparences.* Paris: Seuil, 1984.

Peschel, Enid Rhodes. "Medicine and Literature: Beaumarchais' *Le Barbier [-chirurgien] de Seville.*" *Romance Quarterly* 37 (May 1990): 141–46.

Petrey, Sandy. "Le discours du travail dans *L'Assommoir.*" *Cahiers naturalistes* 52 (1978): 58–67.

Pick, Daniel. *Faces of Degeneration: A European Disorder, c. 1848–1918.* Cambridge: Cambridge University Press, 1989.

Poincaré, Léon. *Traité d'hygiène industrielle à l'usage des médecins et des membres des conseils d'hygiène.* Paris: Masson, 1886.

Pommier, Jean, and Gabrielle Leleu. *Madame Bovary.* Nouvelle version précédée des scénarios inédits. Paris: Corti, 1949.

Ponnau, Gwenhaël. *La Folie dans la littérature fantastique.* Paris: CNRS, 1987.

Porter, Laurence M., and Eugene F. Gray. *Approaches to Teaching Flaubert's* Madame Bovary. New York: Modern Language Association, 1995.

Porter, Ray. *The Greatest Benefit to Mankind: A Medical History of Humanity.* New York: W. W. Norton, 1997.

Poulot, Denis. *Le Sublime ou Le Travailleur comme il est en 1870 et ce qu'il peut être.* 2nd ed. Paris: Lacroix, 1872.

Prince, Gerald. *A Dictionary of Narratology.* Lincoln: University of Nebraska Press, 1987.

———. " 'Le Horla,' Sex, and Colonization." In *Alteratives.* Ed. Warren Motte and Gerald Prince. Lexington: French Forum Monographs, 1993. 181–87.

———. *Narrative as Theme.* Lincoln: University of Nebraska Press, 1992.

Przyboš, Julia. "The Aesthetics of Dirty Laundry." In *Kaleidoscope.* Ed. Graham Falconer and Mary Donaldson-Evans. Toronto: Centres d'études romantiques, 1996. 179–91.

———. "Concerning a Physiological Geometry: The Metaliterary Content of J.-K. Huysmans' 'Sac au dos.' " *L'Esprit créateur* 25, no.4 (winter 1985): 105–14.

Ramsey, Matthew. "Medical Power and Popular Medicine: Illegal Healers in Nineteenth-Century France." *Journal of Social History* 10, no.4 (1977): 560–77.

Reeves, Eileen. "Theatres of Operation." Paper delivered at the 17th annual Nineteenth-Century French Studies Colloquium, University of New Orleans, New Orleans, Louisiana, 1991.

Regnault, Dr. Félix. "Le Mal de Flaubert." *Revue moderne de médecine et de chirurgie* 27 (1927): 345–46.

Reiser, Stanley. *Medicine and the Reign of Technology*. Cambridge, U.K.: Cambridge University Press, 1978.

———. "Responsibility for Personal Health: A Historical Perspective." *Journal of Medicine and Philosophy* 10 (1985): 7–17.

Renan, Ernest. *La Vie de Jésus*. Paris: 1863.

Respaut, Michèle. "The Doctor's Discourse: Emblems of Science, Sexual Fantasy, and Myth in Barbey d'Aurevilly's 'Le Bonheur dans le crime.'" *French Review* 73, no.1 (October 1999): 71–80.

Ricatte, Robert. *La Création romanesque chez les Goncourt*. Paris: Colin, 1953.

Rideout, Blanchard Livingstone. "The Medical Practitioner in the French Novel, 1850–1900." Ph.D. Diss., Cornell University, 1936.

Riffaterre, Michael. "Flaubert's Presuppositions." *Diacritics* 11 (1981): 2–11.

Ripa, Yannick. *La Ronde des Folles: Femme, folie et enfermement au XIXe siècle (1838–1870)*. Paris: Aubier, 1986.

Rosello, Mireille. "Contamination et pureté: Pour un protocole de cohabitation." *L'Esprit créateur* 37, no.3 (fall 1997): 3–13.

Rothfield, Lawrence. "From Semiotic to Discursive Intertextuality: The Case of *Madame Bovary*." *Novel* (fall 1985): 57–81.

———. *Vital Signs: Medical Realism in Nineteenth-Century Fiction*. Princeton: Princeton University Press, 1992.

Roudinesco, Elisabeth. *La Bataille de cent ans*. Vol.1 of *Histoire de la psychanalyse en France*. Paris: Ramsey, 1982.

Ruderman, David B. *Jewish Thought and Scientific Discovery in Early Modern Europe*. New Haven: Yale University Press, 1995.

Russett, Cynthia Eagle. *Sexual Science: The Victorian Construction of Womanhood*. Cambridge: Harvard University Press, 1989.

Sachs, Murray. *The Career of Alphonse Daudet*. Cambridge: Harvard University Press, 1965.

———. "The Role of the Blind Beggar in *Madame Bovary*." *Symposium* 23 (spring 1968): 72–80.

Sainte-Beuve, Charles-Augustin. *Portraits contemporains*. Paris: Didier, 1846.

Salières, Dr. François. *Ecrivains contre médecins*. Paris: Editions Denoël, 1948.

Salomon-Bayet, Claire. "Histoire des sciences et histoire de la médecine." In *Pour l'histoire de la médecine: Autour de l'œuvre de Jacques Léonard*. Ed. Michel Lagrée and François Lebrun. Rennes: Presses Universitaires de Rennes, 1994. 49–55.

Sandras, Agnes. "Sous le scalpel des gens de lettres: Représentations littéraires du médecin (1850–1900)." Thèse d'histoire, Université de Toulouse, 1992.

Schor, Naomi. "For a Restricted Thematics: Writing, Speech and Difference in *Madame Bovary*." In *Modern Critical Interpretations: Gustave Flaubert's* Madame Bovary. Ed. Harold Bloom. New York: Chelsea House, 1988. 61–81.

———. "Sainte-Anne: Capitale du délire." *Cahiers naturalistes* 52 (1978): 97–108.

———. *Zola's Crowds*. Baltimore: Johns Hopkins University Press, 1978.

Scott, Malcolm. *The Struggle for the Soul of the French Novel*. Washington DC: Catholic University Press, 1990.

Shaw, George Bernard. *The Doctor's Dilemma*. New York: Brentano's, 1909.

Shortt, S. E. D. "Physicians, Science and Status: Issues in the Professionalization of Anglo-American Medicine in the Nineteenth Century." *Medical History* 27 (1983): 51–68.

Showalter, Elaine. *The Female Malady: Women, Madness and English Culture, 1830–1980*. New York: Pantheon, 1985.

Siler, Douglas. "La Mort d'Emma Bovary: Sources médicales." *Revue d'Histoire Littéraire de la France* 81, nos.4–5 (1981): 719–46.

Silverman, Willa Z. "Anti-Semitism and Occultism in *Fin-de-siècle* France: Three 'Initiates.'" In *Modernity and Revolution in Late Nineteenth-Century France*. Ed. Barbara Cooper and Mary Donaldson-Evans. Newark: University of Delaware Press, 1992. 155–63.

Slott, Kathryn. "Narrative Tension in the Representation of Women in Zola's *L'Assommoir* and *Nana*." *L'Esprit créateur* 25, no.4 (1985): 93–104.

Spackman, Barbara. *Decadent Genealogies: The Rhetoric of Sickness from Baudelaire to d'Annunzio*. Ithaca: Cornell University Press, 1989.

Stein, William Bysshe. "*Madame Bovary* and Cupid Unmasked." *Sewanee Review* 73 (1965): 108–209.

Stivale, Charles. *The Art of Rupture: Narrative Desire and Duplicity in the Tales of Guy de Maupassant*. Ann Arbor: University of Michigan Press, 1994.

———. "Guy de Maupassant and Narrative Strategies of Othering." *Australian Journal of French Studies* 30, no.2 (May–August 1993): 241–51.

Sullivan, E. D. *Maupassant the Novelist*. Princeton: Princeton University Press, 1954.

Tarde, Gabriel. *Les Lois de l'imitation*. Paris: Alcon, 1890.

Tardieu, Ambroise. *Dictionnaire d'hygiène publique et de sobriété*. Paris: Baillière, 1852.

Terdiman, Richard. *Discourse/Counter-Discourse: The Theory and Practice of Symbolic Resistance in Nineteenth-Century France*. Ithaca: Cornell University Press, 1985.

Thomas à Kempis. *The Imitation of Christ*. Trans. Leo Sherley-Price. London: Penguin, 1952.

Toussenel, Alphonse. *Les Juifs, rois de l'époque: Histoire de la féodalité financière*. Paris: G. de Gonet, 1847.

Veysset, Georges. *Huysmans et la médecine*. Paris: Société d'édition "Les Belles Lettres," 1950.

Vial, André. *Maupassant et l'art du roman*. Paris: Nizet, 1954.

Voltaire. *Candide*. Oxford: Basil Blackwell, 1966.

Waddington, Ivan. *The Medical Profession in the Industrial Revolution*. Dublin: Gill and Macmillan, 1984.

Wajeman, Gérard. *Le Maître et l'hystérique*. Paris: Seuil, 1982.

Wallon, Armand. *La Vie quotidienne dans les villes d'eaux (1850–1914)*. Paris: Hachette, 1981.

Watroba, Maria. "*Madame Gervaisais*, roman hystérique ou mystique?" *Nineteenth-Century French Studies* 25, nos.1–2 (fall–winter 1996–97): 154–66.

Weber, Eugen. *France Fin-de-siècle*. Cambridge: Harvard University Press, 1986.

Wetherill, P. M. "*Madame Bovary*'s Blind Man: Symbolism in Flaubert." *Romanic Review* 61 (1970): 35–42.

Whorton, Michael. "Of Sappho and Syphilis: Alphonse Daudet on and in Illness." *L'Esprit créateur* 37, no.3 (fall 1997): 38–49.

Whyte, Peter. "Maupassant et le réflexe conditionné." In *Maupassant conteur et romancier*. Ed. Christopher Lloyd and Robert Lethbridge. Durham, U.K.: University of Durham, 1994. 173–84.

Williams, Michael V. "The Hound of Fate in *Madame Bovary*." *College Literature* 14, no.1 (winter 1987): 54–61.

Williams, Roger. *The Horror of Life*. Chicago: University of Chicago Press, 1980.

Wing, Nathaniel. *The Limits of Narrative: Essays on Baudelaire, Flaubert, Rimbaud, and Mallarmé*. New York: Cambridge University Press, 1986.

Wohnlich-Despaigne, Isabelle. *Les Historiens français de la médecine au 19ᵉ siècle*. Paris: Vrin, 1987.

Zeldin, Theodore. *France 1848–1945: Intellect, Taste and Anxiety*. Vol.2. Oxford: Clarendon Press, 1977.

Zola, Emile. *L'Assommoir*. Trans. Margaret Mauldon. New York: Oxford, 1995.

———. *Œuvres complètes*. Ed. Henri Mitterand. Paris: Cercle du Livre Précieux, 1960.

———. *Les Rougon-Macquart*. Ed. Henri Mitterand. 5 vols. Paris: Gallimard, Bibliothèque de la Pléiade, 1961–67.

Index

𝒢

Page numbers in italics refer to illustrations on those pages.